MARIJUANA

GROWING AND BUSINESS

2021

A Complete and Simple Guide to Growing and Selling
Your Own Cannabis (3 BOOKS)

by ELIA FRIEDENTHAL

CONTENTS

CHAPTER 11: OPENING A DISPENSARY ____________ 361

MARIJUANA

GROWER'S HANDBOOK

BUSINESS PLAN

Techniques & Facts Regarding the Cultivation of Cannabis

—

INDOORS AND OUTDOORS

by ELIA FRIEDENTHAL

CONTENTS

INTRODUCTION

BACKGROUND. If we take a look at the origins of the cannabis plant, we will find that they reveal much of the history of humanity. Substantial changes have recently occurred, indicating greater acceptance of the plant on a social level. Further progress needs to be made, but we can look back and admire the progress made so far. Following in the footsteps of a significant plant like cannabis can be helpful in learning more about the company that uses it. Marijuana contains chemicals that interact with cannabinoid receptors found in the human body.

This fortunate connection has given rise to numerous religious and spiritual traditions related to cannabis use. Cannabis seems like a heavenly substance, but let's take a look at the interesting journey it has made on Earth. At some point in history, the cannabis plant started growing in the wilderness. It is possible that it was born in the areas of passage of hunter-gatherers, rich in nutrients.

The farthest point in time that we can confirm the presence of cannabis is roughly 11-12,000 years ago. It would appear that the plant first grew in the mountainous areas of Central Asia, particularly Mongolia and southern Siberia. Humans began to grow two different varieties, using them for various purposes.

The "Cannabis sativa" plant offered humans a unique psychoactive high. The one classified as "Cannabis sativa L.", however, is the common hemp, a non-psychoactive plant but used industrially to produce oil, rope, paper and other materials.

It is difficult to pinpoint the exact moment when humans discovered how to use psychoactive plants. At some point, someone will have decided to smoke some cannabis, to see what happened. Had it not been for this pioneering spirit, perhaps the amazing properties of these two plants would have remained unknown to humanity. Later, two other psychoactive cannabis strains were discovered: Cannabis indica, with a physical and comfortable high, and Cannabis ruderalis, with softer effects and a shorter stature. But to analyze in detail the characteristics of each variety, we must first understand how the plant spread from the mountains of Central Asia to the rest of the world.

History of the use of cannabis.

Always used in China for the manufacture of ropes and fabrics, in the Po Valley, cannabis has been present since Roman times for the production of textile fiber. It fell in the 1930s, when a 1937 law, the Marijuana Tax Act, outlawed it in the United States. With a domino effect this happened in many other countries around the world. In past centuries, Italy was the largest exporter in Europe, and the economy was based on hemp, especially in Piedmont, Emilia-Romagna and Campania, while families used it to make ropes and yarns.

Hemp has been present in the Bolognese plain since the 14th century as a specialized crop, so much so that in the first quarter of the 20th century, 53,000 ha were planted to grow 450,000 quintals of fiber (half of the national production). It was harvested at the end of July by uprooting or mowing at the foot, dried, beaten and raised upright in conical piles, then collected in sheaves by drawing, and they extracted the fiber by maceration in pulp. Each farmhouse had its own pulp, a large basin up to 2 m deep, in which the bundles of hemp (rods) were sunk (with 3-7 kg river stones) to facilitate the separation of the fiber from the woody material (hemp): it was the "first transformation", which lasted a few days (smelly). The actual detachment of the fiber from the hemp took place directly on the farm with the scutching, initially performed by hand and finally with rudimentary machinery.

Every year the pulp was emptied and cleaned of algae and various residues, a bacterial flora that caused the hemp fiber to yellow and diminish the quality. The rubble was near the house because it also had ancillary functions (bathroom, swimming pool, laundry, breeding of fish, frogs and water birds, irrigation and ice).

From the end of the 1950s, production fell due to the hardness of the first processing work and the competition from synthetic fibers, until prohibition in 1971 with the approval of the legislation on drugs (which in fact also prevented the cultivation of textile hemp). It remained only in France, China, Russia and Eastern European countries, which today are the world's largest producers, while Germany, Austria, Great Britain and Spain are also appearing among the major producers. The term "prohibition" refers to that particular ideological and legislative orientation that tends to prohibit the use of certain substances based on their alleged or ascertained danger.

This orientation stems from the idea that organizations and states have a duty to protect the health of citizens and the social order from the consequences of the use of the substances themselves. In practice, prohibition means limiting individual freedom for reasons of health, public order, morals, or respect for traditions and / or religions. Given these premises, it is not surprising that the discussion on the prohibition of certain substances has been on the agenda since the dawn of time. In the United States, the term Prohibition indicates in particular the period between 1919 and 1933. In a period of increasing Puritanism and an increasingly conspicuous presence of social unrest caused, according to prohibitionists, mainly by alcohol, in January 1919 the federal government of the United States ratified, through the XVIII amendment, the law that "the production, sale and transport of alcohol is prohibited."

Many US citizens strongly disagreed. Many did not stop drinking. It is true that within four years the national average of alcohol consumption, at least officially, dropped from twenty-seven liters to four liters per person, but many continued to use alcohol illegally, either at home or by finding themselves in special clandestine bars. Prohibition created the phenomenon of gangsterism: Mafia-type criminal gangs dedicated to alcohol smuggling. Discontent, unrest and the crime caused by this law prompted the legislator to decree the end of Prohibition after only 14 years: in December 1933, alcohol became legal again. In the US, Prohibition completely failed.

As in the US nearly a century ago, prohibition is practiced in many countries around the world today. In some countries with a Muslim majority, alcohol is prohibited, but in almost all countries of the world, the consumption of soft drugs is prohibited, so the sale, purchase and/or possession of these substances are crimes. In some countries, the crime is punished with the death penalty.

CANNABIS AMONG THE ANCIENT PEOPLES

The Cannabis plant, also known as marijuana and ganja (from Sanskrit: गांजा - gañjā), is an extraordinary plant: it is the only plant in the world that can be used as a drug or as a fiber at the same time. Considering its specificity, it is not surprising that its cultivation dates back to at least 10 thousand years ago. Evidence has been found on the island of Taiwan, as well as in some caves in modern day Romania.

First found in Asia, probably in Central Asia, cannabis has been used for medical, spiritual, religious or recreational purposes (via inhalation or vaporization) for at least 5,000 years. We know for sure that the Aryans smoked cannabis and it may have been the Aryans who taught the properties of cannabis to both Indian peoples (probably we refer to cannabis when in the Vedas, the sacred Hindu texts, we speak of intoxicating hallucinogens) and to the ancient Assyrians. A Chinese pharmacology treatise attributed to Emperor Shen Nung, dated 2,737 BC, contains the first reference to the use of cannabis as a medicine.

The Ancient Greeks loved and idealized wine and did not use marijuana for recreational use, but there are many texts attesting to their trade with peoples who ate or inhaled cannabis. Herodotus in 5 BC writes that the Scythians (a semi-nomadic population of Iranian origin) cultivated and then vaporized cannabis. On another occasion, Herodotus again writes that the inhabitants of some Mediterranean islands threw cannabis on the fire and then, "sitting around in a circle, they inhale and are intoxicated by the smell, just like the Greeks with wine, and the more they throw away the more they become intoxicated, until they get up and dance and sing."

Other passages by Pliny, Marco Polo, Abu Mansur Muwaffaq and The Arabian Nights demonstrate beyond a shadow of a doubt that cannabis was grown for both its fiber and its psychoactive properties throughout Asia, the Middle East and much of the area of the Mediterranean since the dawn of time. For example, the sails of the Phoenicians' ships were made of hemp fiber.

The date when cannabis was introduced in central, northern and western Europe is unknown, but it probably dates back to at least 500 years before Christ, as an urn containing cannabis leaves and seeds was found in Berlin dating back to around 2,500. Years ago. Also a few centuries before Christ, before the advent of the Roman Empire, various European peoples such as the Celts and Picts cultivated and used cannabis.

Since then, cannabis cultivation has been common, if not massive, in Europe for centuries. Hemp clothing has been very common in central and southern Europe for centuries. But the Europeans obviously also knew the plant's recreational potential. Although a papal bull in 1484 forbade its use to the faithful, Francois Rabelais wrote extensively about it in the sixteenth century. In the following centuries, despite the condemnation of the Church, the use of cannabis for recreational purposes became a real fashion among intellectuals, so much so that the Club des Hashischins or Club of hashish eaters, was founded in Paris, frequented by poets and writers such as Victor Hugo, Alexandre Dumas, Charles Baudelaire, Honoré de Balzac and Théophile Gautier.

From ancient times to industrialization, hemp was also used to make paper. The famous Gutenberg Bible, the first book printed in Europe with the movable type technique, was printed in 1453 on hemp paper specially imported from Italy. At the end of the same century, the sails of the ships of Christopher Columbus' caravels were made of hemp. The use of cannabis was also widespread in Africa centuries before European colonization. In the black continent, cannabis was cultivated, used as a fiber and as a medicine, inhaled and sometimes worshiped in very different areas: from South Africa to the Congo to Morocco.

In the eighteenth century, cannabis was widespread in North America. Most of the land of the founder of the United States, George Washington, was planted with hemp. Thomas Jefferson also had a large and profitable hemp crop. In 1850 in the United States there were 8,327 hemp plantations (each plantation had at least 2000 acres of land), used mainly for the production of fiber. The United States Declaration of Independence was laid out on hemp paper.

HEMP

Italy was a world leader. Italy was also a very important producer of cannabis for centuries. The reason is simple: the climate of the peninsula is particularly favorable for the cultivation of this plant. In particular, Italian farmers produced cannabis for two reasons. On the one hand, because it grew on soils that were difficult to cultivate with other industrial plants (sandy soils and marshy areas in the river plains), on the other hand because there was always a need for "oily" (sativa, light), "fibrous" plants (textiles, paper, ropes) and feed (leaves) for productive livestock. They excelled in the hemp lands of Bologna and Ferrara. The major Bolognese agronomist of the seventeenth century, Vincenzo Tanara, testifies to the vitality of the Canapacola economy with a long, accurate description of the cultivation technique. Thanks to the quality of its hemp, Italy became the second largest producer of hemp in the world and the first supplier to the British navy. The decline began with the spread of coal ships, when a slow agony began for the hemp-producing areas, which lasted for a century, forcing the restructuring of all agrarian rotations.

The demonization of CANNABIS

During the Second World War, however, the Middle European and Mediterranean production began to increase rapidly, because textile fibers and sativa oils became more expensive. In addition, there was a need for raw materials containing a lot of cellulose from which explosives could be obtained by producing nitrocellulose. But the Marijuana Tax Act of 1937 gave the final blow to hemp cultivation, banning it in the US. Cannabis was pseudo-scientifically accused of making people violent and maddening or dying. As a result, hemp was banned in much of the rest of the world in the following years.

The director of the American Federal Bureau of Narcotics, Harry J. Anslinger, was an ambitious, racist and bigoted man who justified the prohibition with the following words:

*There are 100,000 marijuana smokers
in the United States of America. Most
of them are Negroes, Hispanics,
Filipinos and artists. Their satanic
music, jazz, swing, are the result of the
use of marijuana. Marijuana causes
white women to want to have sexual
relations with blacks, artists, and
others.*

*(...) The first reason for banning
marijuana is its effect on degenerate
breeds.*

Marijuana is an addictive drug that produces insanity, crime and death in users.

Marijuana leads to pacifist and communist brainwashing.

Spinels make niggers think they are like white men.

Smoke a joint and you'll probably kill your brother.

Marijuana is the drug that has caused the most violence in human history.

In addition to bigotry, there were economic interests behind the prohibition campaign. Famous paper/publishing house Hearst, the biggest supporter of the anti-cannabis campaign via its newspapers, had just made huge investments in tree paper. Its owner William Randolph Hearst, paper tycoon and character who inspired Orson Welles in the figure of Citizen Kane in the movie of the same name, declared the following nonsense in the newspaper, Tycoon:

"Marijuana is the shortest way to the asylum, smoke marijuana for a month and your brain will be nothing more than a repository of hideous specters Hashish creates a killer who kills for the pleasure of killing." Hearst newspapers carried out a huge disinformation and prohibitionist propaganda campaign

against cannabis for years, falsely attributing to it a myriad of "social evils", from murder to communism, from pacifism to marital infidelity, up to sexual relations between "white women and inferior races".

Headlines like this were often read: "THREE QUARTERS OF CRIMES in this country are CAUSED BY MARIJUANA". At the same time DuPont patented nylon. According to some scholars, all these were not mere coincidences. Since 1937, 20 million Americans have been arrested and jailed for possession or use of the world's most popular and least harmful drug.

LET'S START

The collection of quality flowers is done manually, to preserve the delicate trichomes of the flowers that contain the desired bioactive parts.

DRYING

Stems / Fiber / Canapulo

The drying of the stems to obtain fiber and hemp usually takes place in an open field. A few weeks after harvesting, depending on the weather conditions, the drums are usually ready to be packed and sent to the centers for the first processing of hemp straw.

SEEDS

Given the high fat content and the presence of green plant parts, hemp seeds are susceptible to rancidity and mold if they are not dried properly. Generally, within an hour of threshing they are prepared for drying which can take place in dryers with dehumidified air screw and at max 35C, or laid on the ground in a clean, covered and ventilated place where care must be taken not to spread it too thickly.

The correct humidity for good drying is below 10%.

FLOWERS

The hemp flowers are left to dry in the dark because the UV rays of the sun ruin the precious bioactive components of the trichomes. Usually, they are kept with the branches that support them and hung on horizontal wires or vertical nets, or detached from the branches and placed on special baskets or horizontal nets, guaranteeing in both cases, a good exchange of air and humidity around 60%. With these parameters, in about 7-10 days the flower has an optimal drying. For faster drying, dryers can be set up that can achieve drying results in a few hours. Fast drying, however, is not recommended for hemp because it causes residues of chlorophyll to remain in the plant parts and the organoleptic qualities and bioactive components may be altered.

The drying and proper storage of marijuana is the final stage of the cultivation process. It is also among the most important, since they make the gems, if properly dried and stored beautiful, tasty and pleasant in taste and intoxication. The drying method is easy but it is also fundamental, in order not to ruin all the work done previously, since an incorrect drying would ruin the quality of the gems, both in terms of smokability and high.

By reading this guide, we will see how to cure it, how to dry it, the necessary timing, the equipment we need and the conditions we must provide to obtain perfect and tasty gems.

INTERPRETING THE SIGNALS

When ready to harvest, female cannabis plants send out clear signals. The grower will need to sharpen his eyes and monitor the behavior of the plants in the final weeks of flowering. Falling and yellowing of the leaves are the first visual signs, as the cannabis plant is now going through its period of senescence. Also, bud size and resin production stop increasing. The pistils curl up on themselves and dry, showing predominantly orange/red and brown colors (although some still retain a certain turgor and a whitish color). Pay close attention to these signs in the final weeks of flowering.

Step One:

Stop feeding fertilizer seven to fifteen days before harvest. The latent accumulation of nutrients in the foliage gives it an aftertaste of fertilizer. The fertilizing substances must be leached from the substrate seven to ten days before harvesting. Some growers continue to fertilize for up to three days before harvesting. There are products that accelerate the elimination of chemicals accumulated in cannabis plants.

Step Two:

If sprays have been applied during the last week (not recommended), you need to wet the plants abundantly to wash away any unwanted residues from the foliage. Such a bath will not affect resin production. To shake away the deposited water, gently rock the plants. To prevent fungi and top rot, it is advisable to water the garden early in the morning, so that the excess water can dry before sunset. In case there is a threat of mold buds, (botrytis) DO NOT WASH buds.

Step Three:

Maybe you want to try giving the plants 24 hours of total darkness before harvesting. Many growers do this and say the buds get slightly more resinous.

Step Four:

Harvest in the morning when the THC level is at its highest. You can harvest the whole plant or one branch at a time by cutting near the base with shears. Tearing up the ball of roots is useless and creates great chaos. All THC is produced in the foliage, not the roots.

Step Five:

There is no need to hang the plants upside down for the resin to drain through the foliage. Once formed, the resin does not move. However, it is very convenient to dry a whole plant upside down. When the branches are left intact, drying takes place much more slowly.

Step Six:

To dry whole plants and / or whole branches:

A. Remove the larger leaves a day or two before cutting the plants themselves. The leaves can otherwise be removed even after cutting the plants. By picking them first, they are out of the way and facilitate and shorten the tanning operation.

B. To collect whole plants, cut at the base before carrying out the tanning.

C. Otherwise you can cut each branch to a length of 15-60 cm. It is best to clean up the newly picked inflorescences early, eliminating the surrounding leaves with shears or scissors. The branches thus tanned should be hung until they are dry. At that point, the buds can be cut off the branches, taking special care in handling the tender buds with the utmost care.

D. Alternatively, you can leave the primary leaves on the branches to protect the buds. The tender resin glands remain protected from bruising and shattering until the final tanning, which is however more laborious and slower if dry leaves are cut.

PINKING

After harvesting, the buds are carefully cleaned, cutting off the large leaves where they are connected to the stem. If you leave the petiole (the stem of the leaf), mold could settle there. The smaller, less potent leaves around the low resin buds are scrapped off, leaving a beautiful, high THC bud. Topping is easy when the leaves are soft and flexible, immediately after harvesting. Cutting away the leaves at this point also speeds up drying. If you wait for the foliage to dry before cleaning the buds, it will be dull and long.

The easiest topping is achieved with well-sharpened and pointed scissors, to be able to easily scissor away the petioles of the leaves attached to the main stem. When curing cannabis for hours, an ergonomic pair of scissors is essential. The buds should be cleaned on a thin screen-printing sieve (see Chapter 15, "Hashish") or on a glass table. Scrape off any resin glands that have fallen onto the table or under the sieve. This potent resin can be smoked directly or pressed into hash blocks. Wear cheap rubber gloves to pick up finger hash.

After tanning for a few hours, you can remove the smoke from the fingers of the gloves using a small amount of isopropyl alcohol. Place the alcohol loaded with hashish on a counter and let it evaporate overnight. Otherwise, put the gloves in the freezer for a few hours. Once cooled, it will be easier to scrape and rub the sedimented hashish off the gloves. Scrape off the residual resin from the scissors. To detach it from the blades, you can use a small knife. Ball up the small pieces of resin by squeezing them between your fingers. The hashish ball will grow with the advance of the preventive topping long enough to collect and trim your plants. To properly trim 454g it takes four to six hours by hand with scissors and two hours using an automatic trimmer.

Step by step guide for drying cannabis or marijuana

The most common and reliable method for drying our grass is air drying. To dry it in the best possible way, carry out the processes illustrated below.

- Once harvested, we will taper the tops, that is, we will remove the excess leaves and this will reduce the drying times.
- We will hang our buds in a dark room, tying them with a thread, a clothes pin or anything that supports their weight at the end of the stem, and we will make sure that they do not touch each other.

How to dry our grass?

If we have chosen a strain for its potency, proper drying will guarantee we get the most out of the buds we grow. If we want to dry in a shorter time, we should make sure that we have cured our buds in the right way, that is, that we have removed all the excess leaves.

What will I need after it has dried properly?

While drying, the buds need darkness and a cupboard is the perfect place. If we don't have a cupboard, we could use a cardboard or wooden box, equipped with suitable air holes to ensure circulation air inside it. We will be careful to hang the branches so that they do not touch any surface since they will drop the resin wherever they are placed.

To fix our buds we will use a fishing line, dental floss or anything that can support the weight. The easiest way to hang the marijuana is to have a pin on which to fix the ends of the branches on it with a strong enough wire. It is strongly not recommended to dry the grass in the place where we have grown it, given that the buds need darkness and very low humidity to dry.

- We will use a fan to ensure air circulation. We will be careful not to point the fan directly on the buds, so that they do not dry out too quickly, since this would ruin both the taste and the power, as mentioned above.

- We will leave it to dry for 5/9 days, checking daily that mold or other problems such as too much dryness develop. We will turn the branches from time to time in order to guarantee a homogeneous drying. Of course, we will be very careful in turning them and we will do it from the end of the stem in order to avoid dispersion of the resin.

What are the optimal environmental conditions for drying my marijuana?

The conditions that we are going to illustrate below are perfect to guarantee perfect drying.

- Temperature - between 18 and 24C

- Humidity - between 45 and 55%

High temperatures increase the humidity in the air, and consequently the time required for drying and the risk of developing molds that are harmful to our buds. In fact, the high temperatures decrease the drying time and make it dry too quickly, reducing its quality.

Light and heat are the most bitter enemies of the correct drying of marijuana. We will dry our beloved flowers in a dark room, taking great care to keep them away from hot surfaces. We will try to handle the buds with care, that is, being very careful not to shake them and not to lose the precious veiled sugar scattered above, as this would damage the power of the same.

• We will leave it to dry for 5/9 days, checking daily that mold or other problems such as too much dryness do not develop. We will turn the branches from time to time in order to guarantee a homogeneous drying. Of course, we will be very careful in turning them and we will do it from the end of the stem in order to avoid the dispersion of the resin. Our sprouts are ready when the buds are dry and the stems bend easily without breaking. What are the optimal environmental conditions for drying my marijuana? How to properly store and mature our buds? A good conservation and maturation of our cannabis allows us to dry it gradually in order to remove the moisture little by little and consequently increase its potency. Proper storage guarantees us good quality, excellent taste and a lower risk of developing mold. What do we need to keep our cannabis buds healthy? For proper storage and to reduce the risk of developing mold during the drying process, it will be good to use hermetically sealed jars, since once sealed, no air or other factors that could damage our precious buds. If we do not have jars available, we could always use any other airtight container but we will avoid using bags as moisture could enter them.

We will keep our ganja in a cool, dark and dry place, and we will take great care to avoid it being exposed to direct sunlight as this could evaporate the moisture too quickly and increase the risk of mold.

HOW TO STORE OUR MARIJUANA STEP BY STEP

The technique we are going to illustrate is probably the best and most commonly used for storing marijuana, even if the only flaw is that you need to be patient. Using this method, we will ensure that we have nice looking buds that are tasty to the palate and with the maximum potential for high or amazing effect that can be obtained from them. We will dry our weed for 5/9 days until we feel it dry to the touch on the outside and the stems bend easily without breaking. We will place our precious gems in an airtight container, taking care not to crush them together so as not to damage the resin glands and to allow them to breathe. We will open the container every 2 or 3 hours and let it breathe for a few minutes in order to let out the humidity and promote air exchange.

We will follow this pattern for the first week, naturally keeping the container closed at night when we sleep. We will continue as illustrated until the buds are dry to the touch, that is, for about 10 or 15 minutes, before closing and letting it rest for another 2 or 3 hours.

After the first week, the buds should no longer be too exposed to the risk of developing mold and should already be dry enough so that they can be left closed in their jar or container for longer times. Every 12 hours or less we will remember to let the jar breathe until the sprouts reach the desired drying.

We will continue with the process outlined above for at least another three weeks. In the fourth week, our sprouts will be reduced by 75%, compared to the beginning of the drying and curing process, and we will finally be able to start enjoying them or continue to store them.

This process can be carried out for six months, in fact many growers claim that the longer the drying phase is, the tastier our weed will be. But we will follow the indications illustrated above and we will certainly not be disappointed by the quality of our gems.

Marijuana storage

We will keep our marijuana in a container similar to the one we dried it in. It will be good to keep the container in the fridge, in order to guarantee a low temperature and consequently avoid the degradation of THC. We will make sure that the container is airtight and we will check from time to time that there is no humidity that could stimulate the appearance of mold. We will be very careful to keep the jar away from sources of light and heat that could ruin all the work done so far.

POSSIBLE PROBLEMS DURING THE DRYING PHASE

WHAT SHOULD I DO IF MY GRASS GETS WET? It must be remembered that THC is not soluble in water and therefore does not affect the potency of our buds. However, it does stimulate the appearance of mold, so we will make sure to dry the shoots in a dark and well-ventilated room.

WHAT SHOULD I DO IF I HAVE DRIED MY GEMS TOO MUCH? If we have dried our buds too much, we can try to wipe them gently with a cloth. Although the best thing would be to introduce a peel of any citrus fruit in the container where they are kept, in order to increase the humidity and also provide a very sweet citrus aftertaste Popular wisdom has always held that the geographical area and environmental conditions, in short, what is defined as 'terroir', were decisive in the sudden increase in THC that occurs in some hemp plants. Temperature, amount of water, composition of the soil, cultivation area, were considered factors capable of causing the so-called 'heating' in hemp which leads to an increase in the THC content, as happens for example when plants are kept in bloom longer than recommended.

HOW DO YOU GET ADVANCED CANNABIS SEEDS?

How to make the most of advanced cannabis seeds

If your goal is to grow sinsemilla (the quality marijuana you use to smoke, vape, eat, etc., rich in cannabinoids and free of seeds), you will hardly want your plants to ripen seeds to save. However, it is possible that you have some left over, either because you haven't used all of them or because you may have found some at the bottom of a weed bag, but it could also happen that some plants accidentally produce a small amount. In the latter case, if the plants were to experience severe stress during the vegetative and/or flowering phase, you could be faced with a hermaphroditism problem. This phenomenon causes the accidental pollination of female flowers, which will begin to produce seeds instead of inflorescences. The same can happen if you allow male plants to pollinate females. This is why plants grown from regular seeds must be kept under strict control, in order to check their sexual traits during flowering and promptly eliminate the males before they release the pollen, ruining the entire crop. Hermaphroditism occurs because cannabis plants have the ability to produce male and female flowers on the same specimen. Unless you have chosen to grow feminized seeds (which guarantee crops exclusively composed of female plants), you may end up with some hermaphroditic specimens if your plants experience one or more of the following forms of stress:

• Light Stress: Caused by unwanted or poorly considered changes in the photoperiod, a malfunction of the timer or too brightly lit hot areas.

• Water stress: Caused by poor quality irrigation water, excess or shortage of water, unbalanced pH and wrong water temperature.

• Environmental stress: Caused by adverse levels of temperature and humidity within the growing environment or by parasites and fungi affecting plants.

• Nutritional stress: Caused by too high or too low nutrient concentrations, unbalanced pH, inappropriate fertilizers for the growth phase.

5 WAYS TO MAKE THE MOST OF ADVANCED CANNABIS SEEDS

However, you ended up with a handful of cannabis seeds after harvesting your plants, here are 5 alternative ways to make the most of them instead of just throwing them away.

USE THEM TO EXPERIENCE DIFFERENT CULTIVATION PLANTS

Have you forgotten those seeds that you saved up long ago?! Perfect, now you have a good excuse to use them! Take the opportunity to do some experiments by adopting cultivation systems that you have never used before. For example, you could try a simple and inexpensive hydroponic system, or try guerrilla cultivation or any other technique that you have never dared to try. Pay attention to your budget, but don't be afraid to venture into new growing techniques! The seeds you have are still "in reserve" and will give you the opportunity to learn by experimenting, without the fear of wasting precious or expensive seeds if something goes wrong. You have nothing to lose by using them, so why not take the opportunity to learn new cultivation techniques? Then you have an additional advantage: if all goes well, you will have grown a few more plants to harvest!

TRANSFORM THE ADVANCED SEEDS INTO A DELICIOUS SNACK

Hemp and cannabis seeds are among the most nutritious seeds on the planet. They are rich in protein, fiber, healthy unsaturated fats (omega-3 and omega-6 fatty acids) and vitamins A, E, D and B. In addition, they contain a wide range of minerals such as sodium, potassium, iron and magnesium. You can eat them raw (with or without shell) or roasted. You can use them as they are or eat them as a side dish. Neither hemp nor cannabis seeds contain detectable traces of THC, so you can eat them without any risk of getting high.

ANIMALS ALSO LOVE THEM

Guess what?! Cannabis seeds are not only good for humans, but also for animals. Your furry or feathered friends can benefit greatly from all the nutrients we just mentioned. Mix the seeds with the food they usually eat and let their digestive system do the rest. Don't have pets? It doesn't matter, leave them to wild birds or rodents in an outdoor feeder. The passing animals will be grateful to you!

SELL OR GIVE IT TO FRIENDS

Getting certified seeds from a reputable seedbank is by far the best option, because if you opt to buy or sell them on the street you will find yourself in no man's land in terms of quality and legality. The regulations in force vary from country to country and the utmost attention must always be paid in these cases. Another option, perhaps safer, is to give the leftover seeds to friends, without putting money in the way. This, coupled with transparency in telling where your seeds come from, can be a great way to inspire someone to embark on their own cannabis growing journey.

START YOUR OWN PRIVATE SEED BANK

This is perhaps the most ambitious project you can aspire to with advanced cannabis seeds: hybridization. This involves a lot of patience and precision to find the best characteristics of the different cannabis strains and the seeds associated with them.

Over time, you will have a stocked collection of genetics that you can cross, perhaps keeping some mother plants alive, etc. And if you start with seeds from unknown sources, then back to our first tip: use them to experiment and expand your horizons as a grower.

A good drying and curing process is an essential step in producing high quality cannabis. During this process you can lose, preserve, or improve the smell, taste and potency of cannabis. An incorrect drying process can ruin even the best quality sprouts. It's a time-consuming process, but the patient grower will be rewarded with buds that will have a much better flavor and height.

Drying of fresh cannabis buds

During the drying process the water content of the shoots must be reduced from 75% to 10-15%. To do this takes 10 to 14 days. The most popular method is to cut off the branches with the shoots, remove the leaves from them and hang them upside down in a room or closet. Make sure that the branches do not touch each other to avoid drying out with an odd shape. It is best to get rid of as much moisture as possible during the first 3 days. After this period, the drying process should be slightly slowed down.

To dry fresh cannabis buds the right way, the following circumstances are required:

• **Temperature**. During the first 3 days the best temperature is around 20 degrees Celsius. This way the sprouts will dry quickly, but not too much. After the first 3 days the temperature should be lowered to around 17-18 degrees Celsius in order to slow down the process.

- **Humidity**. During the first 3 days, the relative humidity should be around 50%. After three days the relative humidity should rise to around 60%, again to slow down the drying process.

- **Air recirculation**. It is very important that there is enough air circulation in the room, so it is advisable to use an electric fan. A ventilation device can also come in handy for controlling temperature and humidity. However, do not aim the appliance directly at the buds, as this could dry out the cannabis buds improperly.

- **Dark**. The room should be relatively dark as light, especially direct sunlight, degrades THC.

Sprouts are dry when you can easily break the stem. If it curves, it means more time is needed. You will know when the time comes ...

It is very important not to dry the sprouts too quickly. During drying, not only humidity but also chlorophyll and other pigments present in the plant tissue evaporate and leave the shoots. If the sprouts are dried too quickly, some of these pigments don't have enough time to leave the sprouts and will end up in the final product. When cannabis contains a high amount of chlorophyll it often has a bitter, "green" taste and smell, which many compare to smelly hay. That's a good enough reason not to speed up the process too much. Here we are with one last important note on the drying of cannabis. When fresh cannabis buds are drying, they release an extremely strong smell, especially in the first few days. So, if you don't want to attract attention, get yourself a decent amount of deodorant.

The treatment of dried cannabis

When the sprouts are properly dried, it is time to process and store the finished product in an airtight glass jar. Even after a proper drying period of 10-14 days some chlorophyll and other pigments may remain and continue their process. The entire treatment period is 2 weeks to 2 months, depending on how the grower wants the sprouts. And how much patience he has. There are cannabis experts out there who only smoke cannabis that has been treated for at least 1 year.

Cannabis must be placed loose in a jar and the jar must be filled to a maximum of 2/3, as the buds need air to breathe. The jar should be placed in a cool, dark place. During the first 2 weeks, it is very important to check the sprouts at least once a day to change the air and check growth and mold. After 2 weeks the jar should only be opened and checked 1-2 times a week. Treating good quality cannabis is like aging exquisite wine. It takes time to develop that intensity of flavor. It takes time to achieve that rich, lingering flavor. It takes time to reach that refined and complex philosophical height. Surprise yourself and your friends; give yourself plenty of time to dry and process your cannabis.

DRYING

After harvesting, the inflorescences must be dried before they can be used. Drying converts THC from the raw, non-psychoactive acid form to the neutral and psychoactive form. In other words, green and fresh marijuana will not be very potent. Drying also converts at least 75% of the freshly harvested plant into water vapor and other gases. When cutting a plant or a part of it and hanging it up to dry, the transport of fluids inside the plant continues, albeit at a slower pace. Since the stomata close almost immediately after harvest, obstructing the escape of water vapor, drying is slower. The natural processes of the plant stop slowly as the plant dries up. The outer cells are the first to dry out, although fluid continues to flow from the inner cells to supply liquid to the outer, dry ones. When this process takes place correctly, the plants dry out evenly in each point. Eliminating large leaves and thick branches at the time of harvest can reduce times, however uneven levels of humidity remain in the tops, leaves and "dry" branches.

When the buds are dried too quickly, starch and nitrates, as well as chlorophyll and other pigments get trapped in the plant tissues, giving a "green" taste and an unpleasant taste to a "ganja" which, moreover, will burn badly. When it is dried slowly, over five or seven days, the moisture evaporates uniformly in the air, giving homogeneously dried florets, with a minimum loss of THC. The buds dried in this way have a sweet taste and are soft to smoke. The flavor and aroma improve with the decomposition of the pigments. Slow and uniform drying - the same in the branches, in the foliage and in the tops - leaves sufficient time for the pigments to deteriorate. If you hang whole plants to dry, you allow this process to take place gradually over time. To speed up drying times, remove the leaves and the largest branches at harvest time. When the leaves are fresh and supple, it is easier to work with them.

Plants with still intact "fan-shaped" outer leaves take longer to dry and require much longer topping. The outer leaves, if left intact, form a sheath that helps protect the delicate trichomes during drying, although using this method the cut of the dry leaves doubles and becomes uncomfortable and messy. The fans and extractors for the exchange and movement of the air serve to keep heat and humidity at bay, keeping them at acceptable levels. To further limit humidity you can also use a dehumidifier. An air conditioner is ideal for setting the temperature and humidity in hot climates. In large drying rooms, it will sometimes be necessary to heat to reduce humidity and increase the temperature. Do not direct the fans directly onto the plants: they would cause uneven drying.

The ideal room temperature is between 18 and 24C, with humidity between 45 and 55%. Temperatures below 18C stop drying and often cause humidity to rise, which exceeding 80% prolongs the duration of the process and increases the risk of mold. Temperatures above 24C could cause the buds to dry excessively quickly and the humidity would drop below the ideal level of 50%. Those that go above 29C cause the buds to dry so quickly that they end up in a harsh, bitter smoke.

With a relative humidity of less than 30-40%, the buds dry out too quickly, keeping the chlorophyll inside, which leaves a "green" taste. In addition, the quickly dried buds crumble easily and remain crumbly. Too little humidity also causes a loss of flavor and fragrance. If the humidity is between 30 and 40%, the movement of the air must be minimized to slow down drying. A thermometer with minimum / maximum function and a hygrometer as accurate as possible must always be used, to ensure that the temperature and humidity parameters are preserved in terms of an ideal excursion.

Small crops can be placed to dry in a wardrobe, bedside table or cardboard box, proportionate to the size of the cultivated area. Larger harvests require more space: if there is no place to dry, you can decide to plant in stacks, or you can plant both early and late flowering varieties, in order to produce a staggered harvest, which leaves some free space. as the buds dry out.

To dry large crops outdoors and indoors, you need spacious rooms. You could use the growing area as a drying room if it is not being used for its original purpose in the meantime. While it is not recommended to dry the plants in the same indoor room used to grow them: you need different climates to cultivate, and to dry. Mushrooms and red spider mites could breed, migrating from dead plants to living ones. It is necessary to inspect the buds that dry every day to identify any traces of problems, such as mold or fungus, or red spiders.

A cardboard or wooden box turns out to be an ideal dryer in which to hang small crops. The flow of air within the confined space is obstructed and the tops and leaves must be turned daily to ensure leveling and discourage molds. To pull the threads to hang the tops, you can use dental floss passing it from one end of the box to the other. If this is not very high, the wires can be placed at different heights. Keep the box closed to protect from light, and open it daily for air exchange. Check the drying processes every day. If the buds dry out too quickly, the opened box can be placed in a cooler place.

Hanging the plants saves effort and allows for a slow and smooth process. To shorten the period by a few days, if necessary, you can remove the large and damp stems, and hang the smaller branches, using clothespins or office staples. Alternatively, you can cut the branches so that they form a hook, and thus hang them on the wire. To create a mobile and practical drying room, a portable and foldable clothesline can be used. Just open it and hang the tops on the threads, and then cover them with a black sheet or cloth, which will allow the air to pass and the tops to remain in the dark. By directing a fan towards the outer side of the sheet, the air circulates under the sheet and dries the tops.

Building a small dryer is easy, just fix plywood nails at right angles and hang wires inside the perimeter created. Alternatively, you can use a black cloth, nailed or attached to the walls with adhesive tape. To save space, on large volumes, it may be useful to use racks for buds. To make them, mosquito nets for windows or fine-mesh plastic nets are used. By spreading the rack on a wooden surface and securing it with staples, you get several drawers stackable one on top of the other. However, it is necessary to hang the cleaned buds for a couple of days, before placing them on the nets, to allow the bulk of the liquids to dissipate. Once the buds are spread on the nets, they need to be turned over daily to dry them evenly.

To check the consistency and dryness of the buds, you can gently squeeze and check for resistance; for the twigs it is sufficient to fold them to understand if they are ready: if the branch breaks instead of bending, it is ready for tanning. The top should be dry to the touch, without crumbling; when properly dried, it should burn well enough to be smoked.

Light (UV rays), heat and friction accelerate the biodegradation processes and are the worst enemies of dry or drying marijuana. It is advisable to keep dry marijuana away from heat sources; friction and clumsy and abrupt handling deteriorate the resin glands. Even if it has been dried and cured properly, it can lose THC if handled roughly.

Millions of tiny resin glands are being shattered every minute in the world, by clumsy and / or careless hands! To preserve the flawless quality cannabis, store it in an airtight glass container and place it in the refrigerator. The common preserving jars allow you to admire the peaks, as well as protect them. The glass containers impart no plastic or metal odors and retain the pungent fragrance of fresh cannabis buds.

TANNING

The tanning allows the inflorescences to continue to dry slowly. The first week of tanning affects potency, eliminating liquids from the grain evenly, so that virtually all the THC present is psychoactive. Thanks to the tanning, moreover, the flowers dry so well that they prevent the growth of mold during the subsequent storage of the buds. Well-tanned inflorescences burn making uniform embers and soft smoke. Even the plants, branches and / or inflorescences that have been dried for 5 to 7 days in a specially designed room (on nets or hung), although dry, still contain liquids. These liquids affect the flavor and power of the effect. The tanning serves to eliminate this residual moisture, allows the flower to dry evenly and converts practically all the THC into its psychoactive form. Cut the branches into manageable lengths - 30/40 cm - and place them in an airtight container.

Airtight glass containers with a rubber seal or similar are best. Avoid zip lock bags and other types of leaky plastic bags. And in general, growers try not to use plastic containers, so as not to give an unpleasant taste to the buds. However, on large quantities, containers of this kind can be useful, due to their available sizes. Closing the inflorescences in a container creates a microclimate that allows the liquids to be distributed evenly in the flowers. The humidity will move from the inside to the dry parts of the flower. Try to put as many buds as possible into a container, without forcing them and therefore damaging them. The containers should be stored in a cool, dry and dark place.

After two or four hours it is advisable to check if the buds have "oozed" moisture. In this case, proceed as follows: squeeze the florets slightly, to feel if they are wetter than a few hours before. Crush the buds carefully - the resin glands shatter easily. If, when folded, the twigs flex rather than break, with inflorescences that remain moist to the touch, remove them from the container and place them gently on the bottom of a paper bag. Up to 15 cm of tops can be stacked in the bag. To close the bag, simply fold it, and check the buds two or three times a day. Gently turn the bag over to expose all sides to drying. Return the buds to the container when they become too dry.

Check the tanning container several times a day, leaving the cap open for five or ten minutes, to evacuate the water vapor. Depending on the liquid content, the buds should be completely dry within a few days (maximum two weeks). When completely dry, they can be stored in an airtight container. To find out the approximate level of water contained in the dry buds, a bud is weighed at random after harvest, when it is not yet dry. It is weighed later during the drying and tanning phases, to know how much liquids it has lost. For example, a rope weighing ten grams per time of harvest, it will weigh two and a half grams, having lost 75% of the liquids. In general, a dry bud will weigh 75% less than its "wet" weight at harvest time.

KINDS OF CANNABIS

Cannabis has always been one of the most debated topics, starting with the distinction of the varieties commonly present in nature which, phylogenetically, are considered distinct even though they belong to the same species, thanks to the similar characteristics both under the morphological and chemical and still linked aspects to the growth and development of the plant. However, it is useful to know that cannabis varieties can vary their phenotype according to the cultivation area, the peculiarities of the soil, the climate and the altitude and although marijuana plants can be easily crossed to obtain male and female individuals, it is possible to distinguish three common types, each of which differs not only in use but also and above all in properties: we are talking about cannabis sativa, indica and ruderalis of which, through this guide, we will show all the varieties available, legal and otherwise.

Cannabis indica is traditionally considered one of the most potent marijuana strains available in nature. Mainly used for indoor and hydroponic cultivation, it can have THC levels that can easily reach and exceed a concentration of 25%, which varies according to the cultivation methodology. The plants generally take on a triangular shape similar to a conifer, maintaining small dimensions of up to 1.5m. Originally developed in the mountainous areas typical of India and Nepal, they are particularly robust and relatively simple to cultivate and able to tolerate any problems during development and growth, without suffering stresses.

Types

The seeds produce particularly dense and large inflorescences with chalices that appear massed together and the intake of these results in a bodily effect defined by a status of well-being and relaxation capable of involving the body and mind. However, the woody trunk does not make the species suitable for the textile industry but rather for use in the therapeutic field thanks to good concentration, albeit variable, of CBD or cannabidiol. Cannabis sativa generally has an approximate height of 1.5m, differing from the indica hemp species due to its significantly shorter branches.

Native to tropical areas such as the Caribbean and Thailand, it produces quite a significant number of buds and, although they appear dense and less compact, they can define a quantity even higher than 1.5Kg for each marijuana plant once dried. The effect given by its intake is mainly cerebral: it acts mainly on the mind through different states ranging from psychedelic perception to the creative state, this in relation to its power and concentration of active ingredients. Also known for the characteristics of the fibers commonly used in the textile sector, until a few years ago, it was also particularly widespread for the production of paper material. Instead, its use in the medical and therapeutic fields is limited, since cannabis sativa has a reduced THC content of around 1-2%, reaching a maximum concentration of 5% with difficulty. Cannabis ruderalis, also commonly referred to as Russian, ruderal or American hemp, unlike the varieties illustrated above, is not intended for the production of marijuana due to the reduced content of THC and CBD, in both cases irrelevant both in the medical and recreational fields.

Originally from Russia's inaccessible and inhospitable areas of Siberia, it is distinguished by the characteristic small plants which are around 0.5m, by the sturdy stem without lateral ramifications and by the presence of insignificant peaks, often even absent. Generally, its use is limited to crossings, in order to increase the strength of a new plant, making sure that it can produce inflorescences according to age as well as the hours of light available.

First of all, there is a note to be made, marijuana and cannabis are the same thing, in fact the term marijuana was coined by Mexicans to distinguish cannabis for recreational use. Marijuana is a family of plants with two primary classifications: **Sativa and Indica**.

Their aesthetic similarity makes it difficult for the less experienced to distinguish between marijuana and hemp, which are very different in their biological structure. Marijuana features broad leaves, dense buds and a short, bushy appearance. Cannabis contains a variety of different compounds called cannabinoids, the best known are certainly Tetrahydrocannabinol (THC) and Cannabidiol (CBD). Both cannabinoids have been shown to provide great benefits to the human body, however, THC induces psychoactive effects unlike CBD. In marijuana, the concentration of THC is between values ranging from 15% to 30%. The presence of Tetratidrocannabinol plays a very important role on the legality of the plant in the various countries of the world, where the permitted quantities differ from state to state. In the United States, for example, the maximum amount of THC allowed is 0.3% while in most of the rest of the world it is 0.2%, which is why cannabis is illegal in many states, while hemp is not.

HEMP

Unlike marijuana, hemp has narrow leaves that are concentrated for the most part on the upper part of the plant, which reaches considerable heights, often touching 2 meters. Hemp has a lower THC content and a higher CBD content for this reason its sale is allowed in most countries of the world.

Precisely for this reason hemp is used for industrial purposes, hence the name Industrial Hemp, in fact it can be used in various fields, such as construction, clothing, food and energy.

Cannabis, marijuana and hashish are synonymous with each other, but basically, they mean three completely different things. Let's shed some light on it, indicating what cannabis is, its derivatives and various uses.

What is cannabis?

Cannabis is a plant that has three subspecies: sativa, indica and ruderalis. It can grow to almost three meters in height and its leaves are toothed. It's one of the oldest plants, which has accompanied human civilization with different uses. The most famous uses are in the textile, pharmacological and psychotropic fields.

With cannabis, the resin is produced which can contain up to 60 cannabinoids, 100 terpenoids, 20 flavonoids. In recent years, numerous studies have been carried out, especially on cannabinoids, but the strong cultural and ethical debate influence this pharmacological research.

WHAT IS THC?

THC is the main psychoactive substance found in cannabis. When this is used, smoking it, vaporizing it or ingesting it, it interacts with different receptors located in our brain and in the rest of our body causing different effects. Some research has shown that the prolonged use of THC can cause harm, but it has also been shown that its low toxicity must be consumed in very high doses to cause harm.

In addition, research has also highlighted effects positive from the intake of THC, such as:

- Treats reactions from chemotherapy drugs;

- The reduction of symptoms of multiple sclerosis;

- Treatment of glaucoma.

WHAT IS CBD?

CBD is the second most common cannobinoid in cannabis. Cannabis rich in CBD provides therapeutic benefits without the euphoria or lethargy that TCH causes.

CBD is present in legal marijuana, which is currently available for purchase in Italian stores. CBD can help treat a variety of medical symptoms, such as:

- Chronic pain;

- Inflammation;

• Anxiety;

• Muscle spasms.

Scientific research has also proven its ability to stop the spread of breast metastases and other cancers.

CBD, as we said, is present in legal marijuana, sold in stores. Recently, the Superior Health Council has given a negative opinion on the sale of legal marijuana. But from the documents presented there are concerns about its use in conjunction with other drugs, breastfeeding or progressing states of disease.

The differences between Cannabis, Marijuana and Hashish

These three terms are usually not used appropriately. We make the difference:

• Cannabis: indicates the plant as a whole: stem, roots, leaves, flowers, without distinguishing between plants with a high THC content and those of textile use;

• Marijuana: indicates the flowers of the plant, they contain a high concentration of active ingredients. They are dried and smoked for recreational or medical purposes;

• Hashish: is a cannabis resin and pollen product that can reach high concentrations of THC and CBD

VARIOUS USES

Hemp is a plant that is back in fashion thanks to its multiple uses and a very economical and ecological culture. However, this plant suffers from the bad reputation of its little sister, cannabis. So, what are the differences between THC cannabis and CBD hemp use? What is hemp? Hemp is a cultivated plant belonging to the Cannabaceae family. Sometimes called "hemp", hemp is a so-called annual plant, meaning that it only lasts a year between germination and seed production, and which lives between four and five months.

The large size of these canes makes it a popular vegetable in many sectors and this since the Neolithic era. It is a multipurpose plant thanks to its seeds and fibers. It is also a very resistant plant to climatic dangers and diseases. It requires little energy and water, which is an ecological advantage. It is also a very effective plant for preparing the earth for other crops: it suffocates weeds, purifies and aerates the earth thanks to its deep roots. Today hemp is recognized as the all-purpose plant and this sustainable sector creates jobs.

Hemp is therefore used for the manufacture of fabrics and ropes, the cosmetic industry, the production of oil, construction, stationery, animal feeding. It is a plant that is also consumed in human food in the form of oil or seeds. These products are appreciated for their many nutritional benefits. Rich in minerals, vitamins and fiber, they are excellent for arterial health and for lowering cholesterol levels. It is also a very popular plant in the cosmetic industry due to its moisturizing and soothing properties.

Hemp and cannabis: what's the difference? Hemp is often confused with cannabis. However, hemp has a low THC content. Botanists and industrialists also make a distinction between hemp as a plant fiber and cannabis, which designates the psychotropic substance. The regulations on the use of cannabis hemp date back to the 19th century. The United Nations (UN) established the "Single Convention on Narcotic Drugs", the first in a long series to ban the use of cannabis. The difference between the term "hemp" and "cannabis" therefore derives from the content of THC (delta-tetrahydrocannabinol) and CBD (cannabidiol). A plant with a high concentration of THC, a potent psychotropic agent, will be called "cannabis".

The plant containing a high level of CBD will be called "hemp". Hemp Cannabis, also known as Indian hemp, is native to Central Asia. It is a plant grown in tropical regions. Cannabis is therefore known by over 350 different names around the world. It is also one of the most widely used drugs on the surface of the globe. According to the United Nations, over 20% of the adult European population has already used cannabis in their lifetime. Cannabis use, whether smoked, inhaled or injected, seems completely and increasingly uninhibited, despite very strict legislation. So, the big difference between what is called "hemp" and what is commonly called "cannabis", but also "marijuana", "hashish" or "weed" comes from the THC content. THC is the substance responsible for the psychotropic effects of cannabis.

This substance was isolated in 1964 and its effects on the brain were quickly updated: modification of the brain rhythm, modification of neuronal activity, action on the psyche, behavioral change. It takes from 26 to 36 hours to eliminate the substance from our body but some traces are detectable up to a month after consumption. The negative effects of THC are undeniable and can be serious: memory, coordination, reasoning disturbance, tachycardia. In high doses or with regular consumption, THC kills neurons.

Likewise, THC causes the secretion of the feel-good hormone dopamine, which gradually leads to addiction and addiction. Cannabis also contains several volatile components, responsible for its typical and easily recognizable smell: monoterpenes and sesquiterpenes. These are the components that police dogs are trained to recognize. Today, several seed companies genetically select hemp plants to minimize their THC content, preferring plants rich in another molecule: CBD.

Hemp and CBD

Another of the substances in the use of hemp is CBD, or cannabidiol. This molecule is the same whether we are talking about hemp (the plant) or cannabis (the plant used as a drug).

The big difference with THC is that CBD is not psychoactive. On the contrary, it acts against THC and its effects. This health-promoting substance, unlike THC, has been known for thousands of years in many countries for anti-inflammatory effects, relaxing and soothing effects, sleep aids and many more. To learn more, you can read our chapter on CBD and its benefits.

CBD is 100% natural and occurs naturally in hemp, more particularly in viscous resin. With CBD, there is no risk of being "stoned" or having trouble with the law. CBD hemp contains only 0.3% THC,

USES OF CANNABIS

The best-known uses of cannabis sativa are of an illegal nature or otherwise for recreational activities. Few people know that hemp is a plant with infinite properties, known for its most diversified uses but demonized by many.

Let's find out what are the most common uses of cannabis sativa, to make us re-evaluate the properties of this wonderful plant

The uses of cannabis sativa in the food industry are many. Starting from the plant we can obtain edible seeds, flours, oils and subsequent processing such as high protein pasta or bread. These products, generally distributed by organic brands, are naturally THC-free and therefore do not carry any hallucinogenic effects.

On the contrary, they are foods with excellent nutritional values, rich in B vitamins, provitamin A and vitamin E, a powerful natural antioxidant. Hemp oil is also rich in omega3 and omega6 fats, optimal for reducing cholesterol and improving our heart efficiency.

Another industry that has been able to exploit sativa marijuana in an optimal way has been the cosmetics industry. Among the uses of cannabis sativa, we find that of an ingredient for personal care, treating the skin thanks to the vitamins and anti-oxidants in which it is rich.

Cannabis creams generally perform an anti-wrinkle, regenerative and nourishing action, perfect for giving new life to the driest and most mature skin. With its complex vitamins and natural antioxidants, some cosmetic companies have harnessed the power of this plant to produce organic cosmetics with 100% natural ingredients.

Hemp seeds are an extremely nutritious and complete food because they contain all eight essential amino acids, the same ones that the body cannot synthesize independently and which must therefore be introduced through food. In addition, they are composed of 25% protein and also contain minerals and vitamins.

Extremely easy to digest, they are often recommended by doctors to people with difficulty in assimilating food. From hemp seeds it is possible to obtain precious flours or hemp oil, which has excellent properties because it strengthens the immune system, protects the cardiovascular system and lowers cholesterol levels, providing the body with essential fatty acids and, as we have already said, proteins and vitamins A, E, and B. Hemp seeds and derivatives are perfect for those who adopt a vegetarian or vegan diet. In the textile sector, the long fiber of the hemp plant is mainly used as a replacement for cotton and synthetic fibers. Its advantages are different: first of all, its cultivation requires few pesticides and fertilizers, unlike cotton which requires a lot of them and is considered one of the most polluting crops on the planet. Then, the fabric made from hemp remains cool in summer and warm in winter, it is extremely resistant to tearing and wear and has various antibacterial and antifungal properties.

With the tow and the woody part of hemp, or the waste resulting from the extraction of seeds and fiber to make fabrics, it is possible to produce thin and resistant paper, of high quality but also for daily use. The really positive factor of hemp paper is that the plant is not cultivated specifically, but the waste from extractions for other productions is recovered from it. The advantage is economic and environmental, since the cellulose present in one hectare of hemp is equivalent to that present in 4 hectares of forest.

Furthermore, the chemicals to be used for the treatment are very few. The use of hemp to produce paper dates back thousands of years. Suffice it to consider that Gutenberg's Bible was printed on this type of paper, as well as the originals of the American and French Constitution. Thanks to the content of tocopherols, omega 3 and 6, and the presence of y-linoleic acid, hemp has excellent natural antioxidant properties, which make it perfect as a favorite ingredient for certain cosmetics. In addition, this plant fights premature aging thanks to vitamin E, it also has anti-inflammatory and regenerative properties.

DEEPENING

In the second half of the last century, its main active principle consisting of delta-9-tetrahydrocannabinol was identified and, subsequently, receptors and endogenous ligands called endocannabinoids were identified. The effect of cannabinoids, the active ingredients of cannabis, has long been recognized in the wasting syndrome in AIDS, as well as in the treatment of nausea and vomiting during chemotherapy for cancer. Furthermore, cannabinoids possess analgesic properties, particularly interesting as regards especially central neuropathic pain. The chapter examines current knowledge on the subject and sets out the practical indications and procedures for prescribing cannabinoid drugs.

NEUROPATHIC PAIN

Neuropathic pain can be caused by an injury or disease of the somatosensory system and is estimated to affect up to 7-8% of the European population. The most recent systematic review of epidemiological studies reports an estimate of the prevalence of pain with neuropathic features between 6.9 and 10 percent. It is considered one of the most difficult chronic pains to treat and with a devastating impact on psychological well-being, social life and other aspects related to quality of life. Neuropathic pain can originate from lesions of the peripheral nervous system, from toxic insults and from diseases, and can be considered a maladaptive response"... in the sense that pain neither protects nor promotes healing". The therapeutic approach remains a significant problem, as this pain responds poorly to current therapies. In randomized clinical trials, no more than half of patients respond significantly to pharmacotherapy, considering that partial pain relief is defined as successful, and the response to many drugs is not predictable, moreover side effects can limit the dosage and contribute inadequate symptom reduction.

The nervous system can be damaged both peripherally and centrally. Central pain may be due to lesion of the somatic pathways in the spinal cord, brain stem, thalamus or other brain structures, and it is generally believed that the lesion must involve the spino-thalamo-cortical pathways; any pathology affecting these structures can be at the origin of central pain.

Damage to the central nervous system (CNS) can be due to trauma to the spinal cord, such as a cross section, but the cord could also be affected by compression, siringomyelia, vascular lesions, tumors and multiple sclerosis (MS). Similar lesions can be found at the brainstem level, such as the Dejerine-Roussy thalamic syndrome, due to ischemic or hemorrhagic insults in the thalamus. Other causes of central pain are Parkinson's disease, HIV infection and iatrogenic causes (post-actinic myelopathy and nervous system interventions such as chordotomies).

In particular, patients with multiple sclerosis frequently suffer from acute pain than chronic, which was considered the most common symptom, with a prevalence that reaches, according to recent estimates, 83 percent. It is responsible for a large part of their handicap and is sometimes the main cause of the interruption of their professional activity.

The causes of pain are difficult to differentiate, but certain types of pain are common, such as trigeminal neuralgia, present in 5 percent of patients, and spasticity in 50 percent. More than half of the pains seen in patients with multiple sclerosis are neurological, with dysesthesia, painful trigeminal anesthesia, burning sensations in the limbs and trunk, electric shocks and twitches. In less than one out of five cases, the pain occurs during an access and regresses with the treatment of the latter.

Mostly the pain of the central type is persistent, evolves independently of the seizures and is often accompanied by other subjective disturbances of sensitivity (paraesthesia) and more rarely by a sensory deficit. It has also been reported that the incidence and prevalence of central neuropathic pain reaches 8-10 percent of patients affected by cerebral ischemic-haemorrhagic events at the thalamic level, 30 percent of patients with multiple sclerosis and up to 30-60 per cent of myelopic sufferers.

CANNABIS AND CANNABINOIDS

Hemp, in Latin "Cannabis sativa" is a plant that belongs to the order Urticales, Cannabaceae family. The name derives from the Assyrian qunnubu or qunnabu. Botanists have established that there is only one species of Cannabis, as no decisive variations have been found between the various types, and thus eliminating Cannabis indica from the classification, a variety that contains in greater quantities active principles. In Europe, the spread of Cannabis dates back to the nineteenth century, on the occasion of Napoleon's military campaigns in Egypt.

The first studies date back to 1839: O'Shaughnessy, an Irish doctor, administered cannabis to subjects suffering from various diseases, from epilepsy to rheumatism, finding an anticonvulsant, analgesic, antiemetic efficacy.

During the nineteenth century and in the first decades of the twentieth century, cannabis was a medicine of common use in clinical practice, even in Italy, until the availability of other types of treatment (the active ingredients had not yet been discovered and there could be no standardization of the basic drug or of the extracts) and, "importantly, the socio-political pressure", did not lead to its decline. Still in 1962 Benigni and collaborators, in their historic treatise on phytotherapy, wrote: "Its therapeutic uses are mainly related to the analgesic action of this drug, an action very similar to that of opium of which Indian hemp can be considered a substitute".

Shortly thereafter, in 1964, the Israeli group led by R. Mechoulam isolated the most important active principle of the plant, laying the foundations for its scientific re-evaluation. In the late 1990s, one of the fathers of pain therapy, Patrick Wall, wrote: "This is another herbal remedy with a very bad reputation. But today it is undergoing an incredible re-evaluation as a therapeutic analgesic that repeats after twenty years the history of the passage of opiates from drugs considered a social danger to therapeutic tools with a scientific basis".

Active principles

The Cannabis sativa plant contains hundreds of substances with various chemical structures. Of these, up to now, about 66 compounds belonging to the cannabinoid family have been identified, united by a particular structure of 21 carbon atoms, grouped into a chemical class, that of terpenoids, aromatic hydrocarbons containing oxygen, non-polar and with low solubility in water. Delta 9-tetrahydrocannabinol, " δ9-THC " was isolated as the active ingredient in Cannabis in 1964.

Research into its potential use in the medical field has recognized it as being primarily responsible for the plant's pharmacological properties, although other compounds contribute to some of these effects, in particular cannabidiol, devoid of psychoactive effects, but with antipsychotic, analgesic and anti-inflammatory activity. When THC is co-administered with CBD there is a reduction in anxiogenic, dysphoric effects and potential effects on memory.

ENDOGENOUS RECEPTORS AND CANNABINOIDS

The brain receptor for cannabinoids, called CB1, is found mainly, but not exclusively, in the central and peripheral nervous system, in parallel with the brain structures, whose implementation justifies many of the effects of cannabinoids. They are also present in some organs and tissues, including endocrine glands, reproductive, urinary, and gastrointestinal systems. Subsequently, the CB2 receptor on immunocompetent cells was identified. Its distribution is central and peripheral, in particular in the cells of the intestine, liver, spleen, tonsils, lymphocytes and monocytes and in particular in mast cells. The discovery of these receptors followed, in 1992, the identification of endogenous substances "binding" to these receptors, called endocannabinoids. This term, which was coined by Italian researchers in 1995, identifies a new class of neuromediators united by the ability to interact with cannabinoid receptors.

These endocannabinoids are derived from arachidonic acid, a polyunsaturated membrane fatty acid. The endocanna-binoids identified so far are seven, of which the most important are anandamide (N-arachidonoil ethanola-mide "AEA") which owes its name to the Sanskrit word "Ananda", which means "state of grace", and 2-

arachidonoyl glycerol "2-AG". The AEA not only binds to the CB1 and CB2 receptors, but it also acts on the vanilloid receptor "PV1".

Endocannabinoids, unlike other chemical mediators, are not produced and stored in the micro vesicles, but are produced "on demand" by their predecessors and then released from the post-synaptic side, reaching the pre-synaptic where they activate the receptors. They then mediate a retrograde signal from the postsynaptic to the pre-synaptic. After their release, they are rapidly deactivated by uptake in cells and metabolized. The activation of CB1 receptors leads to a retrograde inhibition of the release of histamine, serotonin, glutamate, acetylcholine, dopamine, GABA, cholecystokinin, D-aspartate, glycine and noradrenaline.

These complex interactions explain not only the large number of physiological actions of cannabinoids, but also the pharmacological effects of cannabis preparations.

Pharmacology of cannabinoid receptors It has been noted that, interestingly, our first knowledge on the pain system came from research on analgesic substances derived from plants, namely opium (Papaver somniferum) as regards morphine, chilli (Capsicum annuum, C. frutescens, C. chinensis) for capsaicin, willow (Salix spp.) for salicylic acid, and cannabis for THC, CBD and other cannabinoids. The antinociceptive properties of cannabinoids have been demonstrated in various animal model acute pain, for example using thermal, chemical, mechanical, and visceral stimuli. Chronic ligation injuries, partial sciatic ligation, spinal nerve ligation, and other forms of experimental injury have been studied. In addition, they have also been shown to be effective in both chronic inflammatory and neuropathic pain. Cannabinoids have been shown to inhibit pain "potentially in any paradigm of experimental pain" in the supraspinal, spinal and peripheral sites.

The areas of the CNS responsible for pain control are very rich in cannabinoid receptors and the stimulation of these receptors activates a circuit that reduces pain. CB1 receptors have been identified on three structures: primary afferent neurons and on type fibers C than on type one S.

Aß / d, dorsal root ganglia, spinal and terminal intrinsic neurons (in the dorsolateral funiculus, in the dorsal horn and at the level of the lamina X '), and neurons that project to the brain (ventro-medial rostral medulla, periaqueductal gray matter, amygdala and thalamus). The cannabinoid-induced antinociception acts on the various levels of the pain sensory pathway by activating the antinociceptive pathways. At the spinal level, the analgesic effect of cannabinoids appears to be obtained from the activation of the opioid k receptor. In fact, the analgesic effect is canceled both by the intrathecal administration of a k-receptor antagonist and by the antiserum for the k-receptor.

Again, at the spinal level, cannabinoids block the expression of c-fos in response to noxious stimuli, act on wind-up mechanisms and reduce hyperalgesia through inhibition of the calcitonin gene-related peptide.

The periaqueductal gray matter PAG is one of the area's most heavily involved in mediating cannabinoid analgesia. This may be due in part to the direct inhibition of GABA release in the PAG and bone marrow, in part it may be related to the inhibition of glutamate release. In fact, the hyperalgesia induced by the CB1 antagonist is attenuated by the administration of NMDA receptor antagonists. In the ventral-posterolateral nucleus of the thalamus, cannabinoids are ten times more active than morphine on wide-dynamic range neurons involved in pain; the CB1 receptor system is tonic and its activity increases in response to noxious stimuli.

A cannabinoid-activated mesencephalic circuit has been shown to reduce pain sensation in the ventromedial rostral medulla (RVM). In fact, inactivation of this region prevents cannabinoid analgesia. Cannabinoid-induced antinociception at the level of the descending pathway may be related, at least in part, to the release of noradrenaline. it has been shown that the antinociceptive effect can be attenuated by yohimbine administration, but is not affected by methysergide. Another cannabinoid-induced analgesic mechanism is mediated by the action of dopamine on D2 receptors being potentiated by agonists and attenuated by selective antagonists.

The endocannabinoid system is also involved in stress analgesia. In addition, the cannabinoid and opioid systems exhibit receptor-mediated synergism at the spinal and supraspinal levels. As discussed, at the spinal level, cannabinoids activate k receptors while opioids activate the µ and d receptors. At the supraspinal level, synergism occurs by activation of the µ receptors, indicating that morphine analgesia, which is mainly mediated by the µ receptor, can be increased by cannabinoids through the activation of the k receptors.

The use of cannabinoids has been shown to reduce the need for morphine. THC is able to reduce the minimum effective dose (ED50) of morphine by 55%, methadone by 75% and codeine by 96%. CB1 receptors are 10 times more frequent in the CNS than the more studied receptors involved in pain, the opioid receptors μ. An advantage of cannabinoids is that their specific receptors, unlike those of morphine, are absent in the areas of the brain that control breathing, so there is no risk of respiratory depression.

Unlike opioids, cannabinoids do not lose their efficacy in the treatment of neuropathic pain as fewer receptors disappear in this situation (destruction of primary afferent fibers with rhizotomy or with neonatal administration of capsaicin reduces the expression of CB1 receptors less than those opioids).

Conversely, there is less expression of opioid receptors in the posterior horns. Cannabinoids are also involved in the system of immune and inflammatory responses, which can act on neurogenic inflammation by inhibiting the secretion of substance P and activating the vanilloid receptor (VP1) of the terminals of both central and peripheral afferent fibers. Endocannabinoids are also related to the cyclooxygenase system; anandamide and 2-acyl glycerol are in fact metabolised by COX-2 to give rise to pro-inflammatory prostanoids, although the predominant pathway of metabolism is that of Fatty Acid Amide Hydrolase (FAAH). In the course of inflammation there is an increase in COX-2 activity, which can therefore lead to a reduction in endocannabinoid tone, and COX-2 inhibitors could reduce pain also thanks to the reduction of the transformation of antinocycetal endocannabinoids into prostanoids. nociceptives. The endocannabinoid system is also active in the periphery, where stimulation of CB1 reduces pain, inflammation and hyperalgesia.

Cannabinoids have recently been seen to have a greater effect on neuropathic pain. In animal models of neuropathic pain there is an up-regulation of CB1 receptors in the nerve structures involved in pain processing such as the surface of the ipsilateral dorsal horns or the contralateral thalamus, thus increasing the analgesic effects of cannabinoid receptor agonists. The upregulation of central CB1 receptors after nerve injury indicates a role of these in these pathologies and also explains the effects of cannabinoid receptor agonists on chronic neuropathic pain. It is hypothesized that Ad fibers are more involved in neuropathic pain, which are myelinated, of small caliber, connected to the mechanoreceptors involved in the transmission of tactile sensation to pressure and present only in the skin. On the Ad fibers there is one predominance of cannabinoid receptors over opioid receptors prevalent in C-fibers. This may partly explain the greater potency of cannabinoids in the treatment of neuropathic pain. Furthermore, the pathways used in cannabinoid-mediated analgesia at the local level dorsal roots are different from those characterized by μ-opioid-mediated analgesia, and this may explain why cannabinoid receptor agonists remain effective, unlike morphine, in animal models of neuropathic pain. CB2 receptors are present on the microglia, a population of macrophage cells found in the CNS that are functionally and anatomically similar to mast cells.

Microglia secretes pro-inflammatory factors and induces the release of various mediators (such as nitric oxide, neurotropic, free radicals) which are associated with the formation of new synapses and in neuronal plasticity. During the development of chronic neuropathic pain, the number of CB2 receptors on the microglia increases, a sign that the cells are trying to capture as much cannabinoids as possible in the vicinity for pain relief.

Microglia appear to be involved in the development of neuropathic pain through the release of several cytokines, which are known to produce sensitization at the spinal level. Interestingly, stimulation of CB2 receptors attenuates activation of microglia, and release of cytokines from activated microglia. Accordingly, CB2 agonists induce analgesic effects in neuropathic pain models and experimentally reduce microglia activation in neuropathic pain. Laboratory data demonstrate the crucial role of CB2 cannabinoid receptors in regulating central immune responses during this pain.

Cannabinoids have shown greater therapeutic potential than opioids in treating diabetic neuropathy. Delta-9 THC showed increased antinociceptive therapeutic efficacy in diabetic rats, where morphine had reduced efficacy; furthermore, a non-nociceptive dose of delta-9-THC, administered alongside morphine, increased the antinoycective properties of morphine in both diabetic and naive mice. A recent functional brain imaging study in volunteers investigated how THC influences capsaicin-induced hyperalgesia. The study suggests that "peripheral mechanisms alone do not account for the dissociative effects of THC on pain that have been observed. Instead, the data reveal that the activity of the amygdala contributes to the response ... and suggests that the dissociative effects of THC on the brain are important in pain relief in humans ".

In other words, cannabinoids, and THC in particular, can have differential effects on sensory components (such as intensity and quality) from the affective (unpleasantness, suffering) of the pain. An alternative approach to exploit the therapeutic potential of cannabinoids is to maximize the effect of endocannabinoids, the action of which is interrupted by re-uptake and metabolism by various enzymes, such as Fatty Acid Amide Hydrolase (FAAH), monoacylglycerol lipase (MAGL), and type 2 cyclooxygenase (COX2). Preventing metabolism or uptake of endocannabinoids increases the concentration of these compounds in the tissues and has produced analgesia in experimental pain models. Future selective agonists for peripheral CB1 and CB2 receptors could reduce central psychoactive effects. Research on the endocannabinoid system has recently evolved towards the concept of "endocannabinoidoma", ie a complex system that includes other mediators similar to endocannabinoids and their often redundant metabolic enzymes and "promiscuous" molecular targets. This peculiar complexity of the endocannabinoid system has not discouraged efforts aimed at its pharmacological manipulation which, however, seems to require the development of multitarget drugs, or the re-examination of natural compounds with more than one mechanism of action.

In fact, these molecules, compared to "magic bullets", seem to offer advantages in modulating the "endocannabinoidoma" in safer and therapeutically effective ways. As it was written "the history of the pharmaceutical industry of the twentieth century ... it was the history of highly targeted single molecules based particularly on the goal of obtaining a" clean "drug profile, thus reducing side effects and improving the risk/benefit ratio. This holy grail has not yet been achieved at the moment.

Adverse drug reactions are the fourth leading cause of death in the US and cause around 25,000 deaths per year in the UK ... Our response to this paradox is to still consider plant extracts as drugs, whereas extracts from these plants have a long history of popular use with apparent low risk of serious adverse effects. Cannabinoids provide an excellent example that this approach is combined with the regulatory authorities' demands for high quality standards". The re-evaluation of the concept of synergy as developed in herbal medicine (the interaction between the different components, with enhancement of beneficial effects and attenuation of undesirable effects) and of which cannabis is a typical example.

In fact, in addition to THC and CBD, other phytocannabinoids can contribute to the activity. Entourage effect is the term used to describe the increase in efficacy, with improvement of the therapeutic effect, derived by combining phytocannabinoids and other molecules deriving from plants. Cannabichromene, the third most important cannabinoid in cannabis, has an analgesic effect as well as cannabigerol, but terpenoids, such as myrcene, which has an analgesic effect, blocked, unlike cannabinoids, can contribute naloxone. Terpenes may also help mitigate the side effects of THC.

Interesting research has recently shown the action of ß-caryophyllene, one of the major components of the essential oil of cannabis, and which has proved to be anti-inflammatory, selective CB2 agonist and experimentally able to act on neuropathic pain. Hence, cannabis produces at least two entirely chemically different substances capable of acting on CB2 receptors

Flavonoids can also contribute to the analgesic action.

Endocannabinoid system, neuroinflammation and neurodegeneration

In addition to the symptomatic level, it has been hypothesized that cannabinoids may also affect the mechanisms of neuroinflammation and neurodegeneration at the basis of diseases such as multiple sclerosis or amyotrophic lateral sclerosis. There is now evidence that classic neuroinflammatory diseases, such as multiple sclerosis, have neurodegenerative aspects, while classic degenerative disorders such as Alzheimer's, Parkinson's and amyotrophic lateral sclerosis also have inflammatory aspects.

Endogenous and exogenous cannabinoids regulate the function of the immune system by limiting immune responses. Conversely, cannabinoids protect the integrity and neuronal function by preventing excitotoxic damage. There is increasing evidence that the endocannabinoid system is involved in both the inflammatory and degenerative processes typical of these pathological conditions, and not only plays a modulator role in pathological processes, but is also altered by the same diseases.

The effects of CB1 receptors are greater on neuroprotection, while those of CB2 receptors are more important on modulation of the immune response, although there may be potential overlap as well as a non-CB1/CB2 mediated mechanism. Thus, agents capable of modulating cannabinoid receptors or endocannabinoids provide promising therapeutic opportunities in the treatment of inflammatory and CNS disorders.

Cannabis, marijuana, hemp? When it comes to "weed", we often tend to get confused. A plant native to Central Asia, cannabis, also known as hemp, produces real marijuana thanks to its dried female inflorescences. In nature there are different varieties of hemp containing in varying proportions different psychoactive substances, narcotic and non-narcotic. The main active ingredient that causes brain alterations is THC (delta-9-tetrahydrocannabinol) contained in the golden resin released by the inflorescences of the plant. Among the 60 cannabinoids present in Cannabis, in addition to CDB or also called Cannabidiol, THC is the principal present in greater quantities. It is able to bind, once taken and in a very specific way, to receptors present on the surface of the cells present in our organism called CB1 and CB2. These receptors allow the substance to reach the spine, lungs, kidneys, brain, central nervous system and immune system. The receptors stimulated by THC in turn naturally produce endocannabinoids, substances involved in various physiological processes.

The benefits of cannabinoids

There are several debates today about the use of cannabis: can it become a fundamental medical aid or a gateway that leads to the abuse of this substance? Two positions in stark contrast. There is no doubt, however, that THC and CDB have many therapeutic benefits and a pharmacological efficacy now proven by universally shared studies. In fact, if used responsibly, cannabinoids become effective methods to soothe the symptoms of various diseases. While tetraidocannabidiol, responsible for the psychoactive effects of cannabis, has pain-relieving, anti-blood, and appetite-stimulating effects, cannabidiol has analgesic, anti-epileptic, anti-psychotic and anxiolytic effects.

When can medical cannabis be useful?

The pathologies on which the administration of cannabinoids has reported great improvements are many. In pain therapy (neuropathic and oncological) in which opioid treatment, cortisone and non-steroidal anti-inflammatory drugs have proved ineffective, THC has become a viable solution to relieve pain. In fact, several studies have shown that THC is able to block pain signals that reach the brain thanks to their ability to alter the central nervous system. The analgesic effect of cannabis also helps relieve pain in individuals with multiple sclerosis or spinal cord injuries thanks to the potential of THC to block the breakdown of neural connections that lead to worsening of the disease.

The effects of cannabis intake in subjects suffering from anorexia, cachexia, cancer patients and AIDS patients are also evident. The drug allowed them to improve their appetite and proved to be a consistent aid in weight loss.

Contraindications: not recommended for young people and adolescents, more prone to mental alterations, for those suffering from cardio-pulmonary disorders, renal or hepatic insufficiency, for those suffering from mental disorders or familiar with schizophrenia.

Furthermore, if you are already taking drugs with sedative, antidepressant or psychoactive effects, cannabis is not recommended because it could aggravate the effects. Finally, it is forbidden for women planning a pregnancy, pregnant or breastfeeding. If prescribed, the patient should avoid driving or operating machinery: the reaction time is reduced and the concentration is lowered. It is also likely that it will test positive for doping tests and the controls required by the highway code.

Who can access therapeutic cannabis? Cannabis can be prescribed, with responsibility and compliance with current regulations, in all those patients suffering from the aforementioned diseases. The drug can also be prescribed in cases of post-operative pain, lupus erythematosus, chronic inflammatory bowel diseases such as Crohn's disease, psoriasis, fibromyalgia and low back pain, post-traumatic stress disorder caused by a particular type of memory that tends to reliving, glaucoma, sleep disorders and Alzheimer's patients.

Methods of intake and dosage of medical cannabis.

The assumption of the cannabinoids present in the plant, can be carried out by means of vaporization, topically, by inhalation or orally. The choice depends on the pharmaceutical formulation and the desired effect. In any case, in order for the substances present in the plant to be activated, they must undergo a chemical process called "decarboxylation", that is a chemical reaction that involves the molecules and in which the latter are brought to a temperature of over 100 degrees centigrade. As for the dosage for therapeutic use, the amount varies from person to person.

The dosage must necessarily be established by the doctor and varies from a minimum of 1 gram to a maximum of 5 grams per day.

Hemp (Cannabis sativa) represents a fundamental natural resource unfortunately excessively underestimated worldwide and overshadowed by the prohibition period which severely limited its cultivation even in Italy, a country where hemp plantations were flourishing. When we talk about hemp we immediately think of marijuana, but few know that this plant, so versatile in many cases, can perfectly replace oil, for example as regards the production of fuels and plastics, as well as representing at the same time an alternative, ecological cotton for the production of textile fibers, a food resource not to be underestimated and a raw material suitable for the manufacture of paper and building materials. We therefore wish to contribute to the dissemination of knowledge of its possible uses:

1.   **Food: Hemp seeds.**

Hemp seeds are considered a surprisingly nutritious food, rich in polyunsaturated fatty acids considered essential for the functioning of muscles and nerve receptors, such as linolenic, linoleic and alpha-linoleic acids. THC-free hemp seeds (the substance considered a drug) contain all the amino acids considered essential for the synthesis of proteins by our body. They represent an aid in the prevention of high cholesterol, asthma, sinusitis, arthrosis, tracheitis and diseases related to the cardiovascular system. Two additional foods can be obtained from hemp seeds: hemp oil and hemp tofu. In Italy, companies that produce hemp-based foods are beginning to resurface.

2.   Food: Hemp oil.

Hemp oil is obtained from cold-pressed hemp seeds, a valuable natural supplement to be used preferably raw for seasoning food. Just like the seeds themselves, hemp oil is rich in polyunsaturated fats considered beneficial for the proper functioning of the body, with particular reference to the cardiovascular system. It is rich in vitamins A, B, and E and has a pleasant flavor reminiscent of hazelnuts.

3.   Remediation.

Hemp plants can be used for the remediation of soils contaminated with heavy metals through a process called "phytoremediation". Hemp is considered particularly suitable for this purpose, as, through its root system, it is able to carry out its effective chelating capacity against contaminants such as arsenic and copper, as well as solvents and pesticides. It is used for soil remediation processes with particular reference to areas degraded and abandoned, allowing operation through an inexpensive methodology. Currently, the use of hemp for land reclamation is in an experimental phase in Italy.

4.   Fabrics.

The hemp plant is considered more productive than cotton in terms of textile fibers. Furthermore, compared to the cultivation of cotton, the cultivation of hemp requires a much lower use of pesticides and fertilizers. We recall that cotton represents one of the crops with textile purposes with the greatest environmental impact, both for the extensive use of pesticides and for the use of water resources. Resistant yarns are obtained from hemp that can be used for the production of fabrics intended for the production of textile products, accessories and clothing.

5.   Tables.

Hemp can be considered as an important substitute for wood in the construction and carpentry sectors. From hemp it is in fact possible to produce sturdy and resistant boards that can replace common wooden boards. The hemp boards are obtained by using the entire stems of this plant, which are pressed and assembled with the aid of glue. In this way lighter and more flexible boards can be obtained than wooden boards.

6.   Green building.

Hemp is increasingly used in construction as a substitute for concrete and bricks. An all-Italian example is biomattone capable of absorbing Co2. It is a type of brick designed to capture the carbon dioxide emissions that reach the atmosphere and to ensure at the same time an excellent thermal and acoustic insulation, in order to achieve the possibility of building a healthy environment in which to live, also thanks to the complete vapor permeability of the brick itself, able to guarantee excellent living comfort and to represent an innovative tool for green building, both in the construction of new buildings and in the renovation of what already exists.

7.   Plastics.

Especially as regards the production of plastics, hemp can be considered as a concrete alternative to the use of oil, in order to initiate a detachment from dependence on it. The cellulose contained in the plant makes it possible to obtain degradable plastic materials that can be used for the production of packaging and materials to be used with an insulating function.

8. Fuels.

Another important area for which hemp can be considered as a real substitute for oil is the production of biomass fuels. In fact, using hemp as a starting material for combustion would not increase the quantities of CO_2 released into the atmosphere, as the emission of carbon dioxide during combustion would be counterbalanced by the quantity of CO_2 absorbed by the hemp itself during the cultivation of the related plants.

9. Card.

From the tow and the woody part of the hemp left after the extraction of the textile fiber or the seeds, it is possible to manufacture both high quality paper and paper of common use, usable for example for printing newspapers and for production of cartons. The major advantage related to the production of paper starting from hemp is the fact that for its realization it is possible to use the "waste" of a single hemp crop designed for the production of seeds or textile fibers.

10. Mulch.

The chipboard hemp stem can be used to carry out an operation often considered of fundamental importance in agriculture and gardening. This is mulch. It is carried out by covering the soil with materials - for example fragments of bark - useful in order to maintain soil moisture and thus reduce the water needs of plants, raise the soil temperature, prevent the growth of weeds and protect the soil from precipitation and erosion.

STARTING INDOOR GROWTH

The first step to starting indoor growth is to find the best place to set it up. Many first-time growers think that cannabis plants require large areas to grow, but this is not entirely true.

In fact, you will be surprised to know that magnificent marijuana plants can be grown in almost any corner of the house, including closets, garages, basements and empty rooms.

Obviously, larger spaces offer important advantages, such as being able to give more space to plants and work with greater comfort. However, keep in mind that larger spaces also require more lighting and ventilation and, therefore, cost.

When looking for a space where you can grow indoors, remember the following points:

Cannabis plants have strict lighting requirements. In fact, they require periods of total darkness during which no light can penetrate from the outside, because it would disturb their normal development. Otherwise, the stress caused could compromise the health of the plants and their final yields.

Temperature/Humidity: Temperature and humidity are two extremely important factors to consider when growing cannabis. Always look for a space where you can easily control the temperature and humidity levels, in order to maximize the potential of the plants.

<u>Cannabis plants require good airflow</u>. Air circulation helps to keep the temperature and humidity levels constant inside a Grow Room. If it is missing, numerous problems could arise for the plants, such as mold and other diseases.

Once you have found the most appropriate space to set up the cultivation, you will need to adapt it to satisfy the needs of the plants. The first step is to install reflective walls.

The reflective walls help direct the light towards the plants as much as possible, in order to obtain more powerful and abundant harvests of delicious buds. This essentially allows you to increase the power of the lights without increasing electricity costs.

A reflective surface can in fact increase the power of a lamp by up to 30%, as well as being extremely easy to install.

<u>Here are some options for installing reflective walls in a grow space:</u>

<u>Grow Boxes:</u> Grow Boxes are cabinets that are very popular with indoor growers. Internally they are already coated with reflective material and are specially designed to work with indoor lamps. This means that they will never melt due to the heat generated by the lamps and the light will always be reflected satisfying all the above requirements. Grow Boxes are also extremely easy to set up and usually come with everything you need to get great yields. Just avoid cracks or bubbles forming on the inside walls of the grow box, as they could reduce the reflectivity of your grow space.

Latex based matte white paint: Can be purchased at any paint shop and offers high levels of reflectivity (85-95%). It is also very easy to apply and does not create cracks or bubbles (as can happen with the walls of the grow boxes where the reflectivity within the grow space can be compromised).

Panda plastic: Panda plastic is a special type of plastic that can be easily attached to the walls of a grow room, simply using nails or Velcro. It also offers high reflectivity levels similar to those of white latex matte paint (85-95%). Panda plastic, however, is quite expensive, especially if large surfaces are to be covered. Also, this plastic can melt when the temperatures of the lamps are too high. Exactly the same as for the walls of the Grow Boxes, also in this case we advise you to avoid bubbles or creases in the plastic.

Cannabis plants are very sensitive to light, especially during periods of darkness. Any ray of light that enters the grow space during dark hours can disrupt the normal growth rate of plants and cause stress. The possible consequences of light leaks are often discussed by cannabis growers. Some argue that even the smallest light leaks can affect plant growth, while others believe this is overestimated.

All growers should take a few minutes of their time to check for any light leaks inside their grow rooms. Their presence can negatively affect plant growth and the quantity and quality of crops. In some cases, they can also cause hermaphroditism. Checking for light leaks is extremely easy. If you're growing in a room, you just need to turn on the lights and step outside. If you see small glimmers of light coming out then there are leaks. On the other hand, if the light comes out of a room it means that it also enters it.

Then reverse the process. Enter the room with the lights off and check for any chinks coming from outside. Usually, you will notice gaps around doors and windows.

If you are growing in grow boxes, cabinets or any other enclosed space where it is not possible to physically enter, check for any leaks from the outside, looking for all the light rays emitted by the lamp closed inside the grow space.

If you notice any light leaks make sure you cover them. The techniques to be adopted vary according to their size and area. The most common strategies are:

<u>Blackout film tape</u>. It is an inexpensive and easy remedy to apply to small joints around door and window cracks, as well as to cracks and holes in reflective walls.

<u>Panda plastic film.</u> This material is perfect for covering larger light leaks and can be used to cover larger spaces such as entire doors and windows. It is more expensive than blackout tape but also more effective.

INSTALL A VENTILATION SYSTEM

In the first part of this chapter, we mentioned the importance of air circulation in cannabis crops. Installing a quality ventilation system is the best way to supply your plants with fresh air throughout their growth cycle. In nature, cannabis plants are constantly subjected to a light breeze. In this way the plants protect themselves from mold, bud rot and powdery mildew, as well as from soil flies, spider mites and more. Furthermore, good air circulation also helps manage the humidity/heat rates of the growing area, reducing the humidity that could accumulate after an atmospheric disturbance such as rain. Finally, a light breeze urges the branches and stems of plants to become stronger and more robust, as a natural reaction to the force of the wind. Although they are not affected by rain, indoor plants are susceptible to many of the pests and diseases most common in outdoor crops. So, always try to install a good ventilation system to provide your plants with the right amount of air flow.

The simplest way to increase air circulation in an indoor grow is to use fans. Most growers strategically place a number of wall fans to create a gentle, yet steady, breeze over all the tall parts of the plants.

To better manage the heat and humidity within an enclosed grow space, most growers also install an extraction system to suck out the stale, warm air that has accumulated in the room and to make room for fresher air.

Many growers install air extractors above the lamp, where hot air tends to accumulate. In these cases, a few standard fans are enough to keep the air constantly moving around the room.

Here are some tips for installing fans and extractors inside a grow space:

Fans should not aim directly at plants with excessive speeds. Instead, try to create a constant flow of air around the apical parts of the plants.

Check the entire grow area after installing fans to make sure the air reaches all corners of the room/area.

Too strong a draft can cause wind burns and stress the plants. A light and steady breeze is enough.

Lamps are the key to indoor growing. Cannabis plants require a lot of light to grow and produce large, delicious buds.

Lamps should always be installed to cover as many plants as possible. We recommend that you check the position of your plants in advance to ensure maximum light coverage.

Remember that cannabis grow lights can overheat and must be kept away from any flammable materials.

On the market you can find the most diverse lamps for cannabis cultivation. The choice largely depends on the size of your grow room, your cannabis experience and your budget.

Here are some of the most popular lighting options among indoor growers:

Compact Fluorescent Lamps (CFLs): This is perhaps the most popular option for novice growers. They are cheap, but do not reach the same power as the professional lamps listed below.

Fluorescent lighting systems (T5/T8): T5 and T8 fluorescent tubes are normally used for plants that require less light intensity than cannabis. Consequently, it is necessary to install them at a close distance from the apical parts of the plants to make them efficient. However, some growers get good results using these lamps.

LED grow lights: LED lights are much more expensive than their fluorescent counterparts just mentioned. However, they are also more powerful and can provide plants with much lighter when used correctly. If you decide to install an LED light, remember to check the model in order to install it correctly.

Metal halide (MH) and high-pressure sodium (HPS) lamps. They are the best lamps for growing cannabis. They are very powerful, relatively inexpensive and particularly easy to install. Most indoor growers opt for metal halide lamps or high-pressure sodium lamps.

INSTALL THE OTHER ACCESSORIES

So far, we have listed most of the most important equipment to install in a Grow Room. Once you've installed these pieces, you'll need to start looking for and installing smaller accessories and equipment. Here is a list of the extra accessories you will need to place inside your indoor grow: Vases. The size depends on how big you want your plants to grow. Device for measuring pH. It is always recommended to measure soil pH levels to ensure the best environment for plants. Thermometer/hygrometer, to measure the temperature and humidity of the grow room. Soil/growing medium. You can find the most diverse substrates for growing cannabis. Choosing the right one depends on your growing skills and preferences. Shears, to be used for pruning plants. Sprayer, to apply pesticides. Dry Fertilizers, to fertilize plants. Timer, to automate the control of light cycles.

Start by selecting the cannabis strains you like best. There are thousands of varieties on the market, each with their own advantages and disadvantages. The choice is yours alone. It is very important to grow a strain that is good to smoke, but also suitable for your growing skills and grow room. You can easily browse the different cannabis strains using our database.

Once you have chosen the variety you need to consider how to get it. There are several ways to do this:

Growing from seed. This is a very common practice, but you will need to know how to properly germinate the seeds. If you choose this option, we recommend using feminized seeds to avoid male plants (unless you are considering some breeding projects).

Use cuttings. Some growers prefer to purchase the cuttings directly to avoid having to germinate the seeds. If you choose this option, try to always get your cuttings from reliable sources.

SOIL PREPARATION

Hemp is one of the most resistant plants on the planet and we find it growing at almost all latitudes and soils. However, it prefers light and medium-textured soils, rich in organic matter and well-draining. For the best preparation of the soil in the open field, it is advisable to start working immediately after the harvest of the summer crop and within the month of October, possibly spreading manure on the ground, about 1200Kg/ha, and burying it with a plowing of the plot of land. In case of intensive exploitation of the field, it is preferable to intervene by inserting as much organic substance as possible with a sowing for green manure before sowing hemp, also in order to restore in the soil all the mycorrhizal flora, enzymes and probiotic bacteria of the soil able to help and implement the absorption of nutrients and the resistance of the plant species that are grown there. "Natural is better".

SOWING

The sowing of hemp in our latitudes in an open field can be carried out taking into account the characteristics of the different varieties and cultivation methods, from March to late June, providing the right humidity conditions. However, the optimal period is generally around the middle of month of April. For a good multipurpose production of flowers / seeds / stems, about 40Kg of seeds per hectare are sown with a conventional cereal seeder, 15-20cm distance between the rows of seeds placed at 2-5cm distance between them and 1-2cm deep; for an excellent production of textile fiber, even 100Kg / Ha of seeds can be sown; For an excellent sowing to obtain flowers, it is advisable to sow 1 to 4 plants / sqm.

FERTILIZATION

The ideal for crops in general would be an exclusively organic fertilization. The best thing in a rotation would be to start preparing the soil immediately after harvesting the wheat straws in August, spreading manure and sowing broad beans, field beans or other green manure crops at the same time, to be mown and buried in November.

With these practices it will be sufficient to prepare the seedbed and find a rich and fertile field. You can further spread the mineral fertilizer 20-10-10 in the measure of 110, 150 Kg / Ha.

The Harvest of Hemp Seeds / Stems

If you have sown for a multipurpose crop of seeds, flowers and stems, harvesting of hemp varieties generally takes place, in our latitudes, at the beginning of September, when about 80% of the seeds are ripe and the bracts that contain them are open. However, it is important to follow the weather conditions to avoid storms that can be harmful to the crop, causing ripe seeds to fall. In this case it is good to anticipate the threshing to avoid crop losses. Threshing takes place with a normal grain machine with slow speed and high ventilation.

Fiber

If you have sown for the specific purpose of making fiber, you need to have sown long-cycle varieties, giving way to the pinata to develop well in height, obtaining an excellent long fiber for fabrics.

Historically in Italy, fiber hemp has always been harvested before the beginning of flowering, around the month of July, as the stem begins to contain more lignin with flowering, also making the fiber less valuable.

Flowers

If it is sown for a specific crop of flowers in the open field, in our Italian latitudes the early varieties can be harvested according to the sowing period, from June to August. The long-cycle varieties, on the other hand, are generally harvested from the beginning of September to the end of October.

The collection of quality flowers is done manually, to preserve the delicate trichomes of the flowers that contain the desired bioactive parts.

DIFFERENTIATE BETWEEN MALE AND FEMALE PLANTS, TWO METHODS OF IDENTIFICATION FOR BETTER CULTIVATION

If you are growing marijuana, you should know how to identify male and female marijuana plants. Only females produce the coveted shoots needed for medicinal or recreational purposes. Male plants have low activity and very low THC content compared to female plants; they are mainly required to produce seeds. Learn to distinguish between male and female plants, as well as hermaphroditic plants.

RECOGNIZE MALE PLANTS

Look for thicker, sturdier stems with fewer leaves on male plants. A male plant, compared to a female plant of the same strain, usually has a thicker stem. This is because it grows taller than female plants and must be able to support the weight of the buds. They also have fewer leaves than female plants. So male plants will drastically reduce the growing potential of your female plants. This is because, once fertilized, female plants expend energy producing seeds instead of THC. You need to check each plant to determine if it is male or female. In general, male plants show their sex 7-10 days (indoors) or 3 weeks (outdoors) before female plants.

CHECK THE AUCTION INTERSECTIONS

The small spheres that grow on the joints of the stem are the main indicators of male plants. These flowers release pollen and need to be removed for a better harvest. This leads to a smaller harvest. If you are looking to create new plants or reproduce them, you need to leave these bulbs. Female plants will have the same bulbs, but will also have long, translucent hairs. If you only see 1-2 on a plant, wait and watch for development before cutting them.

HERMAPHRODITE PLANTS

Keep in mind that hermaphroditic plants (of both sexes) exist and should be treated like males. Marijuana plants can grow both sex organs at the same time. If you see any of the telltale male shoots, you should prune them as you would a regular male plant. They will still release pollen which can ruin your crop. Hermaphrodites are usually undesirable plants.

DISCARD OR REMOVE MALE PLANTS (UNLESS YOU SPECIFICALLY WANT SEEDS)

Once you have established that a plan is masculine, you must get rid of it or it will ruin your crop. Don't try to remove the buds by hand. While most planters simply discard male plants, some keep them for breeding purposes. If you do, put them in a separate room from the females. And make sure you don't pass pollen to females. Check your clothes and your hands.

RECOGNIZE FEMININE PLANTS

Marijuana plants, male and female, will be identical within the first 6 weeks of life. It is only after they have begun to develop their sexual organs that you will be able to tell them apart. You can also buy "feminized" seeds, which usually create 100% female plants. However, there are occasional mistakes and you should always keep an eye on your plants to make sure there are no males.

COMPARATIVE SHEETS

One of the simplest indicators is how foliage is formed. Male plants have thicker, sturdier stems and very few leaves. A female of the same strain will be shorter and fuller, with more leaves, especially near the top.

SMALL TRANSLUCENT HAIRS

Once the plant is mature enough, a female will start flowering. At the junction where the branches meet the main stem, you will see tiny translucent hairs emerge from a small teardrop-shaped bud nestled in the joint. Often there will also be "growing spikes", which are new branches and groups of leaves.

Male plants will have the small buds (pollen sacs), but they will not have these associated "hairs" coming out of them. Plants can grow both pollen sacs and translucent "hairs". If it does, it is a hermaphrodite and should be treated like a male.

SEPARATE YOUR FEMALES FROM ALL MALE

Only female plants will produce enough THC for use, but they won't create much if they are fertilized. The pistil (translucent hair) is meant to attract pollen. If it gets it, it will create a seed and all the energy of the plants, all the nutrients, will be spent on producing seeds, which will create a shortage of buds and THC ... Your female plants are the only ones producing a crop, but only if they keep away from the males. For pollination (seed) techniques, refer to Ed Rosenthal's brush method. This will give you a minimum number of seeds and full control over reproduction.

10 THINGS NOT TO DO IN CANNABIS CULTURE

HERE ARE 10 COMMON ERRORS FOR BEGINNERS AND HOW TO AVOID THEM

Growing cannabis is pretty easy, even for a beginner. Like any plant, marijuana needs light, soil and water. However, due to the ban, those who want to cultivate in secret are exposed to certain conditions that can be misleading. In fact, these crops are usually grown without sunlight. Conditions must be made perfect for optimal cultivation. It is therefore important to recognize the common mistakes of new growers. From lack of discretion to over-hydration, here are the 10 most common mistakes to avoid.

1. MOTIVATION

Growing cannabis requires an investment of long hours and infinite patience to get a good product. Many cycles that will consume time and energy. Without this, we will get a poor harvest and, moreover, a lower quality one. Achieve your goals and invest with love and enthusiasm.

2. LACK OF DISCRETION

The novice grower is excited to implement their growing medium. They will usually be tempted to spread the word among their friends, but this will greatly increase the risk of exposure. Remain in absolute secrecy, just limit as much as possible the number of people who know the plants exist. Beyond the legal aspect, growing cannabis is an issue that should attract little attention. Like any culture, it is personal and discreet.

3. LACK OF A PRELIMINARY STUDY AND ORIENTATION

Most growers aren't lucky enough to be able to consult a growing veteran. But it goes without saying that he will have to learn to begin with. Do some preliminary research as soon as possible. Don't settle for just one informative video. Read up, take notes and get advice from the most experienced growers.

4. USE HIGHER SOIL QUALITY

Good soil (at each stage of the plant's life) will have a direct impact on the quality of the final product. The selection process is just as important as choosing good seeds. Ignoring such a step will lead to the spread of pests and other nuisances in the soil. Which will end in total failure of your cultivation. The soil must be able to adequately drain the water. For best results, the pH of your water should be kept between 6.5 and 7.5 pH. Some will even say that too acidic soil will lead to favoring males. But most experts disagree with this statement. Either way, don't let acidic soil, let alone pests, ruin your crop.

5. LACK OF ATTENTION TO DETAILS

"The devil is in the details". As your plants grow, they will give you a lot of information about their health. Look closely at all the leaves, keep them healthy. No holes, no tears and no bugs. You will have to prune them but also keep them in the light. Ensure good distribution of the canopy (the upper level of the canopy).

If brightness is lacking, use reflectors, reflective material or an additional light source. Uneven and degraded lighting will negatively affect the quality and quantity of production.

6.   LACK OF FAMILIARITY

Some cannabis strains may require other procedures or even special treatment. It is important to make sure your seeds come from a good seed bank. The good reputation of the seed, and therefore of its quality, will surely lead you to use a specific and recognized method.

While the acquisition of a seed of "dubious" origin could lead the beginner to consider unnecessary risks. Indeed, an uncertified seed can come from any type of culture and its configuration will certainly not be known to the beginner.

7.   SPRAY

Excessive watering is the most common cause of crop failure. In fact, too much water will saturate the earth and mold will take hold. Eventually, the roots will rot in place and the plant will begin to wilt. So, don't "drown" your plant! Lightly water the soil and make sure it is dry next time you water. The drying of the soil must be noticed in the following hours.

8.   IMPATIENCE

Medicinal cannabis plants must be harvested at the right time and with precision. Be patient and wait until the flowering phase is over and therefore optimal. In fact, for some cannabis strains, it will seem very tempting to harvest at times when your plant is growing. And especially in the case of medical cannabis, the "yield" will be interesting before its end.

Don't get me wrong, the information your farmer provides is accurate and must be strictly adhered to.

9. A STIMULATING ENVIRONMENT FOR PLANTS

Just like all animals, plants are also sensitive to the environment in which they grow. Beyond the cycle of light and dark, which must be respected from minute to minute; you will have to maintain a constant temperature. Enhance the atmosphere in which your plant evolves. Some will talk to you about hugs, about music; the main thing is that your plant lives in an atmosphere of joy and love ... Be "communicative" with your plant and the fruits will only be better.

10. USE OF CUTTINGS

I can never repeat it enough: "take cuttings". Cuttings are a great way to preserve your plant's genetics. Additionally, a cutting is efficient in terms of growth and yield. However, cuttings can have genetic diseases and the same sensitivity (to pests) as the mother plant. When your seeds are reliable and growth is going well, don't hesitate to cut the "right" plant.

And because of that, you will be in control of virtually every aspect of your plant

BEGINNER'S GUIDE: THE RIGHT TEMPERATURE FOR AN OPTIMAL CANNABIS HARVEST

Cannabis likes a comfortable room temperature when grown indoors, or a little warmer - not too dry, not too humid. For many indoor growers, this is all you need to worry about. If you feel too hot or too cold for you in your grow area, it's probably too hot or too cold for your cannabis plants.

IDEAL TEMPERATURE

The best temperature for growing cannabis is usually between 68-77 degrees (20-25 Celsius). If the ambient temperature around the plant falls well below 20-25 degrees, the plant's growth will slow down and its potential yield will be inhibited or even stopped altogether. Consequently, the plant never ripens ... It is important to note that temperature is very important throughout the "daily" cycle, when you let your plant receive light. This is where photosynthesis and growth potential come into play. Also, there shouldn't be any major temperature changes between day and night.

If your plant's temperature exceeds 77 degrees (25 degrees Celsius), the plant's metabolism will accelerate. So, it will therefore require additional elements: lighter, more water, more carbon dioxide and more fertilizer, etc... Make sure you adjust things according to the temperature.

In other words, the ideal temperature

It is advisable to invest not only in a thermometer, but in a thermometer connected to a ventilation or heating system, in order to automatically manage the temperature in the grow room. An automatic system can also produce excellent ventilation for fresh air and avoid carbon dioxide deficiency.

VEGETATIVE AND FLOWERING TEMPERATURE

Vegetative stage: Young cannabis plants growing in the vegetative stage prefer warmer weather than the flowering stage, in the range of 70 to 85F (20-30C). Learn more about the timing in the vegetative phase.

Flowering phase: In the flowering phase (when cannabis plants begin to sprout) it is best to keep the climate slightly cooler, around 65 to 80F (18-26C) to produce the best color, trichome production and smell. There should be a difference of 10 degrees between night and day for best results. This is particularly important in the flowering phase for the development of top-quality buds.

TEMPERATURE TOO LOW

When the temperature approaches freezing, it is too cold for a cannabis plant to survive without damage. The colder weather will tend to slow growth. Temperatures below 60F (15C) tend to disrupting plant growth and freezing temperatures shock or even kill a cannabis plant.

Plants are more susceptible to certain types of mold when cold, especially if they are also wet. Warmer weather and large temperature fluctuations contribute to excessive leaf size and can also reduce photosynthesis.

A plant that is grown in a relatively cold climate can survive, but it will never grow as quickly as a plant that receives adequate temperatures. Indoor plants tend to be much more sensitive to cold than outdoor plants.

TEMPERATURE TOO HIGH

While cannabis plants don't usually die from heat, temperatures that are too high will cause plants to grow much more slowly. Note that temperatures above 26C (80F) in the flowering phase will not only slow down bud growth, but may reduce the potency and odor of your buds. Room temperature control is especially important in the flowering phase! In the heat, cannabis is also more susceptible to many problems, including mites, powdery mildew (especially if it is also wet), root rot, burning of nutrients (from increased sweating of water), increased stretching, and wilt caused by root oxygen. Deprivation and reduced "odor" of the buds (as terpenes can burn at higher temperatures).

HUMIDITY

The ideal humidity in the cannabis plant's environment is between 40-70%. A hygrometer is needed to measure humidity. An electric hygrometer is probably the best choice for most growers. It often has automatic features that offer more control than just humidity. Which is always good for indoor cultivation?

If your plant's humidity drops below 40%, the plant will have an accelerated transpiration rate. There will be no major consequences. Your plant will simply consume water faster. As long as there is plenty of water in the reserve, there will be no problems. On the other hand, if the humidity is too high, your plant may develop fungi, especially during the flowering period. And then, things rot very quickly ... You will definitely need to dehumidify manually, in order to solve the mold problems and the consequences that come with it.

WHERE TO MEASURE?

The temperature must be measured at the level of the canopy and in the shade of the leaves. The canopy means the tops of the plants, as close as possible to the lamp. The highest temperature is evaluated.

The temperature peak is (inside) near the cover. When measured in the shade, it represents the heat of the ambient air. Here we measure the heat of the air. This measurement is performed by the stomata. A stoma is a small orifice in the epidermis of the aerial organs of plants (on the underside of the leaves more often). It allows gas exchange between the plant and the ambient air (oxygen, carbon dioxide, water vapor, etc.). In addition to the adjustment of osmotic pressure. Focus on cannabis stomata. Then we measure on the stomata of the horizontal leaves, remaining however on the upper epidermis which is directly illuminated. We notice that when it reaches 28/29C, then the stomata begin to close. Therefore, the temperature must be below this fateful limit. And therefore, we take the measurement of the temperature where the stomata are located. Namely in the shade of the leaves.

GROW YOUR CULTURE WITH THE SCROG METHOD

The SCROG (Screen of Green) method is a culture training and improvement technique. It's a bit like the SOG file but smaller. SCROGGING is usually done with a plastic or wire mesh. This growing technique aims to significantly improve the productivity of your crops. The principle is the same as in the SOG, i.e. we grow small plants evenly, trying to maximize the number of buds for a given area. Here is the guide to growing SCROG the easy way.

THE SCROGGING

By analogy with SOG (green screen), we call SCROG a cultivation technique dedicated mainly to indoor cultivation. The SOG method has been popular for years, however the SCROG method is based on the same principles. Growers add a screen mesh that will maximize light exposure. This is how SCROGGING is defined. For this, we have a wire mesh over the plants. When they reach the fence level or a little higher, they are folded to force them to stay under the fence. So let's move on to flowering. Then we continue to hold the plant under the matrix, until growth stops and the buds start growing. If the job is done right, we have a canopy of leaves and a field of buds ready to explode.

THE ADVANTAGES OF SCROG

Optimization of internal space: The intertwining of the leaves allows the unfolding of the branches of uniform size. Under these conditions almost no space will be present on the upper layer of the vegetation. With this network, the most effective results can be obtained in terms of optimizing interior spaces. And this is the most important parameter of the SCROG method

Uniform canopy and level control: One of the most common problems in growing cannabis indoors is keeping the plant uniform while growing. Despite the understandable desire of the growers to provide for wild growth and fill the room with a very large plant, it is important to remember that it is necessary to keep a distance from the light source.

Especially when it comes to an HPS lamp that can burn out all your growing hopes in just a few hours.

Maximum light exposure: The SCROG device naturally allows you to expose all the stems of your germinating plants. For these reasons, the holes of the net are considered a multitude of receptacles exposed to allow the buds to receive light.

Branch support: This positive point is the physical support of the network. This support is essential, especially during the flowering phase when the same massive branches develop within a few weeks.

WEAK POINTS OF THE SCROG

Long Term Growth - The SCROG method has an inherent need of at least 4-6 weeks to have growing branches properly distributed over the net. Of course, the parameter of the number of plants is important. Therefore, 2 plants will take longer to cover an area of one square meter than 4 plants.

The Mobility Problem - During the first few weeks of cultivation, you can usually handle the plants and do proper maintenance. But once the branches emerge from the crevices of the mesh, it will be difficult to reconfigure your growing medium. This obviously does not negate the necessary maintenance; you will have to use a sprayer to wash your plants or fight pests with. Show some ingenuity and inventiveness.

Use feminized cuttings or seeds - Today, most home-growers use feminized seeds or cuttings. In the case of the SCROG method, it is a must! Unless you are a veteran, you will need to establish a homogeneous culture, cuttings are therefore used a lot.

EQUIPMENT REQUIRED

All basic equipment is needed for SCROGGING - i.e., lamp, ventilation, culture medium, controls, etc. But we'll add some essentials:

Cannabis plants - SCROGGING generally involves 2 to 4 plants per square meter. But sometimes you can get to more than 6 plants. As long as the right growing conditions are not altered, the plants shorten the vegetative transition time and their flowering period.

The grid or the net - the net is in fact the only external equipment (almost) necessary for the implementation of this growth technique.

In hydroponic garden stores, you can get nets that conform to the design of the canopy. Most of the ingredients can be found in stores that specialize in building, treating animals, etc.

OTHER NETWORKS

Nylon net - easy to use and highly maneuverable as needed.

Plastic mesh - not the best choice ... Make sure of the quality.

Chicken coop - the cheapest, the most available and widely used. Its main flaw is that it is awkward to work with and it rusts and can eventually damage the plant.

Fishing Net - Although this is a relatively robust material, it is also quite accessible and available. But many growers complain that the net is too thin and would tend to cut the plant.

String - mainly suitable for mounting small spaces.

Wire mesh - you can buy ready-made metal chains and arrange them like a mesh. However, it is recommended to make sure the metal is coated to prevent rust.

Fibers: Another possibility is to form a network of threads with fibers such as cotton, jute, sisal (Agave), coconut, hemp ... You can improvise from almost any material whose characteristics correspond to the size of the holes, i.e., from 5 to 15 square centimeters.

REPAIR To install the desired height of the mesh it is necessary to establish the walls of the growing cavity. For this reason, you can do this using the installation feet, the wooden frame or simple nails (depending on the type of mesh and the convenience of the tower). The recommended position for the height of the net is between 25 and 50 cm (base plant).

THE GENERAL PASSAGES OF THE SCROG METHOD

The vast majority of SCROG fabric: 75% to 85% will be covered with vegetation. To achieve this, it is important that branches are spread across the network during the growth period. Therefore, some general steps are required:

NOTE: When deploying vegetation on the net, identify the main branches and redirect to the outer frame.

This is to allow less developed plants to get better lighting. Also, this prevents your upper branches from being hurt by your lighting device.

ADDITIONAL TECHNIQUES To maximize your plant's coverage rate of the net and to optimize the production offered by SCROGGING, many growers tend to integrate other farming techniques. They are particularly viable in the first half of the growth cycle: Cutting - the size of the plant during the first few weeks of its life is important. Cutting is usually performed after the bifurcation of the third or fourth branch. Then we will have two new growths, which help promote full width growth.

Pruning - one of the most important actions during the SCROG method. Pruning involves removing the vegetation in the lower third of the plant. This makes it possible to strengthen the development of the upper regions. Pruning takes place during growth, but will be even more necessary when your plant is in the flowering stage, no light will reach the underside.

Liens - This technique reveals more art and a certain mastery of SCROGGING. However, it allows you to create the desired shape, by means of ligatures that will be imposed on the branches.

VARIETIES RECOMMENDED FOR SCROGGING

Another very important parameter for the success of SCROG is a selection of suitable cannabis strains. In general, we will take those who respond well to this growth technique. The main characteristics we are looking for are those with laterally extended growth and which have flexible branches.

The cannabis strains that meet these characteristics are generally Sativa varieties. But as their long flowering period is a handicap (10 to 12 weeks), we preferred hybrids suitable for SCROG culture. Among these most commonly used varieties are Satori, AK47, Lemon Haze, and C99. Do not hesitate to consult Community producers using the SCROG method to find the right strain at the moment.

THE "V" SCROG One of the most interesting ideas for improving SCROG is to establish a curved network. This leads to a larger operating surface and thus to a better harvest. It should be noted that the more sophisticated SCROG methods are not recommended for beginners. It is best to start with the simplest (flat) format, repeat it until you have fully mastered it. SCROGGING is a technique that necessarily leads the experimenter to professionalization.

CURIOSITY

Determining the real potency of a cannabis bud isn't easy. Once the strain to grow is chosen, a number of factors emerge that can affect the THC content of buds. The main external factors influencing the potency of a bud are: growing location (e.g., indoor or outdoor), growing medium (e.g., soil or hydroponics), nutrient concentrations, light source, temperature & humidity and carbon dioxide levels. While there are numerous cannabis growing techniques, all of them have advantages and disadvantages. For example, if you want to take advantage of a light with a UVB spectrum, either grow plants in mountainous areas close to the equator, or buy LED lights with UVB emission. In both cases, however, some problems have to be faced: LED lights are quite expensive and growing marijuana plants on a mountain can require enormous sacrifices. A plant's potency is also affected by its genetics. This, in fact, contains all the information about the plant: the amount of THC and CBD it is able to produce, the smells and flavors it releases, its growth behavior, etc. Cannabis expresses the traits inherited from parents, just like humans.

Stable genetics allows predictable characteristics to be handed down from plant to plant, while unstable genetics can give rise to plants with unpredictable characteristics, very often difficult to manage. Today, growers have the ability to select growth characteristics, appearance and effects. This allows them to find the variety that best suits their needs. That said, when starting to grow it is very important to take all of these factors into consideration so that you know which strain is best suited to your preferences. Seeds of native or highly stable quality varieties, for example, have been cultivated for centuries and their specific traits have evolved to adapt to a certain natural habitat. In indoor cultivation there is a tendency to grow varieties with less pungent odors, more compact in size and with a marked resistance to parasites. This is why you should always define the objectives to be achieved in a crop, even before choosing the seeds to plant.

MOST POWERFUL CANNABIS STRAINS - 2020 UPDATE

We've had the opportunity to sample potent cannabis strains for a long time, but every day we see new advances in the industry. We are pleased to present an updated list of some of the most potent genetics on the market. The list contains new features including Cookies Gelato and Triple G, and other classic varieties!

Now that we know how to proceed, what are the strongest strains around?

ICE CREAM COOKIES The union of the sweet fragrances of Girl Scout Cookies and Gelato gave rise to Cookies Gelato, a properly named strain that recently earned a place in this ranking. You know, in addition to inheriting sugary flavors from its ancestors, Cookies Gelato also develops copious amounts of THC: around 28%, to be exact. This hybrid delivers a euphoric and slightly relaxing high, so it won't throw you full speed into the stratosphere, even if you're headed for the stars. As you might have guessed, this strain is not very suitable for novice smokers. However, those who have already developed some tolerance will have a very pleasant time in the company of these buds.

ROYAL GORILLA It is only recently that Gorilla genetics have been made available outside the United States. Today, you finally have the opportunity to try this strain through Royal Queen Seeds' Royal Gorilla. These buds display pleasant shades of light green, with THC concentrations of 26%. This balanced hybrid was created by chance by a group of breeders. The high is incredibly euphoric and the delicious citrus flavors are accompanied by hints of pine. Its effects are balanced and particularly suitable for therapeutic use. Order seeds now and try a strain you thought you didn't need in your life.

GREEN GELATO In California alone, there are numerous regions that compete with each other to grow the best quality cannabis. Initiated in the San Francisco Bay metropolitan area, Green Gelato is a must for any sweet tooth cannabis lover. The parents are Sunset Sherbet and Thin Mint Cookies, both famous for their sweet and pungent flavors. Crossing them resulted in an even sweeter plant, with a THC content that can exceed 25%.

HULKBERRY Colorado was one of the first states in the US to legalize marijuana for recreational purposes. The precursors of this state were able to cultivate some of the most impressive hybrids known to mankind. One of these particular cannabis strains has already taken US dispensaries by storm, making its way to Europe and beyond. We are talking about HulkBerry, a plant that became a cult in a few years after its success at the High Times Cannabis Cup in 2014. It truly deserved an award with its incredible potency, powered by a THC content that exceeds 28%. The hybridization of OG Kush with Strawberry Diesel resulted in a potent blend of indica and sativa effects, accompanied by a delicious fruity flavor.

A new study from the Addiction and Mental Health Group has determined that THC concentrations in weed and resin have increased significantly over the past 50 years. According to these new data, street cannabis around the world has grown much stronger. How has the potency of cannabis increased since the 1970s? This study aimed to systematically examine and meta-analyze changes in THC and CBD concentrations in cannabis over time. According to past analyses, trends over the past decade suggest that cannabis is becoming an increasingly potent product in the United States and Europe. The team behind the study, which belongs to the Addiction and Mental Health group at the University of Bath, synthesized data from over 80,000 cannabis samples tested over the past 50 years from street samples collected in the US, UK, Netherlands, France, Denmark, Italy and New Zealand. After deduplication, a total of 3893 chapters were identified, reviewed, and assessed for eligibility, with 122 selected for full-text search. Their findings are published in the Addiction Review and the research was funded by the Society for the Study of Addiction.

EVOLUTION OF THC AND CBD CONCENTRATIONS IN CANNABIS OVER TIME

The researchers studied how levels of THC (the component of cannabis responsible for the euphoric state of users) have changed over time in different types of cannabis. In the case of herbal cannabis, they found that THC concentrations increased by 14% between 1970 and 2017. This is mainly due to the increase in the market share of stronger varieties, such as sinsemilla, compared to traditional herbal cannabis (Ruderalis) which contains seeds and less THC. THC concentrations in the resins, meanwhile, increased by 0.57% each year between 1975 and 2017, an increase of around 24%.

In particular, an analysis of cannabis flowers and hashish found among 199 results suggest that the amount of THC in a typical gram of cannabis increased by 2.9 milligrams per year for all herbal and herbal cannabis. 5.7 milligrams per year for herbal cannabis and cannabis resin. These annual increases in milligrams of THC per gram of cannabis fall into the range of low single doses that can produce mild intoxication, similar to a "standard unit of THC" of 5 milligrams.

Changing THC concentrations over time could also affect the efficacy and safety of cannabis used for medical purposes in the absence of information on the standard dosage of illegal cannabis products. Researchers believe that the increase in THC in the cannabis flower is due to an increase in the market share of high-THC weed or cannabis, and not a general increase in THC between specific strains. Furthermore, they believe that the increase in THC concentrations in hashish products (while CBD concentrations remained stable) can be explained by the increase in THC-rich material at the time of resin production.

The findings of this new study are particularly relevant in light of growing demands for cannabis legalization in an effort to make it safer. The researchers say that increasing the potency of cannabis highlights the need to implement broader harm reduction strategies, similar to those used for alcohol, such as standard units and public guidelines on drug limits and safer consumption.

Although they considered studies from around the world, the authors note that, with most of the studies included in their research coming from the United States, the results are not "globally representative." Additionally, "non-random" law enforcement sampling may have contributed to potential biases in the study.

2021

MARIJUANA GUIDE

GROWING & BUSINESS

REVOLUTION

CONTENTS

INTRODUCTION

Why GROW MARIJUANA

Most cannabis users have toyed with the idea of growing their own weed at home at one time or another, just as many alcohol drinkers have thought of opening their own bar. YOU HAVE A GREATER CHOICE. If you grow your own weed you can choose which seeds to use and how. You will always know what you are smoking and how your ganja was grown, with no chemical additives and no substances used for cutting. So, you can smoke quality weed in complete safety.

SUDDENLY YOU WILL HAVE MORE GRASS. You will be able to produce the grass you need for your needs, even with just 2 or 3 plants.

Whether you smoke for personal pleasure or for medical reasons, you will have all the weed you need while saving a lot of money. And this is certainly not a reason to be underestimated...

You will GAIN KNOWLEDGE OF THE PLANT. Prohibition has distorted our relationship with cannabis, which with its multiple uses has accompanied us from the dawn of our civilization to today. As we will see, cannabis has had multiple uses throughout history, which today are unknown to most. By becoming a cannabis grower, you will get to know and love a truly extraordinary plant.

YOU WILL GET A NEW HOBBY Taking care of your plants will soon become an almost daily chore. Without realizing it, you will spend a lot of time in the company of your plants and seeing them grow to produce "fruit" will be a truly rewarding experience.

PART ONE: CANNABIS BASICS

Marijuana, also known as cannabis or ganja, is the result of the drying of leaves, flowers, stems and seeds, belonging to the Cannabis sativa plant (or Indian hemp). Containing the active ingredient THC (delta-9-tetrahydrocannabinol), marijuana is a well-known psychoactive / narcotic substance, which, however, in recent years, is also gaining importance in the medical field, as a medicine. In humans, the consumption of marijuana for narcotic purposes has physical effects (respiratory problems, circulatory problems, attenuation of physical reactivity, etc.) and neuropsychological effects (mood swings, paranoia, hallucinations, etc.). Furthermore, according to reliable research, it can give rise to a certain addiction, such as illegal drugs cocaine, heroin etc.

The cannabis plant, also known as marijuana and ganja (from Sanskrit: गांजा - gañjā), is an extraordinary plant: it is the only plant in the world that can be used as a drug or as a fiber at the same time. Precisely because of its versatility, it does not seem strange to us that the first crops appeared 10,000 years ago.

The evidence was found on the island of Taiwan and in some places in today's Romania.

Originally from Asia, probably Central Asia, cannabis has been used for medical, spiritual, religious or recreational purposes (via inhalation or vaporization) for at least 5,000 years. We know for sure that the Aryans smoked cannabis and it may have been the Aryans who taught the properties of cannabis both to Indian peoples (in the sacred Hindu texts, we speak of intoxicating hallucinogens) and and to Mesopotamian peoples. A Chinese pharmacology treatise attributed to Emperor Shen Nung, dated 2737 BC, contains the first reference to the use of cannabis as a medicine. The Ancient Greeks preferred wine, but many documents attest to their trade with peoples who ate or inhaled cannabis. Herodotus in 5 BC writes that the Scythians (a semi-nomadic population of Iranian origin) cultivated and then vaporized cannabis. On another occasion, Herodotus again writes that the inhabitants of some Mediterranean islands threw cannabis on the fire and then, "sitting around in a circle, they inhale and are intoxicated by the smell, just like the Greeks with wine, and the more they throw away the more they become intoxicated, until they get up and dance and sing". Other passages by Pliny, Marco Polo, and Arab historians undoubtedly demonstrate that cannabis was cultivated both for practical reasons: to have a strong and resistant fabric and for recreational purposes throughout Asia, the Middle East and much of Europe around the Mediterranean since the dawn of time. For example, the sails of the Phoenicians' ships were made of hemp fiber. The date when cannabis was introduced in central, northern and western Europe is unknown, but is probably around 500 BC. Also a few centuries before Christ, before the advent of the Roman Empire, various European peoples including the Celts and Picts cultivated and used cannabis. Since then, cannabis cultivation has been common, if not massive, in Europe for centuries. Hemp has been the most used woven material in many European regions for centuries. But the Europeans obviously also knew the plant's recreational potential. Although in 1484 a papal bull forbade its use to the faithful, Francois Rabelais wrote extensively about it in the sixteenth century. In the following centuries, despite the condemnation of the Church, to consume cannabis for fun became a real fashion among intellectuals, so much so that Club of Hashish Eaters was founded in Paris, frequented by poets and writers such as Victor Hugo, Alexandre Dumas, Charles Baudelaire, Honoré de Balzac and Théophile Gautier. From ancient times to industrialization, hemp was also used to make paper. The famous Gutenberg Bible, the first book printed in Europe with the movable type technique, was printed in 1453 on hemp paper specially imported from Italy. The sails of the ships of Christopher Columbus' caravels were made of hemp. The use of cannabis was also widespread in Africa centuries before European colonization. In the black continent, cannabis was cultivated, for textile purposes and for healing purposes, inhaled and sometimes worshiped in very different areas: from South Africa to the Congo to Morocco. In the eighteenth century, cannabis was widespread in North America.

In 1850 there were 8,327 hemp plantations (each plantation had at least 2000 acres of land). The Declaration of Independence was laid out on hemp paper. Italy was also a very important producer of cannabis for centuries. The reason is simple: the climate of the peninsula is particularly favorable for the cultivation of this plant. In particular, Italian farmers produced cannabis for two reasons. First, because it grew on soils that were difficult to cultivate with other industrial plants (sandy soils and marshy areas in the river plains), second because there was always a need for "oily" (sativa, light), "fibrous" plants (textiles, paper, ropes) and feed (leaves) for livestock. They excelled in the hemp lands of Bologna and Ferrara. The major Bolognese agronomist of the seventeenth century, Vincenzo Tanara, testifies to the vitality of the Canapacola economy with a long, accurate description of the cultivation technique. Italy became the second largest producer of hemp in the world. The sunset began with the advent of coal ships, when a slow agony began for the hemp-producing areas, which lasted for a century, forcing the restructuring of all agrarian rotations. During the Second World War, however, Middle European and Mediterranean production returned to increase quickly, as textile fibers and sativa oils became more expensive. In addition, there was a need for raw materials containing cellulose from which explosives could be obtained by producing nitrocellulose. But with the Marijuana Tax Act of 1937 the American government gave the coup-de-grace to the cultivation of hemp, banning it. Cannabis was pseudo-scientifically accused of making people violent and maddening or dying. In the following years many countries of the world following this example, banned hemp. The director of the American Federal Bureau of Narcotics, Harry J. Anslinger, was an ambitious, racist and bigoted man who justified the prohibition with the following words:

Marijuana is a drug that produces insanity, crime and death in users.

Marijuana leads to pacifist and communist brainwashing.

Spinels make niggers think they are like white men.

Smoke a joint and you'll probably kill your brother.

That is the drug that has caused the most violence in human history. "

Behind the bigotry, there were economic interests in the prohibitionist campaign. Famous paper / publishing house Hearst, the biggest supporter of the anti-cannabis campaign via its newspapers, had just made huge investments in tree paper. Its owner William Randolph Hearst, paper tycoon and character who inspired Orson Welles in the figure of Citizen Kane in the eponymous movie, declared the following nonsense:

"Marijuana is the shortest way to the asylum, smoke it even for a short time and your brain will be nothing more than a repository of hideous specters;

hashish creates a killer who kills for the pleasure of killing."

Hearst newspapers carried out, for years, a huge disinformation and prohibitionist propaganda campaign against cannabis, falsely attributing to it a myriad of "social evils", from murderers to communism, from pacifism to marital infidelity, up to sexual relations between " white women and inferior races". Headlines like this were often read:

"THREE QUARTERS OF CRIMES in this country are CAUSED BY MARIJUANA".

At the same time, DuPont patented nylon. According to some scholars, all these were not mere coincidences. Since 1937, 20 million Americans have been arrested and jailed for possession or use of the world's most popular and least harmful drug.

Some studies estimate that today about 4% of the world's adult population (162 million people) uses cannabis very sporadically, while 0.6% (22.5 million) uses it daily. This shows that even today cannabis, despite decades of prohibition in the vast majority of countries around the world, remains an immensely popular drug, second only to alcohol, caffeine and tobacco.

However, they are considered legal in almost all countries. In the United States alone, more than 100 million citizens have tried cannabis at least once, and even two presidents (Clinton and Obama) have publicly admitted that they have smoked marijuana.

Numerous scientific studies demonstrate the absurdity of equating cannabis and heroin.

Commenting on the British government tables, Prof. Nutt explained that "the current conception of drugs is ill-conceived and arbitrary." In particular, "the exclusion of alcohol and tobacco is from a scientific point of view, arbitrary". Suffice it to remember that tobacco is the cause of 40% of all hospital admissions and alcohol causes over 50% of emergency room situations. In addition, alcohol has a high rate of social harm (2.2 on a scale from 0 to 3) and is second in this ranking only to heroin. Tobacco is less addictive than heroin and cocaine. Prof. Nutt explains that cannabis is less physically harmful than heroin, cocaine, barbiturates, methadone, alcohol, ketamine, benzodiazepines, amphetimines, tobacco and buprenofines.

In this ranking, barbiturates are third in terms of danger, alcohol is fifth, tobacco ninth, while cannabis is only 11th. Obviously, the results must be used with a grain of salt, also because they refer not to the substance itself, but to its typical use.

Marijuana is obtained from the dried female inflorescences of the cannabis sativa plant, which contain the psychoactive substance THC.

Hashish is produced from the resin of the same plant and contains the same active ingredient in greater quantities.

These substances tend to be smoked in conjunction with tobacco or used as ingredients for various foods.

The active ingredient THC works on the hypothalamus, pituitary gland (or pituitary) and adrenal gland, which regulate the production of certain hormones, in particular the sense of satiety and libido.

THC produces short-term effects such as those on a perceptual level: there is an alteration of the perception of reality, a motor coordination and a lower ability to react and attention. At the cardiovascular level, THC induces tachycardia. THC alters blood pressure, which can drop or rise. It is not clear whether the effects on the respiratory system are caused only by tobacco smoked. But it is certain that smoking marijuana increases the degree of harm of tobacco. On the long-term effects of this drug, it must be emphasized that there are still no studies that agree on what happens. The question of the possible permanent negative effects of this drug therefore remains unresolved. However, in chronic marijuana smokers, cognitive, psychomotor and memory slowdowns are evident.

The benefits, are scientifically proven. In some countries, in certain therapies: it is used as an antiemetic, in subjects with cancer and undergoing chemotherap. Also, in anorexic subjects because it causes appetite and in inappetent subjects debilitated by chronic diseases, such as AIDS and multiple sclerosis. In fact, it causes muscle relaxation that fights the rigidity that this disease causes. It also plays a role in the treatment of glaucoma, since it lowers intraocular pressure.

SATIVA

Sativa, or Indian hemp, as already mentioned, is an annual herbaceous plant, native to Central and Western Asia, grown mainly for industrial and textile use but also and above all by virtue of the known psychoactive medicinal properties that distinguish it. Resistant and particularly robust, it has female inflorescences equipped with multi-cellular secretory hairs in which there is the resin that contains the main active ingredients: cannabinoids, terpenoids and flavonoids.

The derivatives of cannabis sativa intended for recreational or therapeutic use, take on different names (for the different area of origin and for the portion of the inflorescence used): in India the final product is called "bhang", smoked in pure form or mixed with tobacco, in Arabia and in Egypt "hashish" often ingested accompanied by butter and honey and again in Mexico and the USA simply "marijuana", where the so-called weed is traditionally smoked with tobacco.

In India and Arab countries, its curative use has ancient origins: although of course there is also the luxury one, due to the intoxicating and euphoric properties typical of the species. The "narcotic substance", if smoked generally involves a pleasant sensation of euphoria, well-being, excitement, which can however be associated with some side effects such as hallucinations, loss of conception of time and space, personality disorders which are replaced by deep sleep and in particularly severe cases, coma. In ancient medicine, cannabis sativa was essentially used topically as an analgesic and antiseptic: more recently the application has evolved through the use of tinctures and extracts systemically to obtain a sedative and topical action as an antiseptic and in the case of burns and scalds.

In areas where a temperate climate prevails, cannabis sativa is mainly cultivated for textile purposes in the production of hemp fabrics and the extraction of drying oil: this is because the content of "doping" active ingredients is drastically reduced compared to that present in plants grown in the traditionally original areas. However, cannabis sativa is distinguished by the over 400 chemicals that make up its properties: including the cannabinoids, directly responsible for what may be the therapeutic and euphoric effects typical of the species. Unlike cannabis indica, the sativa strain has a significantly higher concentration of THC which however can vary depending on the variety chosen. In the therapeutic field, its possible uses range from treating chronic pain, to nausea from chemotherapy, from lack of appetite due to the main eating disorders to HIV, up to glaucoma, spasticity and tremor associated with multiple sclerosis, to the protection of neurons from those that may be damage caused by stroke or degenerative diseases and not least in the treatment of convulsive and psychotic states. Its multiple effects, purely subjective since they depend on the emotional state of the subject, and on his personality, can however vary significantly also depending on the amount of substance taken, and due to the concentration of active ingredients present in it, specifically THC and CBD.

Euphoria and a pleasant sensation of peace and well-being appear among the main perceptions that follow the assumption: secondly, drowsiness, agitation, dry mouth, dilation of the pupils, and a different perception of space and time, often accompanied by by the presence of hallucinations and tachycardia. However, these manifestations are always to be considered purely indicative and irrelevant in comparison to the real benefits brought by cannabis sativa and are scientifically documented. A well-known scientific research conducted by the National Academies of Sciences, Engineering and Medicine has in fact amply demonstrated the importance of cannabis in the reduction of chronic pain, an area of application within which it has obtained a truly significant response, and where its efficacy for the reduction of muscle spasms, thanks to the strong muscle relaxant properties typical of CBD.

A study published in The Lancet, showed that cannabis would be able to mitigate epileptic seizures, due to its neuroprotective capacity typical of this species. Further research carried out by the Scripps Research Institute in 2006 published in the Molecular Pharmaceutics Journal, showed that THC could act as an inhibitor in the containment of senile plaques and amyloid protein clusters that characterize people affected by Alzheimer's disease, and which act by slowing down or preventing the normal passage of neurons and causing inflammation of the tissues.

The results of CBD against all types of tumor manifestations are significant, a figure that emerged in a study conducted in 2007 which demonstrated how cannabidiol is able to eliminate the ID-1 gene, the main cause of the immortality of cancer cells, preventing the tumor to develop further. To support this thesis, contribute other studies, which confirm the direct effect of CBD in the control of CB2 and GPR55 receptors, also involved in the definition of the life of a cell, showing how CBD combined with THC would counteract the growth of particularly aggressive tumors, acting as adjuvants of radiotherapy. Numerous investigations conducted at the Neuromed Mediterranean Neurological Institute in collaboration with the Department of Systems Medicine of the Tor Vergata University in Rome in 2017, also demonstrated a significant interaction between cannabinoids and dopamine, which would affect the modulation of some related neurotransmitters.

Thanks to the intake of cannabis sativa, it would therefore be possible to modify this modulation thus attenuating the tremors of patients with Parkinson's. And still in other studies it would also emerge that the intake of sativa would represent a valid help in reducing the typical symptoms caused by chemotherapy therapies, manifested by nausea, loss of appetite and vomiting, thus improving the life of patients. It would also reduce the same effects caused by the multiple treatments aimed at stemming the effects of hepatitis C, a thesis developed by a 2006 study published in the European Journal of Gastroenterology and Hepatology. Cannabis sativa has many benefits, which beyond the pleasure of a purely recreational use, could undoubtedly bring significant changes also and above all in the therapeutic fields.

CANNABIS INDICA

Unlike cannabis sativa, cannabis indica causes a sedative effect much loved by those who need to relax or sleep better at night, as well as those suffering from anxiety, chronic pain or muscle spasms. When choosing a cannabis strain, you don't necessarily have to go for an indica or pure sativa. Often, the best option is cannabis seeds from hybrid strains, which can offer the best of both worlds. but how do they differ from each other? The aroma and appearance are more or less the same, which can lead to think that the effect is also similar. But while belonging to the same family, they are two clearly distinct varieties. They exhibit distinct growth characteristics, antagonistic effects and different medicinal applications. And understanding the variations can make a difference for people who have health problems and want to be able to choose the most suitable genetics for their disorder.

In his original classification of 1753, the naturalist Carl Linnaeus identified a single species of cannabis, Cannabis sativa L. or what we know today as hemp, a non-psychoactive plant that was grown in Europe for obtaining fiber for use in production of ropes and sails, among other artifacts. In 1785, then, the eminent biologist Jean-Baptiste Lamarck received some samples of cannabis plants collected in India that caused a euphoric effect when smoked or ingested. Analyzing a number of characteristics, including the texture of the stems, the thinness of the bark and the of the flowers and leaves, Lamarck believed that those plants could not be classified together with the Cannabis sativa that was grown in Europe at the time, and created a new subspecies called Cannabis indica.

This variety continued to develop especially in Afghanistan, more specifically in the mountainous areas, where it adapted to adverse and cold climatic conditions. This need to protect themselves from the unfavorable climate of the mountain regions is certainly the reason why cannabis indica varieties produce large amounts of resin, a characteristic much appreciated by those who love hashish. The name Cannabis indica includes all varieties that come from the dry climate countries of South and Central Asia, including India, Nepal, Afghanistan, Turkey, China (south) and Pakistan. In these regions, the climate is very dry until autumn when the rainy season begins with the arrival of the monsoon, causing an increase in humidity which at the time caused this variety to evolve to bloom early and avoid mold caused by the humidity of the season. Therefore, cannabis indica often has a shorter flowering period than cannabis sativa, during which its height only increases by 25-30%. Another peculiarity of these plants is represented by the reddish and purple hues which, for unknown evolutionary causes, develop in the leaves when temperatures drop.

The classic example of this plant is represented by a compact shrub and a large stem which, unlike the sativa varieties, rarely exceeds two meters. It has the following features:

The foliage is dark green, to the point where in some specimens the leaves appear almost blue or purple. These have short and wide leaf limbs, designed to lose as little water as possible.

They produce more abundant and dense lateral branches than the other varieties, therefore they have a more shrubby, broad and dense appearance, like small fir trees.

The flowers of female plants form very dense clusters around the nodes (points of attachment of the pairs of leaves to the stem and branches). Given their greater density and compactness, these floral clusters are often heavier than those of sativa plants.

Cannabis indica plants are less productive, which is compensated for by their shorter growth cycle. And given their compact structure, which unlike the sativa structure, does not spread out without control, and is particularly suitable for indoor cultivation.

Also, an excellent choice for terraces and balconies, and for those who need discretion or discretion. The harvest takes place in September.

Indica cannabis strains have very varied organoleptic profiles ranging from musk to grapes and berries, typically with more earthy and moist notes compared to sativa strains, which are sweeter and fruitier, with clumpy and spicy undertones.

A recent study found that, compared to sativas, indica-dominant strains are much richer in the terpene myrcene, a compound that accounts for between 60 and 80% of their terpene profile and that, together with the action of THC, it would be responsible for the hypnotic effect characteristic of this plant which has more relaxing and sedative properties than sativa.

And since they contain higher amounts than other sesquiterpenes, they give off a thick and deep aroma that is very recognizable.

Unlike Cannabis sativa, where THC often predominates, it is rich in cannabinoids THC, CBD and CBN. For this reason, the effect of this indica strain often focuses on the body, with physical sensations such as relaxation, dry mouth or red eyes. These effects are defined by the English term 'stoned', which is very different from the high provided by sativa strains. Indica, having greater sedative effects can help you sleep better. However, Cannabis indica isn't just for insomnia, but a valid alternative to opioid drugs in the treatment of chronic pain, and as a muscle relaxant or antispasmodic for diseases such as multiple sclerosis and fibromyalgia. Furthermore, its analgesic properties make it an excellent ally against headaches, particularly in cases of migraine, and thanks to its calming effects, it is recommended for those suffering from panic attacks.

CANNABIS RUDERALIS

Much more similar in structure and characteristics to fiber hemp, cannabis ruderalis is grown not for its low THC content (present almost like cannabis light) but for its cannabidiol (CBD) content, which makes it extremely palatable for research in the medical and pharmaceutical fields.

Not only that: although the CBD concentrations are not equal to its Cannabis Indica cousin, Ruderalis is a very effective catalyst, able to increase the CBD production of the plants in which it is grafted or hybridized. Ruderalis literally means "rubble", a name given to it by its extraordinary ability to grow anywhere, making its way through debris and rocks.

An extremely strong plant, hardened to withstand low temperatures and adverse weather conditions.

Cannabis ruderalis was discovered for the first time in 1924, in Siberia by the Russian botanist Janischevsky, who by studying them, realized that he was facing a new species, more wild and stronger than the more famous Sativa cousin: these plants were in fact able to infest a field very quickly, causing other cannabis plants to succumb.

Although their height never exceeds one meter, these small plants possess a truly surprising tenacity, making cultivation much easier.

Other studies conducted on the plant revealed other characteristics: in reality, cannabis ruderalis cannot be considered as a plant in its own right, not even a subspecies of cannabis sativa.

Its genetic makeup shows it to be a more resistant hybrid, the result of the combination of the genes of cannabis sativa with those of cannabis indica.

The cultivation of Cannabis Ruderalis requires much less effort than the Sativa species, because it is tempered by a much more rigid climate and much less intensive care, with a maturation time of about 10-12 weeks, extremely short compared to other types of cannabis.

It is not photosensitive, and does not follow a rhythm imposed by the cycle of light administered, but rather grows relying exclusively on its internal biological clock. One of the main benefits is its ability to be autoflowering, a flowering that starts without continuous or prolonged exposure to controlled light. This significantly reduces production costs, making it an extremely versatile plant.

This ability to proliferate and spontaneously blossom has made it a flagship in hemp crops, also suitable for less experienced growers. Some biologists are also studying ways to hybridize cannabis sativa plants, giving them this amazing thriving ability.

It is not grown for recreational purposes, as the low THC concentrations make it unsuitable for this use. You can't get high .... however, if well crossed with indica or sativa it can give excellent results in this field too.

But its CBD contents make it particularly suitable for medical and pharmaceutical use, as extremely useful oils are extracted from its inflorescences for a relaxing and medicinal use.

The cannabinoid CBD is in fact widely used to lead to a state of total relaxation, with the loosening of contracted muscles and mental effects of absolute relaxation.

THC AND CBD

The chemical formula of THC corresponds to the famous molecule delta-9-tetrahydrocannabinol, the structure that underlies the main and best-known active ingredient in cannabis. Depending on the amount present, THC is capable of causing multiple effects to those. Now, you are probably wondering how the THC molecule is taken. Well, the answer is very simple: in cannabis, THC is taken by smoking it, inhaling it or dissolved in fatty liquids (such as milk or butter).

THC derives in particular from the hemp plant and, more precisely, from its inflorescences: by drying and treating them, a sticky and dense resin is obtained that can be used by the consumer.

As we have seen, Indian hemp plants are of three different types and differ both in their sizes and in the percentage of THC present. In ruderalis, it is much rarer and less known than the previous ones. What matters for our purposes is that obtaining marijuana from the types of plants we have listed means obtaining different types of ganja, with different concentrations of cannabinoids based on the variety grown. THC is a substance used for various purposes, and depending on the concentration it can be for fun (higher concentration) and healing purposes (lower concentration).

As we have already mentioned a few lines ago, the main types are three:

- sativa, which produces a low / medium THC content (1% to 5%);
- indica (Indian hemp), whose THC levels can exceed 25%;
- ruderalis (Russian or American hemp), insignificant THC content.

Apart from this first classification, it will certainly not escape most experts that cannabis varieties are much more numerous.

Compared to many other plants, cannabis is divided into two genera:

- male, with green bumps;
- female, with white filaments.

In turn, the female plants produce the flowers full of resin where are the active ingredients (THC, CDB, etc.). The male plant does not contain any active ingredients, or almost none.

Who produces cannabis seeds, to obtain a plant with high THC, will cross the cannabis sativa and indica plants? In this way, over 40 varieties of marijuana plants can be created, including Skunk or White Widow. To these are added other cross breeds such as Northern light, X Haze, Haze19, and X Skunk.

Cannabis produces marijuana (also called weed, mary, smoke, reed, joint, straw) and hashish, a resin derivative, extracted from the pollen of cannabis flowers. But is cannabis a drug?

For some years, an increasingly potent type of cannabis has been proposed on the market, with a strongly dissociative effect. Usually, it has 3 to 5% of the active ingredient (THC), but today there are modified plants grown with violent intensive culture techniques with almost 55% THC, and therefore have a high active ingredient and less of other protective active ingredients such as CBD.

Legal cannabis is low in THC, and instead has high percentages of CBD (non-psychoactive) that can reach 14% and cancel the negative effects of THC on heart rate, breathing, blood pressure.

Dr. Pietro Durante, psychiatrist of Santa Caterina Novella di Galatina, explains: "Once it could be considered a light drug, now, no longer. The main psychotropic substance contained in cannabinoids, THC (Tetrahydrocannabinol), is present today in very high quantities, (up to 60% more) much higher than 30 years ago and it is much more harmful." Even the production of home or greenhouse seedlings have changed: it is artificial, ammonia is added more and more frequently!

The high rate of THC in fact causes psychotropic alterations, creates physical dependence and generates all the symptoms of withdrawal, from depression to hallucinations, from delusions to the loss of concentration, then passing through paranoia, anxiety, feeling of physical discomfort.

Medical cannabis is something completely different: with a very low THC content, with relaxing and sedative effects.

Plants that contain THC

Thanks to some research, several plants with cannabimimetic properties have been discovered, able to activate the body's endocannabinoid system.

Let's clarify one point immediately: these plants do not get you high, as they do not contain any psychoactive substances such as THC, but only cannabinoid substances that do not cause negative impacts. Here are some, the best-known ones:

Echinacea, with anti-inflammatory and relaxing properties;

Acmella oleracea, used to treat stuttering, stomach pain or toothache, also known as 'toothache plant', 'electric plant' or 'Brazilian cress';

Helichrysum umbraculigerum (Helichrysum or Paper flower), a plant native to Africa, of the daisy family, with anti-inflammatory, antidepressant and mood stabilizing properties;

Liverworts, of which there are 9,000 species. Among these, the Radula marginata native to New Zealand contains a substance very similar to THC (perrottetinenic acid) which interacts with the CB1 receptors;

Chocolate (Cocoa Tree), which contains N-linoleoyletanolamide and N-oleoyletanolamide, two substances that deactivate FAAH enzymes. This deactivation triggers the give more levels of anandamide, an endocannabinoid called "the body's THC". It seems that anandamide produces feelings of euphoria, happiness and reduces our sensitivity to pain;

Black pepper, with anti-inflammatory properties. Contains high concentrations of beta-caryophyllene, which acts as a cannabinoid by binding to CB2 receptors.

Other plants that contain cannabinoids or cannabimimetic agents are camellia sinensis (tea plant not to be confused with the tea tree), Peruvian maca and Chinese rhododendron.

What is hashish?

So far, we have talked about weed, now we are talking about its extract, namely hashish. Also known by the common name of "smoke", hashish is distinguished from weed because it is the result of a direct extraction from its inflorescences.

It should be noted that there are different methods for extraction, from which two types of hashish are mainly derived: Charas, which has Afghan origins, and the Panetta, the traditional Moroccan compound.

The first type of smoke is extracted by intensely rubbing the palms of the hands on the tops of mature female plants, thus obtaining a black and sticky resin, which is subsequently removed from the hands and then accumulated in spheres and balls of various sizes.

The second type is extracted in a more noble and pure way, because it is obtained thanks to the percussion of the buds against a sieve, which only passes the trichomes and the THC crystals. Under the sieve, a kind of brown / green pollen is formed which is called Kief, which is then deposited in a mold and subsequently placed in compression with a cold press, thus reaching the final shape of a brick (hence the name panetta, or panetto). This last extraction method guarantees a product with more THC and high purity, because during its preparation, direct contact of the Kief with the hands of the producer is avoided (thus avoiding further bacteriological contamination), but above all because it does not contain plant parts, but only the resin that had developed on the flowers.

So, what is marijuana?

The THC formula falls within bile classification of soft drugs and for this reason, all over the world, there is still a fight between those who want to legalize it, thus taking away a large part of the income from organized crime, and those who want to continue to consider it a drug.

Who Discovered the THC Molecule?

The principle of THC cannabis was first discovered in isolation or for the first time in 1964 by Israeli scientists. Those were difficult years, prohibition reigned and only hippies allowed the use of marijuana.

The team of Israeli chemists still managed to illegally procure cannabis with the permission of the ministry of health with the aim of studying it with a scientific approach.

For millennia the hemp plant, and consequently THC, have been considered curative. Today in many countries there are medicines made up of the THC molecule, and they are used to treat many diseases and to alleviate some symptoms of many diseases.

THC has psychotropic properties, that is, it can affect the nervous system and cause some effects, based on its concentration. The difference between a therapeutic use and a purely recreational use should be emphasized.

As for the latter, there is a general relaxation of the body, an analgesic action that reduces any pain, a strong euphoria, the feeling that time passes more slowly, an increase in the feeling of hunger which coincides with the lack of the sensation of satiety, increased sensory sensitivity, drowsiness and slightly hallucinogenic effects.

The onset of these effects is subjective and can vary according to many factors such as: age, psycho-physical state, combined intake with other psychoactive substances and other factors that can alter the effects.

The receptors that bind with the active ingredient of hemp are located throughout the human body, but especially in the brain area. Precisely for this reason, THC has strong psychoactive consequences.

Apart from the various symptoms known as euphoria, excitement, increased hunger and alteration of all sensations related to the auditory, olfactory and gustatory system, THC also has relaxing and analgesic tendencies for which it is present in many medicines and to combat diseases such as:

- multiple sclerosis,
- Tourette's syndrome,
- different forms of cancer.

The anti-nausea properties of this active ingredient also make it usable by people with a depressed immune system such as AIDS patients or those undergoing chemotherapy. Many studies have investigated its composition and possible side effects.

In fact, there have been studies on animals aimed at understanding whether THC was toxic to the body but, in reality, it is necessary to administer very large quantities to cause death on small organisms such as rats, while for larger specimens it was practically impossible to achieve fatal outcomes. On the other hand, a topic that is much debated is what THC can cause in the long term in a human being. THC has many positive effects on the brain as it is a neuroprotector that defends the brain from inflammation and stress. Although many believe that smoking destroys brain cells, scientists have actually proven that THC induces the synthesis of new cells, leading to the phenomenon known as neurogenesis.

IT CAN BE USED AGAINST

- nausea,
- vomiting,
- anorexia,
- spastic muscles,
- cancer,
- multiple sclerosis,
- asthma,
- glaucoma,
- addictions,
- inflammation,
- psychiatric pathologies,
- Alzheimer's disease,
- Tourette's syndrome,
- neuroprotection and autoimmune pathologies.

Having a strong analgesic effect, marijuana is used against pain. This is precisely why many people use

THC-free marijuana and cannabis light to decrease pain and improve quality of life.

THC also has anti-emetic effects so as to decrease the sensation caused by nausea and vomiting. Many studies have found excellent results on people suffering from anorexia and eating disorders as THC induces appetite, with the famous munchies, which leads the subject to eat with taste and to stabilize the weight or to gain a few pounds.

As for spasticity, the beneficial effect can reduce both pain and tremor.

For cancer, it is used not only to reduce pain but also because people undergoing chemotherapy are severely debilitated and therefore need support and help to drive them to eat more than normal. As for asthma, THC has an effect that dilates the bronchi. For glaucoma, the active ingredient reduces the pressure that is inside the eye and thus protects the optic nerve or relieves its painful symptoms. For glaucoma, it acts as a therapeutic element while for others it simply represents prevention.

Healing marijuana for autoimmune diseases

Cannabis has a strong power able to counter this condition and thus decrease the therapy with anti-inflammatory drugs.

The THC molecule regulates the response of the body's immune system and reduces a high inflammatory response. Some subjects also find benefits to treat anxiety disorders, depression, sleep disorders.

As regards the phenomenon of neuro protection, THC activates a receptor that slows down cognitive decline. Precisely for this reason, many people suffering from neuro-degenerative diseases decide to try the therapy to slow down the course of the disease and prevent a series of problems such as hypoxia and convulsions.

'chemical hunger'. The sense of hunger and satiety are in fact altered.

Due to THC, the active ingredient present in cannabis, causes the so-called munchies as it stimulates certain neurons to suppress appetite. In practice, the brain system that controls nutrition is 'fooled' by the action of THC. The two groups of neurons considered basic in food processes are the pro-opiomelancortin (or POMC) prohormone that sends the sense of satiety to the brain and the Cb1r receptors (or cannabinoid receptor type 1) responsible for the sense of hunger. The extent of the munchies is proportional to the type of cannabis consumed (and relative percentage of THC) and the mode of consumption. The higher the percentage of THC, the more munchies will be felt. Additionally, burning releases more cannabinoids. Taking cannabis or cannabis oil through food preparations (edibles) is less impactful than the classic 'joint' (joint or by vaporization).

Even if they cannot be suppressed, the munchies can be avoided at least to avoid gaining weight. First of all, it is preferable to smoke on a full stomach, reducing the feeling of hunger. If this persists even on a full stomach, it is good to divert your mind by practicing physical or recreational activity or reading. Or, better yet, exercising before taking cannabis to burn enough calories and thereby compensate for the calories consumed later to satisfy the munchies. It is also advisable to drink at least one and a half liters of water after taking cannabis or satisfy hunger by indulging in light snacks, healthy foods such as fruits and vegetables, avoiding calorific foods.

THE BEHAVIOR OF THC INSIDE THE BODY

There are many types of cannabis related to illegal drugs:

- hashish, that comes from the inflorescences;
- marijuana, that comes from air-dried cannabis leaves along with flowers and stems;
- hashish oil with a very high THC level, which in some cases can even reach 60%.

All over the world cannabis is called differently: just think of Maria in Italy.

However, these are names that indicate the same substance that behaves in this way: THC penetrates very quickly inside the brain, and here the substances are usually stopped abruptly by the blood brain barrier (that is, that sort of "wall" of protection so that toxic and harmful substances do not penetrate inside).

This process does not happen with THC, which therefore manages to enter and carry out its effects.

A very interesting feature is that THC also spreads to other organs, especially those that are fatty. The THC molecule is able to dissolve in a gaseous substance. (And this dissolution CAN be detectable within the blood fluid even after months. In a nutshell, if you've smoked illegal cannabis, your body retains traces for 30 days or more, resulting in a laboratory investigation as well. Some studies show that there are organs that THC prefers: like the brain and the ganglia at the base of the cerebellum. Do not be surprised by this feeling with the cerebellum! It is in fact the brain, the organ that orients the body within the space and that is why THC alters the sensation and space-time perception of the subject.

Other very sensitive areas are the brainstem, the hypothalamus, the corpus callosum but ... also other brain structures bind in a particular way thanks and to the appropriate receptors. For example, the receptors in the ventromedial air (linked to mental gratification) and this explains very well why smoking THC makes smokers "feel good". Once you get to the brain it is then interesting to understand what happens to the body, when cannabis is smoked in fact there is an immediate presence of THC in the blood within a few minutes, about 15 or 20, with a maximum reached after 30 minutes. Here the subject has an intense symptomatology, which then gradually diminishes and lasts up to 3-4 hours. Sometimes, the symptoms are no longer perceived although the active ingredient continues to have its effects but are so minimal that they are no longer tangible. When the effect wears off, the individual feels the famous munchies that ... never seem to end.

Have you ever smoked marijuana without THC? You will know very well that the munchies induce that continuous feeling of appetite that does not stop even after large quantities of food.

THC and CBD, brothers and enemies

THC is not the only active ingredient present in cannabis, there is also its brother ... CBD, which is an active ingredient that has the task of curbing the excessive effects of THC and inducing the subject to wake up to counteract the sleepiness perpetuated by the other active ingredient.

Today CBD is considered the true cannabinoid of our century. CBD is the active ingredient used for the famous legal cannabis.

This substance brings a number of benefits to the body without causing any kind of psychoactive variation, and currently there are more and more legal companies and individuals who grow hybrid plants rich in CBD and with a negligible content of THC. Not only that: the properties of CBD are anti-inflammatory and analgesic, therefore infinitely useful for relieving the painful symptoms of many pathologies. The combination of these two active ingredients will have a truly optimal therapeutic effect for patients.

The combined effect of THC and CBD is called the entourage effect.

Science is working to improve and optimize this synergy. We are sure that soon we will have some interesting news in this context!

We have seen that THC is the main psychoactive cannabinoid responsible for a state of physical and psychic alteration. CBD (cannabidiol) is the non-psychoactive cannabinoid, the first to be accepted by traditional medicine. It has many medicinal properties but requires a minimal percentage of THC.

But is there THC-free marijuana?

No, it does not exist because even light marijuana (the legal one) contains, albeit in minimal percentages, this active ingredient (it must be less than 0.2% or, in some limited cases, 0.6%).

The active ingredient CBD (cannabidiol) of legal cannabis qualifies as a NON-psychoactive chemical (like THC), which has antipsychotic properties and brings several benefits.

Today it is necessary to recognize quality marijuana but, being managed by illegal markets, it is often contaminated and cut with foreign substances (glass sand, silica, sugar, washing powder, ripe fruit peels, hard drugs, etc.) to increase its weight. These contaminations make it toxic and dangerous to health, so much so that even marijuana not subjected to adequate root washing can be considered contaminated. The chemicals remain within the plant tissues and can enter the body through the lungs or digestive system.

In conclusion, today there are two types of accessible cannabis: legal and medical.

The therapeutic one has a THC content that can reach 22% and is attainable only with a prescription at the pharmacy.

Legal cannabis has a very low THC rate, with a maximum level of 0.2% or, up to a maximum of 0.6%, the legal limit. You can buy legal cannabis in any web or physical store, but be careful: you can only hold 15 grams at home and 5 outside. You can also grow light cannabis at home.

Weed without THC is a topic connected to that of the plant in general, the theme of light marijuana and the political and economic issues of various countries.

We can call it marijuana or cannabis; however, it is a name that we need to identify the same precious plant. Of extraordinary benefit to humans.

The percentages of THC present in cannabis light are so infinitesimal to the point that it can be said that there is none, since among other things there will be no psychotropic effects.

THC (tetrahydrocannabinol) is a psychoactive ingredient that appears as primary in cannabis. Primary among the dozens of chemicals (called cannabinoids) that cannabis plants produce.

Then there is also CBD, (with different percentages) and its use can give rise to various positive effects in people. To tell the truth, it would seem that even animals can take advantage of the benefits offered by CBD, in fact there is CBD oil for dogs (pain reliever, anticonvulsant). Many studies have confirmed that CBD not only has anti-inflammatory properties but also pain relieving and antipsychotic properties.

Unfortunately, from a clinical point of view, experimentation is still minimal. Another interesting difference to "reveal" is that concerning cannabis for therapeutic use.

Legal Lacanapa is a strain characterized by the selection of low THC cannabis sativa inflorescences, which can be grown and marketed.

Cannabis prescribed by doctors for healing purposes is legal weed called "state marijuana".

Marijuana has been an excellent alternative for the treatment of various diseases; for many patients

Today it is ascertained that CBD has beneficial effects on humans; many studies have confirmed the opportunities and properties that this substance offers.

Cannabis is certainly an effective treatment for chronic pain present in adults, but today it is known that CBD can be useful in reducing pain in general and inflammation. They noted, in studies on CBD in humans and animals, that the cannabinoid is well tolerated and has few possible contraindications.

Furthermore, it would appear that CBD can help with arthritis by relieving inflammation.

In a 2017 study, the possibility that CBD could be used to reduce pain from osteoarthritis and joint neuropathy was raised. Based on those results, the researchers were able to demonstrate that the cannabinoid was useful for "protecting the nerves", to reduce inflammation in the joints. In conclusion, legal weed with zero% THC does not exist and the amount of THC that a plant has serves to define the difference between cannabis plants. This distinction, among other things, allows us to establish what is legal and what is not.

RESIN

The cannabis resin, often also called "sap", represents the term that describes the trichomes, or the "pollen" that is commonly present on the inflorescences of cannabis and related leaves that characterize the hemp sativa plant, extracted through multiple methodologies. It is precisely the trichomes that hold the highest concentration of active ingredients THC or tetracannabidiol and CBD or cannabidiol, the same ones that are responsible for the therapeutic and psychoactive efficacy for which cannabis is known.

The cannabis resin represents a real defense mechanism triggered by the plant and is able to help it stay alive during its flowering cycle: this matter, in fact, is the main source of all the cannabinoids and terpenes typical of marijuana, and it helps to preserve the crop from the possible damage caused by ultraviolet irradiation, if dosed incorrectly. The same aromatic terpenes that accompany this pollen are also a valid deterrent against insects, parasites and infestations of various kinds that could seriously compromise the plant's health. Habitual users who consume ganja for fun purposes recognize cannabis resin as a precious derivative precisely by virtue of the massive presence of cannabinoids contained in it.

The cannabis resin is therefore a particular extract derived from the inflorescences produced by the hemp sativa plants still alive, therefore not dried, specifically by ithricomas, small pistils present that have the highest cannabinoid concentration. Generally, it appears as a dark and particularly dense mass, almost viscous while the extraction method used to produce it is aimed at preserving waxes and chlorophylls, thus maintaining the organoleptic profile of the cannabis itself unaltered. The cannabis resin is preferably dispensed with preloaded syringes to replace the common droppers generally present in CBD oil: the administration of this derivative is therefore more complex and, in some respects, more laborious, consequently requiring some suggestions that we will illustrate later.

The effects given by the intake of cannabis resin are very similar to the more common ones that result from smoking a joint. The high presence of THC and legal CBD makes the derivative highly powerful especially at the psychotropic and psychoactive level, generating first of all a marked sensation of high and euphoria accompanied by well-being and greater energy and vitality, all counterbalanced however by the typical relaxing effect of CBD.

However, only one rule is always valid: even the cannabis resin must be used with common sense, without giving in to excesses. It is therefore better to sip this extract, reserving it only for "special occasions"!

How is the resin used? Like CBD oil, the oral intake of cannabis resin allows a remarkable yield of the active ingredients together with a particularly rapid and immediate effect, since in the sublingual area there are capillaries and small veins that allow direct access to the bloodstream. Cannabinoids bypass both the stomach and the liver reaching the blood almost instantly, allowing you to benefit from their known effects. The intake involves applying a few drops of resin under the tongue, the equivalent of a grain of rice, without then swallowing for at least 10 minutes.

Cannabis resin, just like CBD oil, can also be added to coffee and drinks: this methodology in fact means that the active ingredients reach the liver and digestive system, subsequently metabolized in order to flow into the blood. However, the effects tend to occur after a longer waiting period. Maybe you can add more to the drink to have the desired effect.

This cannabis derivative can have a topical use in order to lead to resolution of problems such as dermatitis, acne, itching, psoriasis or skin rashes. In fact, the skin has its own endocannabinoid system where the receptors bind easily to the cannabinoids applied. It is therefore possible to have a real therapeutic balm with a high concentration of cannabis resin, simply by adding a few drops to a common body cream that is usually used, and then apply the preparation by massaging it if necessary.

Unlike CBD oil, however, cannabis resin, by virtue of the rather thick and viscous consistency that characterizes it, does not lend itself to being vaporized using specific devices for vaping. It can also be included among the ingredients of particularly creative culinary preparations, edibles, taking advantage of the countless marijuana recipes available or, alternatively, mixed with a classic marijuana herbal tea to amplify its effects.

The cannabis resin which is the most common, is undoubtedly the so-called "rosin", a solid obtained by pressure and heat, generally using a pneumatic heat press or alternatively a common hair straightener if the amount of cannabis to be treated appears modest, all in order to vaporize the liquid and volatile terpene components until a compact and semi-solid substance is obtained.

The rosin hash method is relatively fast, simple and accessible: it allows anyone to extract resin of high chemical quality and in a rather short time.

What is obtained from the extraction is quite similar to other extracts although in fact it is particularly concentrated. Applying heat and high pressure to the plant material allows its organoleptic characteristics to be preserved intact, restoring a valuable product capable of enhancing all the properties of cannabinoids.

Alternatively, it is possible to extract the cannabis resin, which in this case takes the name of BHO, through the use of chemical solvents such as N-Butane gas.

The cannabis resin contains a high concentration of cannabinoid CBD, suitable for fighting countless ailments, giving the body countless benefits. it can reduce stress and anxiety, providing a marked relaxing and calming effect, thus eliminating the need to resort to conventional psychotropic drugs and antidepressants.

It also helps fight insomnia and all sleep-related problems, promoting rest and relaxation of the body. It can be used for diseases such as rheumatoid arthritis and multiple sclerosis and neurodegenerative diseases such as Parkinson's disease, allergies and dermatitis.

It also helps to strengthen the immune system by preventing, for example, seasonal ailments and, being an effective anti-inflammatory, it relieves nasal congestion. Mixed with common face and body cosmetics, cannabis resin also offers significant topical benefits, relieving itching, eczema, acne, and redness, while also having an antibacterial and antiseptic action.

There are therefore many advantages of this substance which, if deprived of the active ingredient THC, as is the case with therapeutic cannabis, has always found wide acceptance in the therapeutic and medical field exactly as it happens for common plant material or grass. Using cannabis resin can therefore lead to resolution of problems of minor and modest size, without however having to resort to conventional pharmacological therapies.

SECOND PART: GROWING MARIJUANA

Before producing large quantities of cannabis buds, your seedlings must go through several stages of development. If your cannabis seeds fail to germinate, there will be no harvest.

It is assumed that the flowering and vegetative phases are the most critical moments in the life cycle. However, even during germination the chance of failure is high, especially if the timing is not accurately calculated. By giving your cannabis seeds the right care in the beginning, you will be sure to get healthy, robust and productive plants. There are various ways to germinate small and fragile cannabis seeds. All techniques offer different probabilities of success, and have advantages and disadvantages. Even with some experience in cultivation, and using first choice equipment, it is still possible that some seeds do not germinate properly.

This risk of failure is perfectly natural, as seeds are living beings.

ELEMENTS TO CHECK ON CANNABIS SEEDS

Regardless of the origin of the seeds, we advise you to proceed with a delicate inspection. Generally, all seeds germinate. But poor-quality seeds produce weaker plants. Unfortunately, this is a factor that only manifests itself when the plant enters the vegetative and flowering phase.

To avoid disappointment, remember that dark colored seeds are better, while light green or white seeds may not germinate at all. So even if a dark colored seed appears slightly damaged, plant it anyway. It is very likely that it will germinate, even if the outer shell is scratched.

TEMPERATURE PLAYS A FUNDAMENTAL ROLE IN GERMINATION

Before we look at the germination methods, here are some golden rules for proper germination. Of all the factors to consider, temperature is the first. Seeds need moisture, but they use temperature to tell when it's time to germinate.

- The ideal temperature is between 22 ° and 25 ° C
- The growing environment should be humid, but never wet
- The ideal relative humidity range is between 70% and 90%
- Seeds prefer fluorescent (cool white) light
- Try to handle the seeds as little as possible
- In hydroponic / rock wool growing, the ideal pH is between 5.8 and 6.2

The environmental factors that allow the birth of the first tap root are: heat, humidity and darkness. In its constant quest for moisture, a single root will slowly develop into the gorgeous cannabis plant we all love. The seeds begin to develop within 12–36 hours after adding moisture to the environment.

Timing may vary, based on the environment.

GLASS OF WATER TECHNIQUE

This is one of the least effective, but still valid methods. A very simple technique often used by novice growers. A glass must be filled halfway with water at a temperature of about 22 ° C.

After 3–5 days the seed will begin to develop, with thin white roots. When they reach 2–3mm in length, carefully extract the seed from the water and transfer it to a pot filled with soil.

Dig small holes (about 10–15mm deep) and place the sprouted seeds inside. After placing the seeds, install a fluorescent light 13–15cm away to encourage seedling growth. Avoid giving excess water to newly developed seeds. Use a nebulizer for a humid but not wet environment.

WET PAPER NAPKIN TECHNIQUE

This is probably the most used method. The wet napkin technique has many variations. Some growers use cotton balls or paper towels. In this guide we will use the paper towel, which retains moisture well.

Spread a moistened kitchen paper towel on a flat surface. Deposit the seeds, spacing them a few centimeters from each other. Then, cover them with a second paper towel. Both napkins should be moist, but not wet.

With roots grown to 2–3mm, transfer (gently) the seeds to the pots. For planting, follow the procedure described above.

PLANT THE SEEDS DIRECTLY INTO THE GROUND

By planting directly in the ground, you will avoid handling and moving the seeds when they are still fragile and delicate. The first taproot is covered with microscopic filaments, easily damaged. The water glass method and the paper towel method expose the seed to temperature fluctuations. Therefore, this is a much safer solution.

First of all, fill the pots with top quality soil, previously immersed in water. Many growers prefer to add water with a product that stimulates root growth. Make a hole 10–15mm deep. This will be the new home of your seed. Remove the seed from the package, and place it in the hole.

Cover the seed with soil, without pressing it excessively. The roots would penetrate the compacted soil with greater difficulty, slowing down its growth. Spray the soil, so that it maintains the right humidity.

If you don't want to soak the soil, use a sprayer to moisten the holes before planting the seeds. With an adequate level of humidity, the roots should develop equally.

The germination pots must be in a humid environment, at the temperature described above. After 4–10 days, the first shoots should appear, while the roots will continue to develop below the surface. At this point, transfer the plant to a larger pot, where the actual cultivation will begin.

USE CUBES IN ROCK WOOL

Maintaining an ideal temperature (between 22 and 25 ° C), and the right level of humidity can be complicated. Leaving the seeds outdoors or on a windowsill is not recommended; a DIY climate-controlled cabinet would do a much better job. A heated mat maintains a constant temperature but does not solve the moisture problem.

You should therefore invest in the purchase of special equipment but, by using rock wool cubes, you can create a perfect environment for the germination of cannabis seeds. Immerse the cubes in water, as you would with normal soil. Rock wool retains moisture and meets the plant's water needs. After dipping the cubes, glue them to a plastic tray. Large pastry trays are perfect for this purpose. The dome of the plastic container creates a tropical micro-climate, ideal for seeds. By placing all components in a temperature-controlled cabinet, there will be a self-feeding source of moisture. Do not handle the seeds until they become small plants ready to be transferred to the final growing medium. Using the rock wool cube technique, your seeds should germinate within a day or two. Two to three weeks after germination, your young seedlings should be ready for their new home. Once you get here, you have two options: transplant them into pots with soil or face the challenge of hydroponic cultivation. You will know when your seedlings are ready to be transferred as their root system begins to emerge from the rockwool cubes. Until they have begun to surround the bottom half of the rockwool cube, the roots will continue to search for water and nutrients in their new environment and grow downward.

Beyond the methods used, always keep in mind the environmental conditions of a spring day. In nature, cannabis seeds begin to germinate following the climatic transition from winter to spring. Humidity levels are still high, and temperatures rise. Always ask yourself the question: "Does the environment I have created for germination reflect the climatic conditions of spring?" If the answer is yes, your seeds will most likely sprout.

In most cases, the seeds germinate without any difficulty. However, sometimes problems can arise.

LIGHTING

The first problem is the light. Your seeds or young plants only need fluorescent or CFL lamps. Every plant needs light to survive, but excessive lighting in the first few weeks of life can be harmful.

Place the lamps 15cm apart. When the seedling begins to develop its first true leaves (with serrated edges), you can bring the lamps closer up to 5cm. If you are afraid of damaging the seedlings, insert your hand between the leaves and the lamp. If you can't stand the heat for at least ten seconds, push the light away by 2cm. Repeat this until the temperature becomes tolerable.

Young seedlings grow very quickly. Therefore, for best results, you will need to constantly adjust the distance of the lamps. After two weeks of exposure to fluorescent lights, you can switch to high pressure sodium (HPS) or metal halide (MH) lamps.

Have no fear. Wherever possible, the roots of a plant will always grow downward. It is not necessary to try to reposition the seed with your fingers. This is a crucial stage in the plant's life, and disturbing the seed at this stage is more harmful than beneficial. Generally, what emerges to the surface is not a root, but the stem of the cannabis plant.

If you are still unsure, wait a few days and you will see the first leaves (cotyledons) appear. If all the needs of the seed have been met, the sprout will be able to grow properly. In any case, the best solution is to stay calm. Follow our "golden rules", and your young seedlings will be ready to move into larger pots in no time.

BEYOND GERMINATION

WHEN SHOULD YOU START ADMINISTRATING THE NUTRITIONAL SUBSTANCES?

It depends on the growing medium you are using. In principle, it is not necessary to feed plants in the first 2–3 weeks of development. The soil is already rich in nutrients, and even in coir the nutrients only need to be added after about a week. If you choose to grow in hydroponics or coir, the nutrient solutions need to be boosted 0.25 times the base concentration. After the first leaves develop, increase by 0.25 for each set of leaves. For beginners, we recommend using soil as a substrate. It allows you to solve problems related to cannabis cultivation more easily. In addition, it tolerates any mistakes of the grower better. An easy way to assess a plant's nutrient needs is to look at its leaves. If food is scarce, the color of the serrated-edged leaves will turn light green. Over time, the leaves will turn yellow. This is an unmistakable sign of a nutrient deficiency. The plant will not die if its leaves turn yellow, but this symptom will remind you that it's time to feed your seedlings. Nitrogen is the substance most used by the plant during growth. When the sprout receives the necessary nutrition, its leaves will return to normal. Depending on the time elapsed before the grower intervenes, this process can take hours or days.

Cannabis Nutrients: How, When and Why to Feed Plants

SIT DOWN AND RELAX

The first few weeks of sprout development require no special intervention from the grower. The nutrients, as well as the lighting, will need minor adjustments. Now that your seed has germinated, you can spend a few weeks in complete peace of mind. Sit back, relax, and watch your plants grow.

After these initial weeks, you can treat your seedlings as if they were in the vegetative stage by switching to an intensive lighting cycle. During germination, always remember our golden rules. If in doubt, ask yourself the question about "spring conditions". If you are sure that everything is going well, you just have to contemplate the development of your beautiful cannabis plants.

HOW TO MAKE FEMINIZED CANNABIS SEEDS?

Growing from feminized cannabis seeds is an efficient way to make the most of all plants, on all occasions.

PRODUCE FEMALE SEEDS

Cannabis cultivation wants resinous flowers, lots of trichomes and rich cannabinoid profiles. These gorgeous features are only present on female flowers. Having gardens full of sturdy, unpollinated sinsemilla females means jars full of crunchy and tasty buds for body and mind.

The only drawback, unless grown from clones, is that hemp is programmed to produce around 50% males and 50% females.

Wouldn't it be better if only females could be grown from seeds, each time?

Well, this is where the feminizing technique comes in: there are two manipulation methods to produce only female seeds from seeds, every time. Although not really every time. But at least 99% of the time, which is a great result.

The general practice behind feminization is that female plants are forced to produce pollen, which in turn is used to pollinate other female plants. The result? The resulting seeds will be feminized, with no possibility of further pollination.

WHY FEMINIZE?

Feminized seeds are super-efficient for indoor and outdoor growers. No space, time and resources should be given to plants that will be thrown away two weeks after the lights change to 12-12. Likewise, outdoors where a large plant can consume maintenance time and resources before the fall flower show, feminized plants are also a good way to reduce pollination in guerrilla crops. There is nothing worse than finding a male or two who have pollinated every female plant.

INHIBIT THAT ETHYLENE

"Applications that lower the amount of ethylene in tissues or inhibit its action cause the formation of male flowers instead of female ones"

Here are the solutions that can be sprayed on female plants to create male pollen pockets: benzothiadiazole, gibberellic acid, silver thiosulfate, silver nitrate and colloidal silver.

Colloidal silver is easily found or produced. It is non-toxic, non-caustic and can be bought easily online or in a pharmacy.

The other solutions can be dangerous, difficult to find and expensive, with the exception of gibberellic acid, used in nurseries, but not as effective as colloidal silver. If you're interested in experimenting, try gibberellic acid. It is a growth stimulant that makes plants very elongated.

TECHNIQUE 1: COLLOIDAL SILVER

Colloidal silver is a solution in distilled water in which microscopic silver particles are suspended. Due to colloids the particles do not settle and cannot be removed with normal filtering. Colloidal silver is commercially available, and easily reproduced at home. It also has numerous uses as an alternative medicine, to soothe burns, as an antiseptic, and as a digestive.

Make sure the concentration is at least 15ppm, preferably 30ppm. Less than 15ppm produces male sacs with little viable pollen. To begin with, select a plant with the right characteristics to preserve. Feminised clones are the usual practice as the growth, flowering and resin characteristics of the mother are already known. No vegetation time is required once a clone is well rooted. Just plant it in a pot, give it a day or two to recover, and start a 12–12 light cycle right away. A plant grown to produce pollen can be small because cannabis produces large quantities of it.

Tip: Make two clones - one to feminize and one to leave for pollination. This creates a separate breeding space and prevents accidental pollination of other plants, or a sneeze that pollinates an entire grow room.

Plants can be induced to develop male sexual organs for up to four weeks from the start of flowering. For clones it is advisable to do this a week before the light change. If using a plant grown from seed, wait until the plant has developed sex before spraying, to be sure it is female.

Spray the plants to be feminized with argent or colloid them every day and thrice a day if you can. Wet them well. Do this for two weeks, then let the plants grow normally. Some growers report getting results after spraying in as little as 15 days. As sex development begins, male pollen sacs will develop instead of female calyxes and pistils. Male plants mature much faster than females and viable pollen can be produced within 3–4 weeks after sex development. Some growers will spray until the plant shows strong sexual growth. Make sure these plants are well insulated from any flowering females. A single pouch can release millions of pollen spores and requires only one spore per pistil to make a seed.

DO NOT SMOKE

The plants, sprayed with colloidal silver and after the pollen has been collected, are to be eliminated and you must not smoke them. Giving them a thorough rinse won't work. Colloidal silver is a systemic treatment absorbed by the plant through the foliage and not a topical application. Stay safe and throw them away.

TECHNIQUE 2: RHODIUM

Synsemilla is an unnatural state for cannabis. Without human intervention, a non-pollinated female would hardly be found in nature, unless she was sterile. When sinsemilla plants are allowed to go beyond their desirable ripening stage for a number of weeks, the plant, through an incredible process that evolution has bestowed upon it, realizes it has not been pollinated. As a last attempt at propagation, it will then produce sacks of male pollen in an effort to self-pollinate.

It is authentic male pollen with XX chromosomes. With all the genetic information from the female and non-Y chromosome, the use of rhodium-plated pollen creates female-only seeds, although, as with colloidal silver, a male may occasionally appear.

COLLECTION OF POLLEN AND POLLINATION

Various methods can be used to collect pollen.

Cover the top of the pot with plastic or cardstock to collect pollen as it falls, or modify a plastic cup to protect the plant and catch falling pollen.

Attach a clear plastic bag, perforated at the top for air exchange, around the entire plant.

A trained eye will remove each pod before it fully opens wide to make sure you catch any spore.

<u>Pollinating a female is easy.</u>

Using a soft brush, or even a cotton swab, dip it into your pollen crop and gently apply it to the flower of your choice. Even though there will be thousands of viable spores on the brush, enough to pollinate an entire plant, the trichomes of the pistils will greedily glue whatever you offer them. Then dip the brush into your pollen container a couple of times when you brush the flower.

To produce a lot of seeds, put the pollen in a bag and place it on top of a branch or whole plant, shake well and leave for twenty-four hours.

It is possible to pollinate different branches with different pollen and have a mother plant that contains 1, 2 or 15 different crosses.

It is also possible to self-pollinate the plant from which the male parts were generated. This will not produce as many seeds as pollinating a separate plant because fewer female and many non-viable flowers are produced.

Treat feminized seeds as you would any other seed, from germination to vegetative, and then to flowering. Now observation becomes important to have the best plants for your garden.

Plants selected using feminization are homozygous. This can have two effects that cannot be evaluated until the seeds have germinated. The homozygous gene will increase the parent's dominant or recessive traits in the offspring, so the traits you want and don't want can be amplified. Genetics is a strange thing.

Just like with standard male-to-female crosses, a heterozygous process, it will be necessary to grow a certain amount of plants and choose the best ones for the mother plants and for future reproduction. With enough space, hundreds, if not thousands, of new plants can be grown to select the best phenotypes.

By thinking a little ahead, you can set up a effective selective feminization program and always have female seeds of your favorite phenotypes at hand. You never know, you may discover the next big thing!

The simplest and least expensive way, considering how much money is potentially saved by avoiding wasting time growing males, is to purchase a colloidal silver generator, which is the quickest, no-nonsense choice. Or you can make your own silver, which is quite simple and does not require any special skills.

Colloidal silver is produced by passing an electric current from a pure silver electrode through distilled water. This simple electrolysis is all there is to it. Although distilled water does not conduct electricity very well, it passes enough of it to create ionized micro particles of silver. It sounds very technical, but it really isn't.

WHAT DO YOU NEED?

A power supply: 9-12 volts is ideal, or a 9-volt battery. Higher voltages require more caution.

Electrical cable. One piece for the positive and one for the negative.

Distilled water. This is easy to find in the supermarket. Do not use tap water as it contains too many impurities.

Pure silver, at least 99%. Silver coins are ideal and relatively cheap. They are available on eBay or from coin dealers. Results are also obtained with silver wire, and some reports indicate that silver alloys also work, but it cannot be predicted exactly what the behavior of the other metals present in these alloys might be. Pure silver is the best solution.

Small spring-loaded metal tweezers to hold silver.

A ppm meters.

Make sure the power supply is set to 9-12 volts.

Remove the insulation at each end of the wires using scissors or wire strippers.

Firmly connect the tweezers to the wires to ensure good current flow. A weld is best.

Secure the wires to the positive (red) and negative (black) terminals on the power supply still disconnected, or to the battery.

Put a piece of silver in each tweezer. Don't let them touch each other. Fill ¾ a jar or glass beaker with distilled water. 500ml will easily make two lots.

Suspend each of the tweezers in the water on opposite edges of the container.

Plug in and turn on the power supply. If using a battery, the process begins when the electrodes are immersed in water. After 20 minutes, remove the electrodes and test the liquid with the ppm meter. 15ppm (0.5) and above is your goal. The solution should turn a pale gold color.

When done, clean the black silver oxide from the silver electrodes and put away for when you need to use it again.

Store colloidal silver in a dark bottle and in a cool place. It is sensitive to light and temperature, but do not put it in the refrigerator.

PHOTOSYNTHESIS AND THE LIFE CYCLE OF MARIJUANA

Photosynthesis is key in cannabis cultivation. The sinsemilla simply could not survive without it. Photosynthesis is the process by which algae, cyanobacteria and plants convert light into chemical energy. There is photosynthesis: oxygenic and anoxygenic. The latter does not produce oxygen and is used mostly by bacteria, which is why in this article we will focus only on oxygenic photosynthesis. During (oxygenic) photosynthesis, plants absorb carbon dioxide and light and transform them into energy or carbohydrates necessary for growth, releasing oxygen as a by-product: real chemical-biological industries! Most plants, including cannabis, contain chlorophyll, which is responsible for the typical green color of plants. Not only that: this pigmentation allows plants to use their leaves as real solar panels. Chlorophyll absorbs the blue and red radiation of light.

Photosynthetically Active Radiation, or PAR, is a measure of the light a plant can actually convert. Visible light falls within the portion of the spectrum with wavelengths between 400 and 700nm. Photosynthetic Photon Flux Density or PPFD, measured in micromoles per second (μmol / s), quantifies the amount of photons reaching the plant. OK, now enough of the science: the key point is that PAR and PPFD are the most accurate measures of "photosynthetically" usable light. Most

LED lighting systems are marketed under their respective PAR and PPFD.

Unlike LED systems, most grow lights, be they MH or HPS, are commercially characterized by their brightness, and lumens are a measure of this quantity. Unfortunately, cannabis plants cannot photosynthesize with old incandescent lamps as effectively as they do with LEDs. This is why we compare a 300-400W LED to a 600W HPS.

The duration of the light cycle is another determining factor to consider. The length of the day governs the development of the crop and determines when and how much marijuana will yield. It is not just the quality of the light that is important; Mary Jane also needs to get a tan for a few hours a day. Interruptions in the light cycle are particularly stressful for photoperiod cannabis plants.

Photoperiod cannabis strains can stay in a vegetative state by receiving 15+ hours of light per day. Indoor growers prefer an 18-6 cycle or a continuous 24-hour cycle. Whiter lights are preferred to mimic spring sunlight. Most growers use MH lamps, cool white CFLs or full spectrum LEDs.

FLOWERING

The 12-12 lighting scheme has become the standard for indoor cannabis flowering. As the amount of light decreases, we move on to another phase, that of flowering. In the outdoor case, however, the process is slower and more gradual, the days shorten naturally after the summer solstice. At this stage cannabis mainly needs light in the red spectrum to grow buds. Yellow / orange HPS lamps are an old-school imitation of autumn light. Instead, growers using full spectrum LEDs just need to reset the lamp timer.

According to some studies, cannabis sativa thrives in environments rich in carbon dioxide.

Sativa performs best when grown at ~ 1500μmol m-2 s-1 of PPFD and with temperatures from 25 to 30 ° C.

Ruderalis is the rebellious cannabis species that developed the autoflowering trait, having a cycle of about 100 days after germination, there is no need to reduce the hours of light to cause flowering.

While autos can survive in just 8 hours of light a day, they do their best with a 20-4 light cycle. Likewise, summer outdoor crops harvested in July / August usually yield the best buds.

WHERE TO GROW YOUR PLANT

Seen from an external perspective, growing cannabis can seem like a complex and cumbersome process. While there are numerous variables that affect cannabis growth and the success of final harvests, the process itself can be boiled down to something simple. Before diving into a project of this type, a beginner should always set clear goals, set up a structure appropriate to the growth cycle of the plants, and make sure that the most important basic criteria have all been covered.

Skill comes with practice. Later on, you can start experimenting with more exotic growing techniques and different tricks to increase yields, but let's stick to the basics for now. Below is a list of the main considerations and suggestions to reflect on to make the process as smooth and productive as possible. So let's get to work right away!

There are numerous advantages (and disadvantages) to growing both indoors and outdoors. Indoor growing allows you to control almost all environmental factors, including temperature, humidity, water, light and air flow. Conversely, outdoor crops are exposed to the elements and factors such as light and heat cannot be controlled easily. However, the overhead for outdoor growing is minimal because the process requires much less electricity. Additionally, plants grown outdoors usually have much more space to grow, which results in larger plants and higher yields.

Some growers are lucky enough to be able to choose whether to grow indoors or outdoors. Others, however, are limited to one or the other. If you don't have space to grow outdoors, you can start an indoor operation. You will need a good lighting system, a fan and a grow cabinet (although you can grow directly in a room if you can). Select an appropriate room in a relatively secluded area of your accommodation and install your equipment.

If you decide to grow outdoors, choose the best area in your garden. We advise you to place the plants in an area well exposed to the sun, where they can receive as much light as possible throughout the day. Choosing an area with excellent quality soil is very important even if you intend to grow your cannabis directly on the ground.

If you have no choice but to grow outdoors but you live in an area where cannabis is prohibited, or have neighbors who would not approve, you can grow in a secret location. This ploy is called guerrilla cultivation. Some of the most important decisions revolving around this type of cultivation include planting the plants in a spot exposed to sunlight, but away from areas prone to flooding and paths frequented by hikers.

There are literally thousands of cannabis genetics on the market. Many of these are the result of selective hybridization, a process that allows cannabis growers to select the best characteristics developed from specific strains and cross them to create new and extraordinary varieties.

Variety selection ultimately comes down to personal preferences and limitations imposed by available space. Additionally, some strains are better suited for indoor cultivation, while others are better suited for outdoor cultivation. If you grow outdoors, you may want to try a large sativa or sativa-dominant variety that will take full advantage of your space to produce huge yields. However, bear in mind that sativas bloom tends to last a lot longer and that in colder climates with rainy autumns they may not be the best choice. If you are growing outdoors and don't want to attract unwanted attention or if you are growing indoors in confined spaces, try pure indica or indica-dominant strains that reach lower heights. You may also want to consider growing autoflowering strains. These plants do not require changes in the light cycle to initiate their flowering, are naturally very resilient and go from seed to harvest in a very short time. Autoflowers are perfect for growers looking for almost instant speed and satisfaction.

If you want to grow indoors you will need a good lighting system to allow the plants to perform photosynthesis optimally. There are several lamp models to choose from, each with their own pros and cons.

LED lights have become very popular with indoor growers because they are cheap, powerful and generate very little heat.

Compact fluorescent lamps (CFLs) are another popular light source. They are relatively cheap to buy, they work particularly well where space is limited, even if they are not suitable for larger farming operations.

High pressure sodium lamps (HPS) that have been tested for years have always demonstrated high reliability. They are also quite inexpensive and highly effective. The negative aspect is, they consume a lot of electricity.

If you decide to grow a photoperiod strain, which is a plant that requires a change in the amount of light to start flowering, remember to give the plant a different cycle than you would use to grow an autoflower.

Without complicating matters too much, most growers give 18 hours of light and 6 hours of darkness during vegetative growth. Once the plants have reached the desired size, they are given 12 hours of light and 12 hours of dark. A clear message that warns the plants that it is time to start flowering. So, keep this light cycle until harvest time. The lamps can be connected to a timer to automate lighting programs.

Plants need nutrients to survive and thrive throughout their life. Many of these molecules are minerals that allow plants to carry out vital physiological processes. The nutritional needs of plants can be macronutrients and micronutrients. Macronutrients are substances that cannabis plants require in large doses. These include nitrogen (N), phosphorus (P) and potassium (K). Almost all plant fertilizers show this relationship. However, cannabis plants also require micronutrients in the form of boron, chlorine, copper, iron, manganese, zinc, molybdenum and nickel.

With a little experience, you will learn how to prepare your own fertilizers, using compost and other methods. But in the beginning, the simplest way remains to buy prepackaged formulas with all these nutrients.

A very important factor to consider for beginners is the "law of the minimum". This principle states that a plant can also have all the nutrients it needs, but if a single nutrient is present in concentrations below the minimum necessary, the plant will inevitably suffer from a deficiency. Remember this if you prepare your own fertilizer formulas in the future, so that you can avoid any nutritional deficiencies. Avoid over-fertilizing your plants to compensate for the deficiency. Over-fertilization can harm your plants

PROVIDE THE PLANTS WITH A QUALITY CULTURAL SUBSTRATE

In this context, by substrate we mean the substance in which the cannabis will grow. Most often this is soil, which is perhaps the best option for budding cannabis growers. Other growers choose water as a substrate instead, a method known as hydroponics.

Soils are not all the same. Some are of poor quality and lacking in nutrients; others may be loaded with minerals and a different consistency. In general, cannabis prefers dark, fertile soils that are well-drained and unlikely to become muddy.

If you are growing autoflowering strains, it is preferable to use a softer and airier substrate, with less nutrients, more suitable for this type of plants. Autoflowers prefer a blend of compost, perlite and vermiculite.

KEEP THE SOIL SLIGHTLY ACID

Cannabis plants thrive in the most acidic soils. You can measure soil pH using litmus paper or pH probes. Keep the soil in a range of 6 to 7, so that plants can absorb nutrients more easily. If your soil is too alkaline, add some cottonseed meal or iron sulfate. To decrease the acidity, try adding some coffee grounds.

BEWARE OF PESTS

Check for parasites to avoid infestations. Of course, this applies primarily to outdoor growers, always keeping an eye on the lower and upper surfaces of leaves, the surface of the earth and even the tops of plants to check for insects.

But not all insects are bad. Ladybugs can effectively devour your garden's other threats, such as mites and mushroom flies. Always use biological pesticide systems ....

After all, it is you who will smoke the product. For any leaf pest issues, a foliage spray with a neem oil solution should suffice. Ensuring proper plant health can also prevent some parasites from attacking, hindering their ideal reproductive conditions.

For large animals, such as deer and other mammals, chicken coop fences and other structural support systems are a good solution.

KEEP AN EYE FOR SIGNS THAT INDICATE THE TIME OF HARVEST

After dedicating so much time and energy to growing your plants, it becomes essential to harvest the buds at the best time, when they have reached their best point of ripeness. There are a number of warning signs that growers can try to read when it is time to harvest buds, such as enlarging the trichomes to take a closer look. These small glands attend to the production of resin and are distributed on flowers and leaves. To see them it is enough even with a simple magnifying glass. They will appear translucent at the beginning of flowering, but towards the end they will become cloudy and then amber. For maximum yield, harvest the buds when the trichomes have taken on a cloudy appearance. Another trick to tell if your buds are ripe is to look at the tiny hairs known as pistils. They are initially white, but as the buds mature, they take on an orange color. Once around 75% have changed color, it will almost certainly be time to harvest.

LIGHTING FOR INDOOR CULTIVATION

Cannabis Growing Lamps

Knowing the many types of grow lights available can be important, especially for newcomers to cannabis cultivation. They all have the same purpose, but do it in many different ways. Every cannabis grower knows how important adequate lighting is for a successful crop. Along with nutrition and water, it is one of the key factors in ensuring healthy growth and high yields.

While natural sunlight is generally optimal for growing cannabis, many growers prefer to grow indoors for various reasons, as we've already seen. Additionally, indoor cultivation involves choosing a programmed artificial light, which gives the grower more control over the vegetative and flowering phase of his cannabis. With that in mind, we believe the world of cannabis grow lamps is worth exploring. There are many types of grow lights on the market for indoor growing today with huge differences in effectiveness and cost. In turn, some grow lights may be better suited to certain types of setups than others.

Fluorescent Lamps for Cultivation

CFLs, "compact fluorescent lamps," are some of the most common on sale, including in home improvement stores and even grocery stores. They are particularly suitable for small growers and are the cheapest beginner lights you will find. In addition, these bulbs have convenient standard sockets suitable for any regular lamp holder. They do not require special equipment.

You will find CFL bulbs with a blue spectrum of 6500K or red of 2700K. Bulbs with a blue light spectrum are better suited for the early (vegetative) period, while CFLs with a "warmer" spectrum are better for the flowering phase.

Pros and Cons of CFLs

- They have a low cost. They have a low light output (maximum for 2 plants)
- They are easy to install and use. They are not optimal for flowering (produce lower yields)
- They are great for beginners. They last less than other lamps
- They are available in various wattages and spectra
- They use little electricity, so they save energy
- They do not overheat
- To be used for clones and seedlings

Cost of CFLs and Expected Duration

A standard 40W CFL bulb will cost a few euros. This makes them great starter lights for growers on a tight budget! Excellent value for money, as the life expectancy of compact fluorescent lamps is approximately one year.

CFL yield

Expect to get 0.3 grams per watt (around 12 grams with a regular lamp).

HID lamps for cultivation

HID (High Intensity Discharge) grow lights are somehow a reference point for those who want to grow hemp. Many growers support HID lamps and believe they produce the best and largest yields.

Basically, these HID lamps are divided into: MH (metal halide) and HPS (high pressure sodium). MH lamps produce a colder (bluish) light, while HPS lamps are generally red. This makes MH lamps more suitable for the vegetative phase and HPS lamps better for flowering.

Therefore, both types of MH and HPS lamps can be used for the duration of the cultivation process. If for some reason you need to use only one type of HID lamp for the entire growth cycle, we recommend HPS. 600W HPS lamps are the most common type. Generally, it is possible to purchase complete kits that include lamps, a ballast and a reflector.

Pros and Cons Of HID

HID grow lights are definitely cheaper than high-end LEDs. They emit intense heat that can raise grow room temperatures or burn plants

They are easy to install and use. Additional equipment is required for their operation, including an electronic ballast and a reflector

They produce excellent yields. HID lamps degrade over time and you will have to replace them periodically.

They are reliable and offer consistent results. HID lamps are very energy consuming and can significantly increase your electricity bills

Cost of HID Lamps and Expected Lifetime

As we previously mentioned, there are complete HID lamp kits that include a lamp, ballast and reflector starting at € 150. However, the low initial cost will be offset by the ... electricity bill.

The duration of the bulb is about one year.

Yield of HID Lamps

Consider around 0.5–1g + per watt, which is around 300–600 grams / per regular lamp.

LED lamps for cultivation

A few years ago, LED lamps were not suitable for "serious" crops, apart from providing lighting for seedlings or clones but LED technology has come a long way.

Modern LED grow lights, with COB (chip on board) or "Quantum board" technology, can now provide consistent light intensity and penetration, even for the most demanding crops. Today, LEDs can compete with or even outperform other types of grow lights, including HID lights. That said, choose well. These lights, among the more expensive ones, can also save you some money later on.

Most quality LEDs emit light that works for both the vegetative and flowering phase, while some come with a switch to change the light (intensity and color) to the appropriate phase.

Pros and Cons of LEDs

More energy efficient lamps (save money and energy over time). These are high quality devices, with modern models that can seriously weigh on your wallet

LED lamps operate at much lower temperatures than HID lamps, barely producing heat.

They reduce cooling costs - impossible to burn the plant.

The cheap trope models on the market produce inferior results.

Most commercially available LED grow lights are ready for immediate installation - no need for special power supplies. Potentially lower yields than HIDs

Simplicity: they can support both the vegetative and flowering phase

Cost of LED Lamps and Expected Lifetime

There is also a low-quality LED device for growing a single plant at a cost of 120 €. However, for good LEDs from a reputable brand expect to pay several hundred euros, even up to €2,000. With LEDs you will get what you pay for, so do your research before you buy.

A good LED lamp has a lifespan of 5–10 years.

Yield of LED lamps

about 0.5g – 1.8g per watt.

LEC

LEC lamps for cultivation, ceramic metal halide (CMH) or metal halide discharge (MHD) bulbs

The name also suggests the difference between LEC lamps and conventional HID lamps. LEC lights use a ceramic arc tube instead of the quartz version found in regular MH lamps. Gives a more natural color, more lumens per watt and a longer lifespan. LEC lamps include integrated ballasts, so installation is very simple.

While modern LED lamps are becoming the standard in most grow rooms, LEC lamps offer some advantages.

Pros and Cons of LECs

They emit a spectrum of natural light (UV-B light is harmful to humans), safety equipment is required to reduce risk to skin and eyes)

LEC lamps emit UV-B rays which can improve the yield or production of trichomes. They have very high installation costs.

They are simple to install and use

Longer life but less power than HID lamps

Cost of LEC Lamps and Expected Duration

Good quality LEC lamps start at € 250–300, with high-end models going up to € 1,000. The bulbs also cost a little more than regular MH / HPS lamps.

Yield of LEC Lamps

When using LEC lamps, it is possibly getting up to 1.5g per watt.

To choose one of these solutions, you need to consider several factors, including the size of your growing area, the type of grass and, last but not least, your budget.

If you need a lamp for seedlings and clones or have a "micro grow" in a closet, a simple CFL lamp will probably suffice. For slightly larger grows, consider purchasing a good LED lamp that is between 400–600W.

For medium to large growth operations, you can look for high-end LED lamps and LEC lamps, or opt for proven HID lighting solutions.

Since lighting technologies differ in their efficiency, it is not possible to compare them based on their wattage alone. The only type of light in which certain yields can be expected (given a particular wattage) would be HID lights. Honestly, the only way to determine true light output is to look at the specific data provided by the manufacturer. Or better yet, ask other growers for advice.

As we have seen, light is very important for cultivation. If you want exceptional yields, you absolutely cannot avoid buying a HID lamp of at least 600W or more powerful, or LED or equivalent LEC.

Most importantly, don't spend money on a grow light without first getting informed. If the prices for a good lamp are intimidating, you can also look for DIY solutions! online there are all kinds of kits that come with the necessary parts.

GROWTH GROUND FOR OUR SEEDLINGS

Growing cannabis in soil is used to harvest full-bodied and aromatic buds. What are the best soils for growing cannabis?

At this point, choosing the right soil is essential. Unfortunately, it is not always easy to get high quality soil. Specialty cannabis soils, cheap universal soils, pre-fertilized substrates - this vast choice can put novice growers in trouble.

Let's examine the various types of soils.

Not all soils are suitable and not all cannabis needs the same type of soil. Choosing the optimal substrate should be made based on the cannabis genetics you are growing, the climate, the growing environment (indoor or outdoor), etc.

Let's look at the characteristics of the various cannabis soils together:

- Consistency

Cannabis favors soil with a light and airy texture. A not very dense structure favors the development of the roots, allowing oxygen to reach the latter, so that the plant grows healthy and vigorous.

- Draining capacity

The ideal soil must have excellent drainage capabilities. When watering your plants, the water should not form surface puddles. If the soil fails to drain properly, specimens may become ill and offer lower yields, or even die.

- Water retention

Water retention, or the ability of the soil to hold water, is no less fundamental. Good quality soil offers a perfect balance between water retention and drainage.

- pH value

pH is a scale that indicates the alkalinity or acidity of a substance. Cannabis grows healthily only within a certain pH range. An optimal soil has a pH of about 6.0. PH levels between 5.8 and 6.3 are equally valid, but if the value deviates too much from this range, lower yields will be obtained. If the pH is extremely far from these values, the plants will die.

- Nutrients

The soil in which it is grown must contain nutrients suitable for plant development. Fortunately, almost all commercially available soil already contains the ingredients necessary for plant growth. These substances have a shelf life of 3–4 weeks. By the time the specimens begin to bloom, the nutrients contained within the prepackaged soil will be exhausted. It will therefore be necessary to add additional nutrition. Note that without these additional nutrients, the soil must already contain organic molecules such as humus, compost, vermicompost, guano, etc. The microorganisms in the soil will transform these substances into food easily assimilated by plants.

CHARACTERISTICS OF A QUALITY SOIL FOR CANNABIS

The pre-packaged soil mixes are already "calibrated". The situation changes if you are growing organically. There are four types of natural soil: sandy, muddy, silty and clayey. Remember that most soils contain a mix of these soils, in varying proportions. For example, a soil can be clayey and loamy, or sandy and muddy.

SANDY: Sandy soils are coarse with good drainage, but offer poor water retention. When irrigation is done, nutrient molecules such as nitrogen will be rapidly dispersed into the soil. Sandy soils are easy to work, and are a viable option for cannabis growers.

- Coarse structure
- low pH
- Pros: Good drainage, keeps soil ventilated, high oxygen levels, easy to work with

- Cons: Poor water retention, need for frequent irrigation

MUDDY

Muddy soil has a medium coarse structure, with a lot of minerals and organic particles that make it extremely fertile. Offers good water retention and adequate drainage. Muddy soils are extremely easy to work.

- Medium coarse structure
- Pros: Contains minerals and nutrients, retains water well
- Cons: Discreet drainage

LOAMY

Loamy soil mixes with sand, silt and clay, and also contains organic molecules. Optimal substrate for growing cannabis, and offers optimal water retention and drainage. Rich in oxygen and nutrients. Downsides: This type of soil can be expensive.

- Mixture of sand, silt and clay
- Pros: Excellent water retention and drainage, contains nutrients, high oxygen levels
- Cons: It is very expensive

CLAY

Clay soil is made up of tiny mineral particles. This type of soil is heavy and difficult to work. It has significant amounts of nutrients and minerals, making it ideal for growing organically. Clay soil holds water well, but offers poor drainage.

- Very fine particles
- high pH
- Pros: Rich in nutrients, it holds water well
- Cons: Poor drainage, heavy and compact, difficult to work

TO IMPROVE SOIL QUALITY

The soil you are growing may not have an optimal composition for your plantation — at least not from the start. Maybe it may not drain the water properly. However, it is possible to improve the soil by adding soil improvers, which are usually found in normal gardening stores.

COCONUT FIBER

The coconut fiber derived from the shell of coconuts. These fibers offer excellent water retention and can lighten the most compact soils. For their ganja plantation, there are those who use a substrate made entirely of coconut fiber and enriched with specific nutrients. To amend an existing soil, up to 30% coconut fiber can be added, depending on the composition of the base soil.

PERLITE

Perlite is a common soil conditioner. It is composed of very light, bright white rocks and improves the drainage and airiness of the soil. Perlite also offers a fair amount of water retention. You can amend your soil by adding 10–15% perlite. Larger amounts can be added, but with caution: the soil may become too light and nutrients will be dispersed. Good quality prepackaged soils often already contain doses of perlite.

EXPANDED CLAY

Many cannabis growers use expanded clay in their hydroponic plants. By adding expanded clay to flowerbeds or to the bottom of pots, you will increase the drainage capabilities of the soil, avoiding accumulation of water in the saucer — which can promote root rot. Growers also add expanded clay to the soil surface, in flower beds and pots as an alternative mulch. Clay retains moisture within the substrate, preventing excessive evaporation. Mulch made from expanded clay covers the surface layer of the soil, suppressing weeds and protecting beneficial bacteria from scorching sunlight.

VERMICULITIS

Like perlite, vermiculite is also a heat-treated mineral useful for lightening the soil and retaining water. Vermiculite has some characteristics similar to perlite, but the two substances serve opposite purposes: perlite for draining capacity and airiness, vermiculite increases the water retention of the soil. They can be used together. The ideal vermiculite dose is 10%.

VERMICOMPOST

Vermicompost is a nutritional amendment, as it contains many beneficial microorganisms, which promote plant growth. The vermicompost is also able to improve the consistency, the draining capacity and the water retention of the soil. When using vermicompost as a soil improver, add about 25-30%.

NUTRIENTS

If your DIY potting soil is already high in organics, you probably won't need to add any more nutrients. Some growers make the mistake of adding manure and vegetable waste to the soil, to "fertilize" it. But in this way, the soil becomes excessively "loaded" with nutrients and this can damage the development of plants.

To properly reuse your vegetable waste in your garden, you must first compost it. If you need to add nutrients to the soil of your cannabis plantation, you can purchase ready-made liquid solutions suitable for each stage of plant growth.

PHOTOPERIODIC VS AUTOFLOWERING

Before choosing the most suitable soil for your weed, you need to choose the kind of specimens to paint whether photoperiodic or autoflowering. Autoflowers prefer light, low-nutrient soil mixes. The ideal substrate for autoflowering varieties is a 50:50 mix of coir and light peat-based soil, with perlite to aid drainage.

When growing autoflowers, avoid soils with overdoses of fertilizer and soil improvers such as bat guano, as they can overload the plants with nutrients. The same goes for seedlings, which do not want too much nourishment.

PHOTOPERIODIC VS AUTOFLOWERING

Place the autoflowering plants in their final container by digging a hole in the ground. Fill the hole with seedling soil, free from nutrients, and insert the seed inside. This way, the seedling will not be surrounded by overly fertilized soil, which could cause nutrient burns.

If you are growing photoperiod plants, place them in small seedling pots with nutrient-poor soil. Repot the specimens cyclically. Adult plants tolerate high doses of nutrition more easily than seedlings.

PRE-PACKED VS HOME MADE

For starters, your best bet is to buy pre-packaged potting soil from a specialty store. Typically, these cannabis blends already contain all the necessary nutrients, and in optimal proportions. If you wish, you can further enrich the prepared soil with a handful of perlites to improve drainage.

Recipe For Preparing A Basic Soil For Cannabis

Some prefer to make their own substrate themselves. Here is a recipe for making a basic cannabis soil at home.

INGREDIENTS

- 1 part of vermiculite
- 1 part of coconut fiber
- 2 parts of compost
- ½ – 1 cup of vermicompost (or humus)

INSTRUCTIONS

1. Sift the compost to remove larger residues.
2. Soak the coir in hot water. Read the product instructions.
3. Mix the coir and vermiculite in a bucket.
4. Add the compost.

Done. Check carefully the pH level of your homemade potting soil. The ideal value is between 5.8 and 6.3.

With the recipe just described you will have a basic soil suitable for most plantations, indoor and outdoor. You can further enrich the mix by adding organic fertilizers.

Bat guano is an excellent and economical organic fertilizer, suitable for the flowering phase. You can mix it with the soil or distribute it on the surface layer, watering later. Additionally, you can opt for gradual release nutrient solutions such as Easy Boost Organic Nutrition pellets. Add this product to the soil to nourish the plants throughout their life cycle — 100g is enough for 2–3 specimens. and water!

NO-TILL CULTIVATION (WITHOUT PROCESSING)

No-till cultivation is a method that allows the soil to rest (without tillage, plowing, mixing, etc.). Microorganisms in the soil can create a viable ecosystem that enriches the soil with bacteria, fungi and other beneficial organisms. No-till cultivation promotes the retention of organic matter and the absorption of water, as nutrients are continuously recycled.

If you are growing outdoors in sunny climates such as southern Spain or similar regions, be careful not to "cook" the root system. If you are growing in pots, choose white plastic containers, which help keep the soil temperature at acceptable levels, even in the scorching sun. You can also use air pots or smart pots, which keep the roots cool. As an additional protection against temperature fluctuations, cover the ground with a layer of dry straw.

If you're growing in particularly dry areas, where it doesn't rain for weeks, or if you can't always take care of your guerrilla-style clandestine plantation, use super absorbent polymers to keep your plants hydrated! You can buy them in stores that specialize in hydroponic systems or take them out of baby diapers.

If you are growing guerrilla style in particularly dry conditions, dig a hole 60cm deep with a diameter of 30cm. Add a few cups of polymer crystals to the bottom, then fill the hole. After putting the plant watered. During development, the roots will reach the polymers and will be able to absorb water even in case of drought. Tip: Soak the polymers in a light nutrient solution for a double benefit!

HYDROPONIC SYSTEMS

<u>Guide for hydroponic cannabis cultivation</u>

Hydroponics is a method of growing plants in a solution of water and nutrients.

Hydroponics can be scary, but the rewards are definitely worth it.

As the name suggests, hydroponics is a soilless cultivation method that uses water as the primary substrate. In a hydroponic plant, cannabis plants are grown in buckets or baskets filled with an inert growing medium and suspended over a water-filled tank. The water contains everything necessary (nutrients) for the life and growth of plants, while the use of porous stones allows the tank to be oxygenated. Of course there are different models and the choice of plant depends on the preferences of each grower.

At first glance, it might confuse hydroponics with something extremely modern. But is not so. The use of crops in water dates back to the beginnings of human history. There is evidence of these crops dating back to 600 BC. in Mesopotamia.

The Aztec civilization also made use of hydroponic cultivation to ensure the sustenance of their society. After being forced to abandon their lands due to a conflict, this population settled along the shores of Lake Tenochtitlan. Here they began to build floating rafts covered with soil, so that the plants grew on the mantle and the roots stretched into the waters below.

The history of hydroponics has demonstrated the effectiveness of this method in the most diverse environments and scenarios, because hydroponically cultivated plants grow much faster than those grown in the ground. Plants grow 30–50% faster and, in most cases, give higher yields. The nutrients contained in a hydroponic system are much more readily available to plants. The nutrients are suspended in the water and penetrate directly into the root system, as there is no soil to cross. Conversely, soil-growing plants must spread their roots through the substrate to absorb nutrients from the deeper layers. reaching nutrients more easily allows plants to store more energy to spend on growth.

MATERIALS NEEDED FOR A DO-IT-YOURSELF HYDROPONIC SYSTEM

We will list all the equipment needed to build an essential indoor hydroponic system. Always evaluate the product that best suits your needs. By purchasing each tool separately, you can invest money on more important equipment, such as grow lights, reducing expenses in other areas.

Here's what you'll need:

a) Lamps (LED or sodium)
b) Lamp supports
c) Grow tent
d) Tray and tank for hydroponic system
e) Porous stone and pump
f) Growing substrate (e.g. coconut fiber)
g) Vases with mesh texture
h) Seeds
i) Ventilation fans and ducting pipes
j) Carbon filter
k) Oscillating fans
l) Nutrients for hydroponics
m) pH and PPM meter
n) Algometer

THE COSTS OF HYDROPONIC CULTIVATION

When we talk about hydroponic cultivation, images of highly technological systems immediately come to mind: automatic switches, flashing lights, timers and stopwatches. but, the cost of a hydroponic system mostly depends on our budget to invest. The various types of hydroponic systems range from the very simple ones consisting of a simple plastic bucket, to self-draining systems and with automatic irrigation. To save time, purchase a low-cost hydroponic growing starter kit, containing all the material to tackle every stage of plant growth, from germination to ripening. A kit costs around € 235.

1. CHOOSE THE SUBSTRATE WITH WHICH TO START THE CULTURE

We start our hydroponic cultivation by choosing a growing medium, a substance capable of keeping the intersection between the stem and the roots in place. Inert substrates also allow the roots at the top to receive air. The list of substrates used by growers is very extensive, but some are more common than others. Each substrate has its own advantages and adaptability When approaching this world, it is a matter of experimenting until you find the substrate that best suits your needs.

EXPANDED CLAY

Expanded clay is an excellent material that maintains proper oxygenation of the root systems. In some cases, expanded clay requires an intervention to balance its pH. There is also no problem on the market for expanded clay already treated. Pour the clay into a plastic basket suitable for this crop, equipped and perforated to allow the roots to grow.

ROCK WOOL

Rock wool is a material created using volcanic rocks. Rock wool has excellent water retention and keeps the upper parts of the roots moist. Rockwool can be placed inside a hydroponics basket, or directly into the top of a bucket.

PERLITE

Perlite is used to provide greater ventilation.

COCONUT FIBER

Coir is a great eco-friendly alternative to use. This is the fiber that covers the coconuts, which is separated and used to improve ventilation and to retain water and moisture. It also serves to protect the roots from infection.

2. CHOOSE A HYDROPONIC CULTIVATION SYSTEM

Now that you have selected the growing medium, you need to choose which type of hydroponic system to use. All use an aqueous solution enriched with nutrients. However, systems can vary greatly depending on a few factors. Most of the following systems are commercially available, but if you are skilled at DIY, you can easily build your own.

DEEP WATER CULTURE

Deep Water Culture is easy and inexpensive. The plants are placed in buckets filled with a nutrient solution and an air pump that constantly supplies oxygen.

FLOW AND REFLUX

A system of ebb and flow ("ebb and flow" or "tide table") consists, in fact, in making the water flow and flow back. It is made up of numerous buckets suspended on a tray that has an inlet and an outlet for water. Both openings are connected to an external reservoir containing the nutrients, a porous stone to oxygenate the water supply and a pump to move the water into the tray. In these hydroponic plants, the roots are not constantly immersed in water, which, passing through the tray, is enriched with oxygen and nutritional substances. At the end of the pumping cycle, all the water returns to the tank.

The length of time the tray is empty allows growers to look after the roots and harvest plants more easily.

DROP-BY-DROP SYSTEM

The drip system installed in a hydroponic system is very similar to the one used to irrigate soil crops. It is composed of a large tray filled with substrate, such as expanded clay. The plants are directly in the substrate, and each is irrigated by its own drip tube positioned in the immediate vicinity. An external water tank with porous stones and pump provides constant water dripping on each plant. The roots are in contact with the air, and the excess water dripping along the substrate and then returns to the external reservoir.

TECHNIQUE OF NUTRITION FILM

It is the equivalent of a crop of grass set up on a river. The plants stay in an inclined cylinder, so that the water can enter from one side and exit from the other. The roots in the cylinder are exposed to water. The water passes from a tank in which a porous stone and a pump are immersed, and then comes back again.

WICK SYSTEM

A tray is used, under which there is a water deposit, from which numerous wicks come out and enter the growing substrate, filled with expanded clay. Water moving along the wicks passively hydrates the substrate. There is no need for pumps.

AIR PORT

The water is nebulized and dispersed in the air to optimize aeration and hydration. The plants are arranged in the upper part of a large container filled with 25% water. A pump is immersed in the water which pushes the solution towards water diffusers positioned below the roots. The fog created in this way is constantly absorbed by the roots, so that the plants receive air and water at the same time.

3. HOW TO PREPARE A SYSTEM TO OBTAIN THE BEST RESULTS

Water reservoirs are perfect habitats for different families of pathogens. First sterilize all equipment to minimize the risk of contamination. Clean everything with suitable products. Once sterilized, mount the system.

ENSURE REGULAR MAINTENANCE OF THE SYSTEM

All hydroponic systems need careful maintenance to ensure the optimal growing environment. Here are the main factors you need to consider.

A) ALWAYS CHECK pH

Nutrients develop best in a slightly acidic environment. Optimal pH of 5.5–5.8 for the first phase. There are kits on the market for testing the pH. Always check the pH and replace the solution every week. In the flowering phase, ph 6 is recommended.

B) CHECK THE WATER TEMPERATURE.

Hydroponically grown cannabis prefers temperatures of 20 ° C. Use a water thermometer to monitor the temperature and make sure you always keep it around 20 °.

C) GIVE THE RIGHT QUANTITIES OF FERTILIZER

The easiest way to fertilize plants is to buy hydroponic formulated fertilizers that contain all the nutrients for both vegetative and flowering phases. On the product labels you will find advice on dosage and frequency of use.

D) KEEP ALL EQUIPMENT CLEAN

Both tanks and trays need to be emptied and cleaned approximately every two weeks. This process will keep plant roots safe from invading pathogens and disease. Repeat the same procedure described above.

E) SELECT A VARIETY TO GROW HYDROPONICALLY

Variety selection is extremely important in hydroponic cultivation. Plants with hydroponic cultivation grown indoors absorb fertilizers extremely quickly, this leads to uncontrolled and very fast growth. Therefore, selecting a large sativa variety if you install your system inside a cabinet, is not the right choice. For these systems, smaller, more compact varieties are better. A variety of dimensions contained in a small space, gives a greater yield and having more space the plants can grow more flourishing

Here are two examples of plants suitable for hydroponic cultivation.

WHITE WIDOW

This is a hybrid of 50% indica and 50% sativa. With THC concentration at 19%.

Indoor White Widow reaches 60-100cm in height, a size suitable for indoor hydroponic growing. It offers excellent yields of 450–500g / m². The flowering period is 8–9 weeks.

ROYAL DWARF

This Skunk and ruderalis strain offer excellent yields and moderate growth. Given the sativa prevalence it induces a motivating and uplifting cerebral high. THC concentration of 13%. It is imbued with sweet flavors, accompanied by citrus notes.

Indoors, plants reach low heights of 40–70cm, with yields of 200g / m², with an 8-week cycle.

For those looking at it from the outside, hydroponics could be scary and seem too complicated a process. It is indeed a very complex technique. So start as simple as possible, choosing the most appropriate strains and regularly observing the environmental needs of your "creatures". Your efforts will be rewarded by thriving, fast-growing plants that give an optimal yield.

CANNABIS NUTRIENTS: HOW, WHEN AND WHY TO FEED PLANTS

These plants are sensitive to nutrients and great care must be taken to properly feed the plants and not burn them with chemicals.

All the nutrients necessary for the development of cannabis plants are naturally present in the environment. However, to help your plants grow even faster and produce a better end product, you'll need to feed them using fertilizer — a concentrated form of nutrients.

Cannabis plants require three nutrients in abundance. These are nitrogen (N), phosphorus (P) and potassium (K), they are called macronutrients and form the foundation of the health of cannabis plants. As such, these three nutrients are usually present in the fertilizer label with a ratio called NPK. The greater the number for each value, the greater the concentration of that particular nutrient.

However, cannabis needs many other nutrients to grow and thrive. It also relies on secondary nutrients such as calcium, magnesium and sulfur to play vital roles in plant growth:

Calcium is important for cell wall development, can help reduce soil salinity and, as a soil improver, can improve water penetration.

Magnesium plays a key role in photosynthesis and carbohydrate metabolism and also helps stabilize plant cell walls.

Sulfur is necessary for chlorophyll, the production of enzymes and vitamins, and for protecting plants from disease.

Plants also use many other nutrients in small amounts (micronutrients) which are however extremely important. These include boron, chlorine, copper, iron, manganese, molybdenum, and zinc. While these are not the main nutrients plants use for food, they still play very important roles in various aspects of plant health.

There are so many types of cannabis nutrients on the market that can vary greatly.

Typically, cannabis fertilizers vary in four areas:

Nutritional Value: Different brands use different nutritional ratios that they consider optimal.

Ingredients: Different brands of fertilizers can achieve the same nutrient ratios using completely different ingredients, ranging from the most chemical (or "artificial") to the most natural.

Soil or Hydroponics: Soil nutrients are very different from hydroponic (or soilless) nutrient solutions. Make sure you only use fertilizers designed for your growing medium.

Supplements: Many fertilizer brands also produce "supplements". Generally, these products contain low NPK intakes, but contain nutrients designed to promote certain aspects of growth. For example, some supplements are essentially molasses.

We recommend that you focus more on meeting your plants' demands for macronutrients and secondary nutrients before filling them with supplements. Overdoing the nutrients can result in chemical interactions or burns that can significantly affect plant size and yield.

Once you've successfully fertilized your plants with these essential nutrients, try a more complex fertilization program to produce bigger and more potent yields.

NUTRITIONAL REQUIREMENTS OF CANNABIS PLANTS DURING THE SEEDING, VEGETATIVE AND FLOWERING PHASE

The nutritional needs of cannabis change at various stages.

NUTRIENTS FOR CANNABIS PLANTS

Cannabis seedlings obtain all their nutrients from the seed and absorb water through their leaves as their root system develops, so they must always live in a warm and humid environment.

You will not need to start feeding your seedlings until they have reached about 3–4 weeks of age, at which point they have developed 3–4 true leaves.

Vegetative growth stage

Some growers choose to start their plants with a light fertilizer with an NPK ratio of 2: 1: 2 for a week - just as their seedlings begin to enter this phase. This is indeed the time to start with fertilizer and avoid nutrient burn. However, some growers get great results by starting their plants with a 4: 2: 3 fertilizer to kickstart the growth.

By the middle of the vegetative phase (6 weeks from germination), you will need to aggressively increase nutrients for strong and healthy foliage to develop. During this stage, most growers opt for a 10: 5: 7 fertilizer.

These high nitrogen levels will help your plants produce lush green foliage and develop plenty of bud formation points in time for flowering.

When the vegetative phase is about to end, it's a good idea to start reducing nitrogen levels and preparing plants to switch to their flowering supplement. Most growers use a 7: 7: 7 fertilizer in the last week of the vegetative stage.

- Beginning of the vegetative phase: 2: 1: 2 - 4: 2: 3
- Mid vegetative stage: 10: 5: 7
- End of vegetative phase: 7: 7: 7

NUTRIENTS FOR FLOWERING CANNABIS PLANTS

Flowering cannabis plants need less nitrogen and more potassium to encourage the growth of large, resinous flowers. In the first two weeks of flowering, most growers fertilize their plants with a 5: 7: 10 fertilizer. From here on, it is advisable to adjust the amount of nutrients on all fronts, always keeping the potassium concentrations higher than the rest. Mid-flowering, most growers will use a 6:10:15 nutrient solution.

In the final weeks of flowering, growers will reduce their nutrients to soften the transition to pre-harvest rinse. At this point, it is common to use a milder fertilizer, with an NPK ratio of 4: 7: 10.

Tips on fertilizing during the flowering phase:

- Beginning of flowering phase: 5: 7: 10
- Mid-flowering phase: 6:10:15
- Mid / late flowering stage: 4: 7: 10
- End of flowering phase: pH balanced rinse

HOW TO READ A FERTILIZATION SCHEME: HOW MUCH DO I NEED TO FEED MY GRASS PLANTS?

Most fertilizer brands offer their customers a fertilization scheme, with this help you can provide your plants with nutrients in a balanced and timely manner.

Generally, a fertilizer table has a growth cycle of 12–13 weeks. The weeks in the cycle are usually listed along the x-axis of the chart.

Most importantly, your fertilization scheme will indicate which nutrients to give your plants (and in what ratio) during the different weeks of their life cycle. Nutrients are generally applied weekly and most fertilizer brands provide a ratio of fertilizer to water (in liters or gallons). Some fertilization schemes may also provide a PPM range for their solutions. If so, buy a PPM tester and measure the nutrients before fertilizing for greater accuracy.

Once you have fertilized your plants, check the PPM and conductivity of your soil to ensure that the crops absorb nutrients correctly.

HOW TO PREPARE THE NUTRIENTS OF CANNABIS

A potential misstep in fertilization can completely hinder your crop. However, feeding plants can be very simple. Just follow these simple steps:

Prepare your water. If possible, heat the water to around 22 ° C to increase root absorption.

Add your nutrients according to the fertilizer instructions and mix. Use a PPM or EC meter to get correct readings.

If necessary, adjust the pH of your solution using a pH regulator.

Once the PPM, pH and temperature of the water are correct, fertilize the plants and measure the runoff using the PPM or EC meter to know if the crop absorbs nutrients correctly.

THE IMPORTANCE OF PPM, PH AND WATER TEMPERATURE

PPM is a measure of how many nutrients are present in the water or growing medium. To avoid excess or deficiency of fertilizers, always measure the PPM of the soil to check if it still contains nutrients. If nutrients are present in the substrate during fertilization, subtract the PPM of the substrate from the PPM recommended in your fertilization chart to avoid over-fertilizing.

PH and temperature are equally important parameters for plant fertilization. If either is even slightly out of place, your plants may have a hard time absorbing their nutrients. So, whenever it's time to fertilize, keep your nutrient solution at the pH suggested by your brand of of fertilizers and the water temperature at 22 ° C.

Adopt chelation

High-quality nutrients contain chemical chelates. If you are an organic grower, use natural chelates such as fulvic and humic acid to help your plants better absorb mineral nutrients such as iron or zinc. Chelates work by surrounding positively charged nutrients with a negative or neutral charge, so they can pass through the plant's pore barrier.

Try foliar fertilization

Foliar fertilization - that is, the nebulization of cannabis leaves - also serves to prevent nutritional deficiencies or pests / diseases. It can also be used for short-term fertilization with secondary nutrients such as magnesium and calcium, or micronutrients such as zinc, iron and manganese.

Always rinse

Nutrients are extremely important, but they don't have to stay in buds when harvested. So, you need to rinse the plants with neutral pH water a week before harvest. The rinse causes the crops to consume any remaining nutrients they have stored, resulting in a soft, clean smoke.

RECOGNIZE THE NUTRIENT-RELATED PROBLEMS OF CANNABIS

Excess or deficiency of nutrients can stress and damage cannabis plants. Pay attention to the following nutrient-related issues.

PH IMBALANCE

PH problems can be caused by imbalances in your substrate.

PH imbalances can have a dramatic impact on plant health and cause many other problems, such as nutrient blockage, deficiencies and more.

If left untreated, pH problems will greatly hinder plant growth and reduce both yields and crop quality.

NUTRIENT BURNING

Nutrient burn is usually caused by an excess or accumulation of nutrients in the growing medium.

Plants develop dark green leaves with almost neon green tips that bend upward and deep red, magenta or purple stems or branches.

Flowering plants develop yellow-colored calyxes and sugar leaves before dying quickly.

It is typically cured by rinsing the roots with neutral pH water for nearly a week, before gradually reintroducing the fertilizer.

Measuring PPM and EC avoids nutrient burn.

BLOCKAGE OF NUTRIENTS

Nutrient blockage is caused by the accumulation of nutrients around the roots of a plant or by pH imbalances and prevents the absorption of available nutrients.

Blockage of nutrients leads to nutritional deficiencies that can cause yellowing of the foliage, burning of the leaf tips, irregular shape and size of the leaf and brown spots. Symptoms vary depending on the nutrients your plant is missing.

It is generally treated with a wash, pH checks, and nutrient adjustments.

EXCESS OF NUTRIENTS

The excess of nutrients with fertilizers and chemical supplements can burn your plants.

The highly concentrated nature of chemical fertilizers leads, if not careful, to over-fertilizing the plants.

The telltale signs of excess fertilizer include dry, burnt-looking leaves with yellow or brown discoloration, burnt edges and tips bent upwards.

Often, those inexperienced buy other supplements in an attempt to remedy existing nutritional problems, however this makes matters worse.

Excess fertilizer must be resolved quickly with a root rinse, pH stabilization and a new fertilization program.

NUTRITIONAL DEFICIENCY

Nutrient deficiency occurs due to insufficient nutrition or nutrient blockage.

Deficiencies in nitrogen, phosphorus, potassium, or secondary nutrients can cause symptoms such as dry foliage, yellow or brown leaves, and discolored stems. Nutritional deficiencies are treated by increasing / introducing nutrients or, in the event of nutrient blockage, making sure that the plants can receive the nutrients.

ORGANIC VS CHEMICAL FERTILIZER FOR CANNABIS

The use of organic nutrients over chemical fertilizers is always to be encouraged. Unlike synthetic ones, organic nutrients have slow release and are also absorbed more slowly by plants, drastically reducing the possibility of nutrient burns or other feeding problems.

Biological nutrients also benefit the soil itself, supporting the development of a rich ecosystem of microorganisms that protect and work together with the crop. In addition, organic soil improves over time, making it ideal for outdoor growers, it also reduces the impact on the environment, as organic nutrients do not produce toxic runoff.

While we are all in favor of organic products, we understand that we are choosing to use chemical fertilizers as well. First, they are absorbed much faster which means they are better for situations where efficiency is key. In the treatment of a deficiency, they bring immediate optimal results.

Synthetic fertilizers are carefully crafted to establish specific nutrient ratios so as to have greater control over what plants "eat" and in what doses.

UNDERSTAND WHAT ABOUT CANNABIS NUTRIENTS

By choosing the right crop, giving enough nutrients, water and the right light, you will be well on your way to growing great weed. Remember: The biggest weapon in your arsenal is experience, so keep hone your skills and reap your rewards.

THE CHOICE OF VARIETY

Growing cannabis indoors is a truly exciting experience. You have full control over the cultivation environment, you can adjust various variables, such as the frequency of irrigation, temperature, humidity, gas exchanges. However, even indoor cultivation has many problems. Although plants are less prone to pest and disease attack, there are other factors that play a role.

When growing indoors, space is the main consideration. Growers often have to take extreme measures to keep their plantation secret. These potential obstacles can be overcome by strategically choosing the variety to grow. There are hundreds of genetics on the market, each of which develops a distinctive aroma and flavor, and generates certain effects. Growers must therefore evaluate the traits they want to obtain from a variety in order to choose.

Choosing a variety can be difficult.

Sativa

HEIGHT AND SPACE

Indoor growers can usually use limited space. Those who are lucky will be able to put a grow tent in a room, while others who are luckier will have an entire space dedicated to their own plantation. Either way, this space won't be suitable for giant varieties anyway.

As already mentioned, the main subspecies of ganjas are sativa and indica. Sativa strains develop elongated leaves and a slender structure, and grow to impressive heights. Some genetics can easily exceed 3m. In contrast, indica strains exhibit wider leaves, greater lateral growth and a stocky, bushy appearance.

If your space is limited, you can guess which one is best suited to your needs. However, pure strains are quite rare, the strains you can buy are hybrids and contain mixes of genetics in different proportions. If you are looking for an easy-to-manage plant, an indica-dominant strain is the logical choice. These genetics have more indica genes, develop a compact structure and are unlikely to grow out of control.

But indoor growers don't have to choose this one exclusively. They can certainly grow stimulating sativa strains too. However, it's nearly impossible to manage a mammoth sativa strain indoors. You can several autoflowering sativa-dominant specimens using the sea of green (SOG) technique and achieve satisfying yields.

Autoflowers descend from the third subspecies s ruderalis. Pure ruderalis strains offer poor yields, but breeders can cross these genetics with other strains to create potent and productive autoflowers. Autoflowers inherit the compact structure of the ruderalis ancestor and rarely exceed 1m in height.

Height is another key factor when growing in hiding. Some have the privilege of living in cities or states where cannabis cultivation is legal, while others cannot. If you have decided to grow in a country where it is not allowed, you should choose a compact autoflowering variety. These plants can be grown in specially adapted boxes or containers. Just install a carbon filter and your plantation will remain completely hidden.

If you are growing indoors in a tight or narrow space, your best bet is probably Royal Dwarf. This miniature plant usually does not exceed 40cm.

SPEED AND PERFORMANCE

Growth rate and yield are generally negatively correlated. In practice, the faster a variety blooms, the lower the yield. The autoflowering strains go from seed to ripening in just 8 weeks but offer a maximum yield of around 500g / m² under optimal conditions.

Indica strains take an average of 7–12 weeks to flower but can produce up to 600–1000g / m².

Sativa-dominant plants are the queen of productivity. These gigantic specimens offer up to 1kg of flowers per plant, but grow more slowly. Sativa specimens need at least 11–16 weeks to complete flowering! Of course, any grower wants the maximum yield. But this is not always possible. Those who live in areas where cultivation is legal have all the time in the world to raise their seedlings. In areas where prohibition is still in effect, cultivation operations should take as little time as possible. If you choose a fast-growing variety, you can increase your final yields by growing several specimens close together. Autoflowers offer poor yields, but are also very compact. Quick One is a fast-growing autoflower that develops buds in a short amount of time. You can harvest the flowers just 8 weeks after the seeds germinate. If you prefer photoperiod strains, try Honey

Cream. This tasty indica has a flowering time of 6–7 weeks.

AROMA AND TASTE

The smell of the weed stands out immediately. Terpenes are the molecules responsible for this delicious and distinctive aroma. These fragrant hydrocarbon particles are widely found in nature and a plant produces over 200 of them. Each variety develops varying levels of terpenes. Some genetics give off fruity aromas and flavors, while others give off floral, herbaceous, earthy or petrol essences.

Learn about the smell and taste of a variety. To understand if you like a variety or not is to taste it. If you don't get the chance, you're still in luck. Many seedbanks provide a detailed profile of each strain and its aroma and flavor. Some even indicate the levels of each terpene. Find out about the assortment of terpenes produced by a variety before you buy it. Lovers of fruity and tropical flavors should definitely try Fruit Spirit. This terpene-rich hybrid strain is descended from Blueberry and White Widow strains, and intoxicates the taste buds with every hit. Chocolate Haze offers a completely different fragrance. This delicious sativa genetics generate an electrifying high, with a taste of sugar and chocolate.

READY, START, GROW!

Done! After considering all these fundamental details, you are one step closer to the final decision.

Remember, space is essential. Evaluate that the place is suitable for the chosen variety. After that, consider the rate of growth. To harvest quickly, autoflowers are the best solution. After you've made your choice, start planting. Now all you need is love and attention to devote to the plants, to have the satisfaction of being able to smoke buds raised with your own hands.

LIFE CYCLE

Cannabis is botanically defined as an annual. This means that its entire life cycle begins and ends in no more than one year. In general, most cannabis strains complete their life cycle, which can range from 4 to 10 months.

Cannabis is one of the few annual plant species that tend to develop as male or female plants. However, it can happen that some specimens become hermaphrodites (plants with both male and female organs) in times of high stress. But on this particular natural process followed by many plant species, man has no way of intervening.

The initial stage of a plant is when a new living organism is born from a seed. All a seed needs to germinate is a little water, air and heat. Thanks to these three important external factors, the seed will generate the nutrients the embryo will feed on to start its rapid development. This internal growth will push the seed to split, thus allowing the sprout to emerge (the sprout is the organ capable of transforming itself into what will later be the tap root). Once the sprout has come out, it will tend to look for nutrients towards the depths of the substrate, while the upper vegetable part, characterized by two small leaflets (called cotyledons), will begin to grow upwards, making space towards the first rays of light. In fact, a newly sprouted seed has the primary task of reaching the light, to synthesize the nutrients through the two cotyledons.

SEEDLING STAGE:

Once the plant has managed to open its cotyledons in search of the light, the young seedling will begin its development phase and put out a series of leaflets. These will have an oval shape, larger than the cotyledons, with serrated edges and the characteristic "finger" shape of marijuana plants. This initial phase of growth has as its main objective to develop the first leaves, but also to develop a strong and wide root system. When the plant shows the first series of well-developed leaves, a main stem with a diameter of about 4-6mm and a height defined by 3 or 4 internodes, this phase ends and we move on to the next one, that is the vegetative.

VEGETATIVE:

The seedling is ready to develop into an adult cannabis plant. Now it is important that the plant receives sufficient light and all the nutrients necessary for its growth. As we have already seen, however, we must not overdo it with fertilizers. The plant will then be able to start growing upwards, constantly looking for light, producing new leaves and making the branches and stems stronger and more resistant. Once it reaches a certain level of maturity, the plant will begin to develop horizontally, creating new lateral branches. Eventually, as the days go by, the plant's internodes will begin to develop small calyxes. This marks the transition from the vegetative growth phase to the flowering phase.

FLOWERING:

It usually starts in late summer, when the days get shorter. At this time of the year, Cannabis receives a clear message: the life cycle is about to end and all resources must be used to ensure the reproduction of the species. Now the "males" start releasing pollen and the "females" develop the flowers (which will form the buds). When these come in contact with the pollen of the male flowers, the pollination process is initiated, which will lead the buds to inevitably produce seeds. When the latter are ripe and well formed, the plant will open the calyxes of its flowers, releasing the seeds in the surrounding areas.

Cannabis growers always try to prevent female plants from being pollinated, as any seed production could damage the final product intended for therapeutic and / or recreational consumption. To avoid this, when you discover the first male flowers, move the male plants to a completely isolated area,

CLONING

Cloning allows the genetics of a specific phenotype to be preserved over time. Below we tell you what cloning is, the different methods that exist and the advantages inherent in growing from clones or cuttings.

Marijuana cloning or cutting is the method that allows to obtain an exact genetic replica of a chosen specimen. So, you can already know the specific characteristics that the new clone or cutting will have. This method is especially suitable for growers with limited time.

Canada is a nice example of a country that has found itself in the situation of having to grow from cuttings due to disputes between local seed advocates and import advocates, even though growing from cuttings and seeds have almost at the same level in terms of popularity.

Why clone a cannabis plant?

Maybe to preserve rare genetics of extreme quality or to start a commercial cultivation based on well-defined goals and profit margins. These types of operations, which require a license, are ideal for maximizing the number of crops over a certain period.

From an economic point of view, cutting is a truly simple and accessible process which, when properly applied, takes no more than 14-21 days. Growers with mother plants can obtain roughly 100-

250 clones from each plant every 90-100 days, so you can channel the budget originally intended to purchase seeds to meet other growing needs. To get clones, you need to have mother plants at our disposal. These must be kept in excellent health, always at a light / dark cycle of 18/6 hours that allows them to be kept in a constant phase of vegetative growth. Overall, the mother plants have a dense and abundant branching that only develops new branches. Before selecting a mother plant, it is crucial, among other things, to have it cultivated on various occasions in order to know for sure its growth pattern, its resistance to pathogens, its suitability for cloning and its chances of remaining in vegetative phase without producing pre-flowers. The main advantage of cutting is that the beginning of everything is a plant about which a lot is known: the sex, the production capacity ... Also, so strong that growers can preserve cuttings and mother plants for over twenty years. In Europe the culture of cloning is not widespread at all, or perhaps it had to remain hidden for legal reasons. In other countries such as the USA, cuttings are available in dispensaries or nurseries. And the customer can select the clone that best meets his needs in terms of flavor, effect, grower's skill, location of the crop (indoor / outdoor) etc. Marijuana plants are truly versatile and for these there are many methods of making cuttings.

Propagation

For this method, the following elements are required: a propagation greenhouse, rooting hormone, freshly picked cuttings and a substrate (Root Riot, jiffy coir pads or rock wool). After wetting the cutting in rooting hormone, place it in the substrate and close the propagation greenhouse leaving the openings on the lid. Try to keep the temperature between 20ºC and 26ºC with a constant humidity of 75% -90%. The lamps must be placed far enough away not to change the internal temperature of the greenhouse. Keep them on 18-24 hours a day. After 14-21 days, the first roots will have started to sprout and then the clones will be ready.

Aeroponics

Aeroponic cloning is a method that consists of using water, oxygen and a porous stone to provide roots to grow, thus placing the clones directly in hydrogen peroxide results in oxygen covering the stems and contributing to rooting. As for the lighting, here too it must remain on 18-24 hours a day.

The clones will not run the risk of being attacked by anaerobic bacteria causing a softening of the tissues. The advantage of this practice is that it is inexpensive. Water temperature and lighting are determining factors. Try to always ensure optimal value.

This method consists in putting a branch in contact with a moist substrate. During the process, the plant will grow as usual, and the selected branch will start producing roots. The right humidity is needed to ensure that root formation takes place keeping the substratum moist and away from direct sunlight. If these requirements are met, 14-21 days later, the branch in contact with the earth will have emitted roots and it can be cut and replanted.

With this method, large mature cuttings are obtained without having to use any propagator or aeroponic cloning system.

Tissue culture

This is a much more clinical and advanced approach; it is not accessible to everyone because you need a truly meticulous protocol, in an appropriate environment. The main benefit is getting a fully rooted plant from a tissue sample.

COLLECTION

The time has come to get the well-deserved reward after so many months of work. In many cases, the inexperience or the anxiety of tasting these delicious cannabis buds can play tricks.

Don't forget that correct harvesting, trimming and drying are just as important as the previous work.

Once you have reached this last phase, don't rush into it, and end the season by following some simple steps that we show you below

Before the harvest ...

Prepare the space

Choose well where to dry your marijuana plants to get the highest quality buds. Ideally the space should have the following characteristics:

Air: the drying room should have minimal air exchange. You can connect the ventilation system (intraction / extraction) for 5 minutes approximately every 2 hours, a sufficient interval to exchange the air effectively.

Discretion: Choose a discreet space or install an odor filter system for pruning and drying, as this will be the time when the smell of cannabis will be most intense.

Temperature: not higher than 27 °, temperature at which some cannabinoids begin to degrade, and tries to minimize thermal variations. Keeping the temperature in the drying room under control can be somewhat difficult, but you can try with the right tools:

During the 3 days of drying: keep the room at 20 ° in order to obtain a quick drying of the buds.

From the fourth to the fifteenth day: lower the temperature to 17-18 °.

Lighting: As far as possible try to keep the drying room dark, as light leads to the degradation of THC. Light and air are the main factors that alter cannabis flowers.

Humidity: a very humid drying space can cause mold and fungus to grow which can damage the entire crop. With low humidity, the flowers may dry out too quickly and won't have the time to metabolize properly, which will result in a bland tasting end product. Clean the room thoroughly before planting and keep the humidity stable, at levels between 55 and 65% maximum. For a quality final product, it is essential to maintain these parameters and avoid drastic variations.

Calculate the time needed

A good trimming of half a pound of marijuana buds will take you six hours by hand, and about two hours with a pruner. Plan your time well and try to do it on days off so you don't have to quit halfway through.

If you are growing in pots

Do a good root wash to remove fertilizers from plants. Otherwise, you will have a bad-tasting crop, which will not be good for your body either. Remember that everything you give your plants will go directly into your body when you enjoy the weed.

Even if you have used organic fertilizers, it is better that the plant does not retain the remains of mineral salts and other nutrients, so before harvesting (about one, two or three weeks) we recommend that you water the plants only with water.

If the leaf tips are burnt or the whole leaf has a deep, dark green color, it is possible that you have over-fertilized your marijuana plants.

One way to try to hide the unpleasant taste of the fertilizer is to do a root wash to get rid of salts trapped in the substrate and excess nutrients. Washing the roots or leaching consists in watering it abundantly: about 2 times the volume of the substrate (if the pot is 10 liters, we water it with 20 liters). Water with water with a pH adjusted to 6.5 and allow to drain copiously.

Once you have adequate space to dry your cannabis plants, prepare a table to do the trimming and above all make yourself comfortable, this procedure can take you a lot of time (obviously depending on the harvest).

Suitable scissors will be of great help, we recommend scissors for trimming and retractable auto pruning

- Powder-free latex gloves
- A thin string (like the one used to hang clothes)
- Clothes pins

The Harvest Step By Step

Step 1 - Choose the best time

Knowing the best time to cut your plants will affect the quality of the crop.

Regardless of which week of your cycle you decide to cut, always do it in the morning or, if we are talking about indoor growing, when the lights come on.

During the night the plant optimizes its resin production.

Step 2 - Harvest: cut the plants starting from the base and one by one.

You can harvest whole plants and / or bunches, so we recommend removing the large leaves first, so it will be much easier to trim the buds. You can remove the large leaves before cutting the plant, or afterwards, as you like.

Step 3- Trimming: dry or wet?

Some growers are for dry trimming and others consider wet trimming the best option. Ultimately it is a matter of taste, since the two methods have pros and cons.

Dry trimming

After you have removed the large leaves, hang the plants upside down and let them dry for a week. After 7 days, when the top has lost moisture and the surrounding leaves are dry and broken, prune carefully for the flowers. With both this type of trimming and wet trimming, you can store the small leaves covered with trichomes for extractions or hash.

Dry trimming is only advisable with a low or easy to manage humidity level. The main problem with dehumidifiers is that, although they help dry the air, they also generate too much heat, accelerating the drying process and giving rise to a phenomenon: too fast drying is undesirable. The temperature must therefore be between 18 and 23 ºC and the humidity between 55 and 65%.

Pros: the smell and taste are preserved better. Metabolisms take place more slowly because the plant retains more resin.

Cons: Dry, it is easier, unwittingly, to break off the top while trimming. In order to avoid the appearance of diseases, try to monitor the plants closely every day, in order to be able to control fungal attacks.

Wet trimming

Put on your latex gloves so the resin doesn't stick to your hands and start trimming very carefully. Try not to crush the buds, treat them with care to avoid possible damage to the trichomes. Cut off the largest leaves and stem as quickly as you can. Leaving it may cause mold to appear during drying. Cut the small leaves that grow around the top so that the end result is as clean as possible. Wet trimming promotes air penetration into the plant material, which is useful if the humidity in the drying room is too high. Remember to keep the temperature between 18 and 23 ºC and the humidity between 55 and 65%, even with the help of a dehumidifier. To thus avoid fungi such as botrytis and parasites.

It improves air circulation and facilitates the drying process.

<u>Cons</u>: drying occurs unevenly, flavor and aroma are lost compared to dry trimming and leads to greater damage to the trichomes. If the drying is too fast, the metabolization is not carried out correctly, and the flowers retain a completely unpleasant dry grass taste.

How to get your marijuana plants to dry?

When your plants, depending on the trimming used, will be devoid of the largest leaves or totally pruned, upside down. You can also put a string from one wall to the other (attached to two bolts) and tie the plants along the string like when drying clothes. After 15 days (approximately) your buds will be dry and ready to move on to the tanning phase. Plants lose about 75% of their water content in this phase.

HERE ARE SOME TIPS TO FOLLOW DURING THIS PHASE:

Keep the drying room in the dark.

The constant temperature and humidity level must be between 18 and 23 ºC and 55 and 65%, respectively. These two parameters are fundamental.

Use a digital hygrometer / thermometer with memory for minimum and maximum values, so you can check for variations, which could alter the final result.

Program the ventilation system (only the entertainer and the extractor, the fans must not be used), ensuring the correct renewal of the air inside the drying room.

Check the plants harvested daily for any fungi. If you find any infected flowers, immediately remove them from the others, place them in an airtight bag and dispose of them immediately.

You can also take a flower sample at different times to assess the state of maturity of the plants. At this stage you can safely crush the flowers, so you will see if they are ready and you can analyze the aroma they emanate (type of smell, intensity, etc.).

After 15-20 days, you can taste that herb and check its state of ripeness. After a maximum of one month, the flowers should be totally dry and ready for consumption. Subsequently, you can start a second evolutionary phase, called "tanning".

How to cure your cannabis flowers?

The purpose of tanning is to enhance and improve the final product. And once again the fundamental three parameters are temperature, humidity and light.

Place the flowers in airtight glass jars and open them for ten minutes a day for three weeks. When opening, the room must be in the dark. Light can oxidize flowers or alter their quality.

Store the crop in a room with constant climatic parameters: a humidity level of 50-55% and a temperature close to 20 ºC.

Taste the flowers every week to check the gradual evolution of ripening. You can improve the taste (perhaps too bland or too much vegetal) of the flowers by adding citrus peels to the jars, to be collected after about eight days.

In the four months following harvest, open the jars for twenty minutes twice a month. From the fifth month onwards, just ventilate once a month for ten minutes. After six months, you can stop the ventilation.

Starting from the eighth month, the process goes into stalemate, and the harvest begins to lose flavor and taste. As for the effect, it becomes more sedative and physical in most cases, but the quality is still good.

We have reached the end of this long process now you no longer need advice.

TIPS FOR PROBLEMS LIKE LEAF ROT AND PREVENTING CANNABIS FUNGUS

Cannabis, just like other plant species, is susceptible to a wide variety of pests, diseases and fungi, including whiteflies, molds and more. However, there is no more dangerous threat than bud rot, a fungal infection that can attack your precious buds, destroying them within days.

Fortunately, there are several strategies to deal with bud rot and prevent it from recurring in the future.

Bud rot is an infection that can affect cannabis plants. As the name suggests, this is a particularly aggressive variety of mold that attacks and destroys the buds of a flowering plant. Bud rot can be difficult to spot and the first symptoms visible to the naked eye appear when the infection is already advanced. Usually, the first to show signs of decay are the leaves, which turn dry and yellow overnight for no apparent reason (especially after persistent rain).

After they develop, the mushrooms take on a whitish, hairy appearance, like any other mold you might find on top of left-over food left over in the refrigerator. As the infection advances, the buds take on a dark brown, black and sometimes slightly purple color. In the most extreme cases, buds are completely covered with a thick layer of dark powder, becoming very soft and crumbly to the touch. In other cases, buds can dehydrate and take on very dark colors. Opening an infected bud, it can be observed how the fungus has the ability to penetrate the innermost layers of the inflorescence.

Bud rot is caused by the Botrytis cinerea fungus. This fungus initially affects the innermost parts of the buds and then slowly moves towards the outermost ones. It can also attack other plants, such as vines, strawberries, and peonies.

Normally, this fungus spreads from plant to plant through strong winds and rains, the main means of transport for fungal spores. Once a wound has been reached (such as a small cut caused by bending branches or wind, as well as damage from caterpillars or other insects), infection begins. Once the fungus comes into contact with the plant, it becomes infected. It spreads rapidly especially when the buds are particularly compact and the environmental conditions are humid.

Bud rot affects one by one all the buds of a cannabis plant and, as a result, can destroy an entire crop making the final product unusable. Fortunately, there are some simple steps to treat an ongoing fungal infection:

Eliminate all infected buds. The first step in dealing with a Botrytis attack is to carefully examine all the plants for damaged buds. Remember to take a good look at the innermost parts of the buds as well, where they normally start to develop. Once you have identified the parts of the damaged plants, cut them and eliminate them. Do not try to recycle the moldy buds and remove the infected inflorescences with extreme caution, to avoid touching other healthy parts of the plant.

Once you have removed all the infected buds you can proceed to collect the rest of the plant, in order to leave the fungus without resources. Alternatively, you can follow the next step.

If you prefer not to harvest an infected plant immediately, you can try to adjust the environmental parameters of your crop, in order to prevent other fungal spores from germinating. To do this, you need to ensure the plants have greater air circulation, better ventilation, higher temperatures and lower humidity rates. You will also need to prevent the plants from getting wet. It is too risky an eventuality that could help the fungus to spread to the remaining tops of the plant.

HOW TO AVOID IT

Fungal spores may be present on your plants, but they don't necessarily have to germinate and mold the buds. In fact, by making a few simple changes in the environment in which you are growing you can effectively hinder the development and attacks of molds.

Increase Air Circulation: Proper air circulation is essential for healthy and robust cannabis plants. Optimal levels of temperature and humidity are easier to maintain when the surrounding air is constantly moving. In addition, the air helps dry the wetted areas of the plants after irrigation, rain or abundant watering.

Keep temperatures warm: Temperature plays a key role in the germination and spread of fungal spores. To avoid bud rot and any other mold related problems, it is advisable to keep temperatures in the growing area above 20 ° C (68 ° F). Spores germinate more easily at low temperatures.

Keep your plants dry: All fungi require moisture to germinate. The same is true for bud rot. So, to prevent infection with Botrytis and other fungal species, make sure you always keep the humidity rates in your grow space under control. Optimal humidity levels for cannabis range from 30 to 70%, depending on the growth stage of the plants. To keep humidity under control, always cover your plants during a rain and shake them if they get wet, so as to eliminate excess water and speed up the drying process.

Prune the plants: The main target of bud rot is bushy, stubby and compact cannabis plants, where it can easily spread through foliage. If you notice that your plants are becoming too bushy and branching, you may want to try pruning them, especially if you are growing outdoors in a humid and wet climate. You could also use some bending techniques to shape the plants to spread out the branches and keep them from taking on the appearance of a squat bush.

Keep an eye on buds: Inflorescence rot prefers thicker, more compact buds. Be sure to always pay close attention to these parts that are most vulnerable to infection. If you should already notice its presence, take the appropriate measures immediately.

BUD ROT: THE WORST ENEMY OF MARIJUANA

Bud rot can destroy entire crops when not treated effectively and quickly. However, to germinate it needs particular environmental conditions, with precise humidity rates and temperatures. So as long as you carefully monitor your plants, providing them with the right amounts of air, heat and humidity, you won't have any problems with this killer fungus. Cannabis can be attacked by various parasites and pathogens. One of them is powdery mildew, also called powdery mildew. By knowing in depth about this disease and its causes, it is possible to prevent the development of powdery mildew in your plants, and to treat the first symptoms in a timely manner.

WHAT IS POWDERY MILDEW?

Powdery mildew is a fungal infection. It can occur in any type of plant. Cannabis growers often face this type of disease. As you can guess from the name, this infection generates a thin white fluff, which mainly covers the younger leaves. At first the fungus causes the leaves to curl upwards. Over time, the leaf dries up and dies. Powdery mildew is a parasitic fungus that feeds on foliage. Gradually, the affected leaves rot, while the overall growth of the plant stops abruptly. In cannabis plants, powdery mildew can cause a drastic reduction in yield, or even destroy the buds themselves. In severe cases, powdery mildew can kill the plant. Fungal spores are extremely hardy. They can survive in your garden for long periods of time, attacking the next planting.

WHAT ARE THE CAUSES OF POWDERY MILDEW?

Pathogens can only successfully attack a plant if its metabolism is poorly balanced. In addition to environmental factors, nutritional imbalance is a major cause of weakness in plants. This fragility favors the development of powdery mildew.

The most frequent nutritional deficiencies are those of silicon and calcium. These two elements are essential for the formation of the structural tissues of the plant. They act as a natural defense against the attack of parasites and fungi such as powdery mildew. Another cause of weakness could be an excess of nitrogen. This condition can dilute the plant's sap, making it more prone to infection by insects and pathogens.

Powdery mildew is caused by various types of fungi. They especially prefer very humid environments, without adequate air circulation. Excessive humidity levels are an ideal breeding ground for fungi and bacteria. The lack of ventilation only makes the situation worse.

If your garden doesn't get the right ventilation, heat and humidity will build up and create "pockets" around your plants.

These "pockets" represent a perfect habitat for the multiplication and spread of fungal spores.

Highly crowded grow spaces are much more prone to developing powdery mildew infections. When the plants are very close to each other, and their foliage touches or overlaps, this promotes the accumulation of humidity and stagnant air. This environment is optimal for the reproduction of mushrooms.

If an infected plant touches the leaves of another specimen, powdery mildew spores can spread and contaminate adjacent plants.

HOW TO DEFEAT POWDERY MILDEW

Powdery mildew can have devastating effects on your garden, especially if it's not treated promptly. Thankfully, a mild infection can be handled very easily. Below are the step-by-step instructions for dealing with powdery mildew as soon as you notice the first symptoms:

1. CLEAN THE INFECTED LEAVES

Clean all infected surfaces using high pH water. The pH must have a value between 8.0 and 8.2. This will create an inhospitable environment for the spores, preventing them from forming a colony again in the short term.

Use paper towels, a sponge or a tea towel, dip them in cold water and use them to clean the plants. Whichever tool you choose to clean the leaves, always remember to throw it in the trash after use. Fungal spores adhere to any material and can spread to other plants in your garden or home.

2. PRUNE IF NECESSARY

Take a good pair of garden shears, and cut off any dry or yellowed leaves. By doing this you will help the plant to reorganize its energies. Infected leaves will die and fall off anyway. Once again, remember to immediately throw away all the cut leaves, to prevent the spores from dispersing into the environment.

3. DO NOT TRANSPLANT INFECTED SPECIMENS

The fungus spores will also multiply in the new soil, and you risk infecting other plants in the garden or in your home. Cover the surface of the diseased plant's soil with some fresh compost. This will prevent spores from splashing onto other plants when you water them.

4. TAKE CARE OF YOUR PLANTS AND APPLY PREVENTIVE STRATEGIES

Finally, you will need to treat your plants with a suitable antifungal.

Products like essential oils or Green Cleaner, for example, are excellent and also very simple to use. Most antifungals need to be diluted in water and sprayed directly on the leaves.

Alternatively, you can apply neem oil to your plants. But remember not to spray it on the buds.

HOW TO AVOID THE FORMATION OF POWDERY MILDEW IN THE FUTURE

If you have ever faced a powdery mildew infection, you will already know how unpleasant this problem can be. Therefore, you must do your best to prevent any future attacks by avoiding having to fight the disease in its full swing.

Fortunately, reducing the risk of powdery mildew infection is pretty simple. Always remember to monitor the humidity levels in your garden. Also, check that there is adequate air circulation in the room.

The best solution to obtain proper ventilation of the premises is to install fans and a good ventilation system. Make sure that your plants are not too close together and that the air circulates freely throughout the growing space, especially above the canopy (the main point where warm and humid air is concentrated).

To check the humidity, use a hygrometer and try not to exceed these levels:

- 65–80% for sprouts
- 60–70% for plants in the vegetative phase
- 40–55% maximum for plants in the flowering phase
- 35–45% in the last 2 weeks before harvest

Remember that powdery mildew is a very persistent infection. However, a little excess moisture is usually not enough to trigger it. It often takes a lethal combination of stagnant air, lack of ventilation, and a warm, humid environment to encourage the development and spread of fungal spores.

POWDERY MILDEW IS NOT THE ONLY MOLD YOU NEED TO BE CAREFUL OF

Powdery mildew is a common fungal pathogen, but there are others to keep an eye out for as well. Humid environments with low airflow generate a variety of different fungi that can harm plant health.

FUSARIUM

This is a fungal soil disease that is particularly difficult to detect and eliminate. This pathogen causes wilt, stunted growth, root and stem rot, and redness of the xylem (the vessels that carry water in the stem).

Finally, Fusarium can also clog the xylem and prevent water from being delivered to the leaves and flowers beyond the block. This leads to wilting and eventual death of the plant. It's easy to see how this fungus can wreak havoc on a cannabis crop. In addition to being lethal, Fusarium is notoriously difficult to get rid of. The fungus can lie dormant in the soil for long periods of time, emerging during the warm season.

If you notice the above symptoms, it is likely that you are dealing with this pathogen. It is devastating: the only thing to do is to remove and destroy the affected plants as soon as possible. In the future, you will also need to avoid using that area of your garden. Soil infected with Fusarium must be allowed to stand for at least 4–5 years before it can be reused. The other option is to remove the soil and replace it with fresh soil.

SMOKE

Smoke is a type of fungus that can infect cannabis plants after being attacked by parasites. It begins to attack after the insects attack the leaves and expose the sap. These types of molds don't attack plants directly, but they can still be problematic. Overgrowth can block light and prevent photosynthesis.

Smoke takes its name from its close resemblance to the black substance found in fireplaces. This type of fungus can also appear dark brown. The initial growth will appear as a thin layer of dust, however if left untreated it will develop into a thick layer. It can affect plants all year round and is particularly prolific during pest infestation.

Smokiness can be dealt with without the use of chemicals. Just clean the leaves or spray them with warm water to get rid of the infection for a while. Over time, the fungus can reappear, but water is enough to keep it at bay periodically before harvest.

PYTHIUM

Pythium is a genus of fungi that includes over 150 species. Some of them live freely in the soil and are harmless to cannabis plants. Others are pathogenic and infect animals, plants and fungi alike. Pythium fungi can cause considerable damage to plants during their first few weeks of life.

Often called root rot, Pythium is a parasite that hides in the rhizosphere. Its natural habitat makes it remarkably difficult to detect. Brown discoloration near the roots, a bad smell, and collapsing shriveled plants are the signs to detect it.

Pythium thrives when there is an excess of water. Giving your plants too much H_2O creates the perfect environment for mold: that is, excess humidity and lack of air. To prevent Pythium from settling, water your plant only when the top 3cm of the soil surface is dry.

THE AMBIGUITY OF THE INTERNATIONAL REGULATORY FRAMEWORK ON CANNABIS

Now that we know how to grow and produce our weed, let's take a look at the laws in force in various countries: the production, use and consumption of cannabis is extremely controversial. Cannabis has never known a single discipline; there are dozens of different regulations from country to country, cause and consequence of the ups and downs that cannabis seems destined for. Cannabis has been classified by international bodies as a hard drug, but the debate on this substance has always been conflicting and many find this classification unfair. therefore, many states are also changing their laws on the matter by moving towards a more open and permissive regulation. Many countries have started legalization processes, so some states have activated processes of change and the regulation of this matter takes place on the basis of three guidelines: legalization, decriminalization. With "legalization", distribution and possession are permitted.

"Decriminalization" possession and use are no longer a crime. In this case, fines may be incurred, without more severe penalties.

"Decriminalization" means that the use of cannabis is still considered a crime, but is no longer prosecuted.

In the US and Canada, cannabis has been regularized, both for therapeutic purposes and for recreational use. Europe has moved with more caution, but here too the situation has changed a lot in the last three years. Let's see together what happened between 2016 and 2019 and how the legislation that regulates its cultivation, sale and consumption has changed.

Holland, beyond what everyone believes, does not have real legislation that allows its production and sale. By contrast, cannabis is sold freely in the country of tulips thanks to a regulatory vacuum. In fact, Dutch law does not expressly prohibit the production, sale and use of this substance, which makes the sale of marijuana implicitly legal. The only restrictions concern the methods and places of consumption: cannabis can only be bought and smoked in coffee shops and it is strictly forbidden to smoke it in public places.

On the other hand, there are European countries that have come to legalization after an intense political debate. In the Czech Republic, if you are caught by the police with 15 grams of marijuana (or 5 grams of hashish) nothing will happen to you. The state has decriminalized consumption and legalized marijuana for medical purposes.

In Spain it is legal to have up to 40 grams of cannabis, but you can only smoke in private or in so-called social clubs; private clubs where members can smoke. In France, only light cannabis is legal. In Germany it is legal to buy and consume cannabis for medical purposes, while it is illegal to use it for recreational purposes, even for small quantities. Luxembourg is facing a legalization process at the end of which it will be the first European state to allow the sale and use of soft drugs.

Also, in San Marino there is something cooking: attempts are being made to regulate recreational use.

Uruguay was the pioneer of legalization, approved by the Mujica government in 2013. In Uruguay it is legal to buy marijuana for citizens residing in the country, adults registered on special lists, while tourists cannot access the sale of marijuana. On the other hand, no possibility of legal purchase has been provided for foreign citizens.

In June 2018, Canada also said yes to marijuana, legalizing recreational use. The law has been in force since autumn 2018. The goal of this law is to fight organized crime, providing consumers with a controlled and quality product.

The third and final country where cannabis trade and consumption is legal is North Korea. The situation in Korea, however, is not as clear as that of Canada and Uruguay: in the Asian country all narcotic substances are banned, but hemp is not included in the list of prohibited substances, it is considered legal and is used and marketed without any restrictions.

Since January 2018 in California, production and sale for both therapeutic and recreational use are legal. The legal limits set the minimum age for purchase at 21 years, while the maximum quantity for possession is 28.3 grams and up to 6 plants can be grown at home. It can also be bought by tourists.

Cannabis is also legal in Alaska, Oregon, Colorado, Washington and Nevada. Here, American and foreign citizens over the age of 21 can legally purchase and own up to 30 grams of cannabis. However, smoking is not permitted in public places, while consumption must be specifically permitted in private places. Furthermore, marijuana cannot be transported outside the country but must be consumed within state borders.

In Italy it is illegal to grow, own and sell it.

Bangladesh has a regulatory vacuum regarding hemp and it is therefore, in fact, totally legal. Average cost: $0.50 per gram

In Spain, possession and consumption not in public places is legal. There are social clubs where you can smoke it -Average cost: $ 10 per gram.

Portugal; the sale is prohibited but, since 2001, possession is legal. Average cost: $ 5 per gram

Switzerland; use punished with a fine of 100 francs. Possession of less than 10 grams is not punishable. Average cost: $ 10 per gram

Germany; possession within 10 grams is not prohibited, use is legal. Average cost: $ 10 per gram

Australia; remains illegal in some states but decriminalized in others, legal for therapeutic use. Average cost: $ 15 per gram

Argentina; legal possession for private use only. Average cost: $ 5 per gram

Chile; the laws in force do not punish personal and private consumption but sanction group consumption. Average cost: $ 5 per gram

Paraguay; decriminalized possession from 1988 up to 10 grams. Average cost: $ 3 per gram

Peru; allowed up to 8 grams, but about 60% of detainees are in prison for crimes related to simple possession. Average cost: $ 10 per gram

Colombia; allowed possession up to 20 grams, legal medical consumption. Average cost: $ 10 per gram

Ecuador; decriminalized personal use. Average cost: $ 10 per gram

Costa Rica; consumption and personal possession do not represent a criminal offense. Average cost: $ 20 per gram

Jamaica; possession (up to 56.70 grams) and decriminalized use since 2015, cultivation allowed. Rastafarians can consume it in places of worship. Average cost: $ 10 per gram

Brazil; clear distinction between traffickers and consumers, the crime is decriminalized. Average cost: $ 10 per gram

India; use is permitted for religious purposes. Average cost: $ 3 per gram

Cambodia; police are not stopping consumers. Average cost: $ 3 per gram

In many countries around the world, the consumption of marijuana is still illegal and its consumption a criminal offense. The punishments for this type of crime are however very variable, depending on the individual states, ranging from simple fines to prison, up to corporal punishment.

Marijuana is prohibited in much of Europe, in Africa and in almost all countries of the Americas and Asia.

In Croatia, the possession of even just one gramme is severely punished with a fine, risks from 3 to 15 years in prison for cultivation and sale.

Belgium; completely illegal in any form

France; illegal, up to one year in prison

Japan; since 1948 all preparations containing THC are illegal

Israel; illegal, allowed medical use only if authorized by the ministry of health which evaluates it on a case-by-case basis

New Zealand; illegal

Poland; illegal in any form, with sentences ranging from 3 to 10 years in prison

UK; illegal

Cuba; illegal

China; illegal

Russia; personal use allowed

South Korea; illegal

Egypt; illegal

Morocco; illegal

Tunisia; illegal

Algeria; illegal

Arab Emirates; illegal

Mauritius islands; illegal

Denmark; illegal, but permitted therapeutic use.

Lithuania; illegal

BOOK 3: MARIJUANA BUSINESS

MARIJUANA BUSINESS 2021

THE LEGAL CANNABIS INDUSTRY IN THE U.S. AND GLOBALLY

OBJECTIVE MARKET-DRIVEN COVERAGE OF GLOBAL CANNABIS INDUSTRY TRENDS AND OPPORTUNITIES

By Elia Friedenthal

CONTENTS

CHAPTER 11: OPENING A DISPENSARY 361

CHAPTER 12: HOW MUCH DOES IT COST AND HOW TO OPEN A CANNABIS SHOP IN ITALY? 373

CHAPTER 13: CANNABIS LIGHT AND MEDICAL CANNABIS. 377

CHAPTER 14: WHAT TO SELL IN A GROW SHOP 383

CHAPTER 15: OPENING A DISPENSARY IN ILLINOIS COST 387

CHAPTER 16: HOW TO OBTAIN A COMMERCIAL LICENSE FOR CANNABIS IN NEW JERSEY 397

CHAPTER 17: IDEAS FOR WORKING WITH LEGAL CANNABIS 399

CHAPTER 18: HOW TO OBTAIN A MEDICAL MARIJUANA CARD IN THE UNITED STATES 406

INTRODUCTION

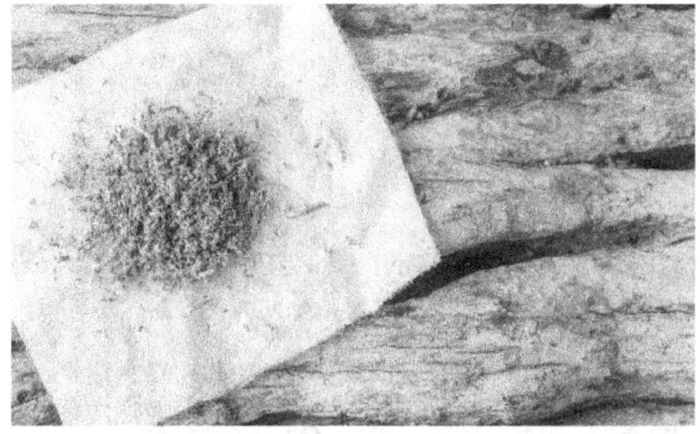

With legalization in Canada and many US states, and with the spread of CBD products like wildfire around the world, the cannabis market has hit stellar numbers this year.

The passion for hemp is gaining momentum globally and, according to statistics, the numbers will continue to rise undeterred.

In fact, according to CNN, in 2019 the cannabis market earned about 15 billion dollars and is destined to reach even higher peaks in the years to come.

Over the past two years, CBD products have mushroomed thanks to the advent of legalization in Canada and the increasingly lax laws enacted in several US states. And with the FDA (US Food and Drug Administration) currently planning a CBD-based epilepsy drug, and the government working to regulate over-the-counter CBD products, the market is expected to expand exponentially.

"The decisions made at the federal level put pharmacies and generic retailers into the market for CBD products in all 50 US states, which has greatly improved the projections on annual revenue," says Arcview CEO Troy Dayton, on CNN.

For the first time, in 2019, Arcview included a section called "Total Cannabinoid Market" in the state's annual sales report, including everything from pharmacy, to dispensary, to online sales.

If the current trend continues, it is estimated that by 2024 the cannabis market will reach $44 billion, of which about half in CBD products, a number that surpasses previous statistics by almost $5 billion.

Only time will reveal whether these forecasts will materialize or not, but with legalization in the US continuing to expand and with Canada preparing for a major supply hike, we expect nothing less than a massive surge in sales of legal cannabis.

As of 2019, legal cannabis has created 211,000 full-time jobs in America.

How many jobs are there in the legal cannabis industry? It's a common question, and one the government refuses to answer. Because cannabis remains federally illegal, employment data agencies such as the Bureau of Labor Statistics ignore all industry-related jobs. It's a shame, because one of the most dramatic job booms in recent history is missing. Over the past three months, Leafly 's data team, which works in partnership with Whitney Economics, has been moving from state to state to calculate the total number of direct full-time jobs in the state cannabis legal sector.

There are now more than 211,000 cannabis jobs in the United States. More than 64,000 of these jobs were added in 2018. Legal cannabis is currently the largest job creation machine in America. The strength of the cannabis business increased by 21% in 2017. It gained another 44% in 2018. 20% of the market's growth was in 2019. This represents a growth of 110% in cannabis jobs in just three years.

The Bureau of Labor Statistics recently compiled a list of industries with the fastest growing employment data. Opportunities for home health aides are expected to grow by 47%. Openings for wind turbine technicians are expected to increase by 96%. The need for solar PV installers is expected to grow by 105%. Such gains are expected to occur over the course of 10 years.

Some states that have seen adult cannabis legalization for some time - Colorado and Washington opened their stores in 2014 - are now seeing the growth of jobs around this industry. Meanwhile, new legal states, such as Florida (medical) and Nevada (adult use), are experiencing booms in cannabis work with jaw-dropping earnings:

Florida increased its cannabis use by 703% in 2018, adding over 9,000 full-time jobs.

Nevada added over 7,500 jobs in the same year.

Pennsylvania finished 2017 with around 90 cannabis jobs. It finished 2018 with almost 3,900.

New York increased its cannabis use by 278%, ending 2018 with over 5,000 jobs.

California, Massachusetts, Oklahoma, Florida and Arkansas are looking for talent and they need it now. Cannabis intake in California remained relatively flat in 2018 due to the disruption caused by moving from an unregulated medical system to regulated and licensed markets for medical and adult use. In rough numbers, this means that 10,261 jobs with good salaries, benefits and advancement opportunities are waiting to be filled.

In Massachusetts, the adult state market is just getting started. We expect to add over 9,500 jobs over the next 12 months. Florida is expected to add over 5,000 jobs, bringing the state's total cannabis employment to around 15,000. Oklahoma is the Wild West of cannabis right now. A year ago there were zero cannabis jobs. Now there are 2,107. In a year's time, we expect there will be 4,407. Arkansas has just started its medical marijuana program, but there is room for growth: from 135 jobs to 960 jobs by the end of the year.

Although Europe followed the European Law 242/2016, cultivation and then trade in cannabis derivatives with low THC content was regulated.

The hemp market is not just a trend of the moment, but a business destined to grow in various fields: from recreation, to medicine, to the world of food and cosmetics, the fields of application are numerous.

This has led to the birth of a new economic sector made up of different parts of the supply chain.

It starts with farms that have seen their earning potential increase, then moves on to wholesalers and intermediaries to get to retailers.

If at the end of 2017 there were a few dozen stores throughout Italy, today in 2019 we have reached almost 1000 scattered throughout the peninsula.

A number destined to grow because more and more people will overcome stereotypes and get closer to the cannabis plant.

Those who want to invest therefore have different strategies: you can open a farm dedicated to the cultivation of hemp, become an intermediary, or open a light cannabis shop.

The light cannabis market is in full evolution, if you are a fan and a connoisseur of this plant, you can use your knowledge to also become a successful entrepreneur.

CHAPTER I: A LITTLE HISTORY OF MARIJUANA

CANNABIS HAS ITS ORIGINS IN ASIA

At some point in history, the cannabis plant started growing in the wilderness. It is possible that it first grew in the areas of passage of hunter-gatherers, rich in nutrients. The farthest point in time that we can confirm the presence of cannabis is roughly 11-12,000 years ago. It would appear that the plant first grew in the mountainous areas of Central Asia, particularly Mongolia and southern Siberia. Humans began to cultivate two different varieties, using them for various purposes. The "Cannabis sativa" plant offered humans a unique psychoactive high. The one classified as "Cannabis sativa L.", however, is the common hemp, a non-psychoactive plant used industrially to produce oil, rope, paper and other materials.

It is difficult to pinpoint the exact moment when humans discovered how to use psychoactive plants. At some point, someone will have decided to smoke some cannabis, to see what happened. Had it not been for this pioneering spirit, perhaps the amazing properties of these two plants would have remained unknown to mankind. Later, two other psychoactive cannabis strains were discovered: Cannabis indica, with a physical and comfortable high, and Cannabis ruderalis, with softer highs and a shorter stature. But to analyze in detail the characteristics of each variety, we must first understand how the plant spread from the mountains of Central Asia to the rest of the world.

GANJA SPREADS AMONG CIVILIZATIONS

About ten thousand years have passed since the discovery of cannabis in Central Asia. During this time, the world expands and the seeds propagate. The first written document attesting to the use of cannabis concerns the Emperor of China Shen Neng in 2737 BC

According to some findings, cannabis may have been used by humans as a traditional remedy for several thousand years. In 2,000 BC, China, Japan, India, the Middle East, Russia and Eastern Europe cultivated the plant for only two purposes: psychoactive cannabis and hemp fiber. Between 2,000 and 1,400 BC the Vedas were written. These are sacred texts of one of the oldest religions in the world, Hinduism. In Atharva Veda, cannabis is mentioned. Some followers of Hinduism drink a cannabis-flavored milk, called bhang, in honor of the god Shiva. In some traditions, Shiva is depicted eating cannabis. According to others, her tears irrigated the Earth, and the cannabis plant flourished there.

HIGHLIGHTS OF THE EARLY HISTORY OF CANNABIS

In 1,550 BC, the Ebers Papyrus of ancient Egypt described the use of cannabis for therapeutic purposes. Over the next thousand years, other cultures acquired this knowledge. Around the 5th century BC, in ancient Greece, Herodotus mentioned cannabis. During his trip to the Middle East, he illustrated the cannabis-infused Turkish bath in which the Scythians participated. Herodotus saw that the Scythians became euphoric and more sociable after breathing in the steam from the bathroom. In 100 BC, the Chinese began to document the psychoactive impacts of cannabis.

During the next millennium, Islamic expansion spread cannabis to North Africa. In the following years, cannabis spread to East Africa and Europe. The propagation of the plant was favored by trade with the Arab world, and by the wide range of applications associated with cannabis and hemp. The hemp rope was solid and strong, suitable for Europeans' long journeys across the seas. When Europeans began colonizing other parts of the world, they brought hemp with them, encouraging its cultivation. An almost extraordinary fact, considering that today the West applies repressive laws against cannabis.

MARIJUANA SPREADS INTO THE COLONIES

As empires gained wealth and enslaved colonized peoples, their fortunes began to consolidate. The more the invasion expanded, the more distant parts of the world connected with each other. In addition to the terrible legacy of colonialism, this link between continents became more solid through the slave trade, and later, by contract servitude. The Indian diaspora was the result of the occupation of India by the British Empire. Workers were sent from India to South Africa or Jamaica. Many carried cannabis with them, and spread it among local populations.

The Africans of the southern regions already knew the plant from 1400 BC For the Jamaicans, however, the introduction of cannabis was a real marvel. Their term " ganja " derives from a Hindu word which in turn derives from the Sanskrit " ganjika ". The Jamaicans ended up developing their own religious tradition which included cannabis. The Rastafarian religion emerged in the 20th century, and included cannabis as a sacrament in contemplative ceremonies. In modern Western culture, Rastafarian iconography is widely associated with cannabis.

This past century has been quite dramatic for cannabis. The United States is a comprehensive example of what nearly all nations experienced during the 20th century.

CANNABIS ARRIVES IN THE UNITED STATES

The British Empire banned the production of cannabis and hemp in Jamaica in 1913, and in South Africa in 1922. In fact, cannabis was beginning to be considered dangerous. The International Opium Convention of 1925 strictly prohibited the export of "Indian hemp" to countries that banned cannabis. Over the years, an increasing number of international laws reduced the production of cannabis to the bone. In 1920, the United States unsuccessfully attempted to ban alcohol consumption. Eventually they retraced their steps, but continued to press what they called "marijuana".

Some revelations about White House policies, particularly under the direction of President Richard Nixon, show that cannabis was targeted for political reasons. Cannabis use was associated with ethnic minorities and the countercultural movement, so it was easy to arrest those who belonged to these groups accusing them of drug-related offenses. Despite the painful consequences of the War on Drugs, American growers continued to develop the plant, especially in the more tolerant and culturally open West Coast area. Cannabis was welcome here, but soon the whole United States would rebel against the criminalization of marijuana.

MARIJUANA MOVES TOWARDS LEGALIZATION

Cannabis was first introduced to the United States from the Atlantic Ocean. Today, American growers offer the world some of the finest varieties. In turn, the world has encouraged America to be more persistent in its fight against legalization.

The Netherlands also became famous for their flexibility towards international drug laws. During the 1970s, the state instructed the police to ignore coffeeshops and their cannabis sales, as long as they followed certain guidelines. This caused a coffeeshop boom in Amsterdam and other Dutch cities. Dutch society did not crumble after giving people a space in which to purchase a substance used for millennia by all of humanity. In fact, the nation has made significant improvements, managing more effectively, drug use by the population.

Various countries have started experimenting with more liberal and lax cannabis laws. In the 2000s, Spanish cannabis clubs were able to take advantage of a loophole in European legislation. In these premises, reserved exclusively for members of legal age, only the consumption and cultivation of cannabis plants for personal and non-profit use was allowed. As other models of decriminalization have emerged, and 2010 was marked by a wave of legalization. The first was Uruguay, which established a cannabis club system. Then Canada legalized the cultivation and sale of cannabis retail, defying international restrictions.

3 December 2020 - The UN deletes cannabis from the list of the most dangerous drugs

A definitive green light for the use of medical cannabis: the news that could finally mark a turning point regarding legalization is in recent days: the UN has in fact chosen to eliminate medical marijuana from the list of the most dangerous drugs, which includes drugs such as heroin and cocaine.

The Commission for Narcotic Drugs, based in Vienna, which includes 53 member states, has finally developed and approved a series of recommendations promoted by the

World Health Organization such as eliminating cannabis from Table IV of the 1961 Single Convention, where hemp sativa appeared from 1961.

This was a long-awaited victory obtained by the UN and perhaps it could finally represent the first step to enhance and improve scientific research on cannabis and its therapeutic use now so widespread.

The legalization of cannabis in Europe

Legalization in Spain

Although Spanish law is quite tolerant and provides a considerable margin of freedom, possession of cannabis in Spain is not always legal. Drug dealing is a criminal offense and, in any case, prison sentences are also given if you choose to follow the path of illegality. The consumption of marijuana for personal use is often tolerated by the police within certain limits. Smoking marijuana is allowed but is considered something strictly private and personal that can only take place in one's home or in places specifically used: otherwise, consumption in a public place is considered a punishable offense at the discretion of the police with fines that can reach €300.

Discreet transport linked only to products packaged and certified by the manufacturer for quantities of less than or equal to 50 grams is also tolerated. However, Spanish cannabis law can vary depending on the location: just think of the freedom of Barcelona or Catalonia. Smoking in public is not permitted except for licensed clubs.

Legalization in France

In France the use of light cannabis is now considered illegal: however, the country has recently started the legalization process aimed solely at medical cannabis in a controlled manner and in anticipation of more radical measures. The imminent start of a marijuana legalization process is therefore desirable in order to provide users with legal access to a specific type of weed for purely medical use without social repercussions, planning such an "experiment" for the next two years.

Legalization in the Netherlands

Coffeeshops have been well known in the Netherlands for over 40 years, a reality made possible by the particular tolerance regime launched in the 70s by the Dutch government and confirmed by successive ones over the last fifty years. Although the production of cannabis and its marketing is formally illegal, the sale of small quantities within the premises is allowed only to adults. However, cultivation and distribution are still illegal and punishable as they are mainly controlled by the local underworld. Hiring in public is also a crime.

Legalization in Sweden

Although Sweden appears among the most liberal countries in Europe, the consumption of marijuana is currently not tolerated in any way. Particularly severe are the penalties therefore for the employers, even the possession of minimal quantities of weed risks heavy penalties and, in serious cases, imprisonment inside the country.

Legalization in Switzerland

In Switzerland, cannabis consumption is now considered illegal as is its sale and production, especially in the form of good weed or hashish. The consumption of hemp by adults is punished with a fine of 100 francs. Possession of quantities of less than 10 grams is not punishable while as regards minors the penalty provided may vary according to juvenile criminal law.

Legalization in Germany

Since March 2017, a law has been passed in Germany that offers the opportunity to prescribe cannabis to seriously ill patients, as a support to pain therapy. However, this law currently has a flaw due to the lack of parameters aimed at indicating and classifying the real severity of the disease. The consumption of light cannabis is usually legal but with obvious limitations related to the quantities in the possession of the user: depending on the region, it is possible to hold an amount ranging from 15 grams in Berlin to ⅗ grams in other regions.

Legalization in the UK

The United Kingdom is still a real laggard: to date, and only since last year, the use of cannabis in the therapeutic field has been authorized while keeping the consumption of weed for recreational purposes illegal. However, significant future changes are desirable in what appears to be the most tolerant country in terms of sanctions.

The legalization of cannabis in non-European countries

The legalization of cannabis in what are non-European countries seems to be a reason for much less heated discussions and debates than in Europe. A radically more open mindset allows jurisdictions a higher margin of tolerance, leading to consider weed, fortunately, no longer a taboo.

Legalization in Australia

In Australia, a recent provision established all the rules related to the consumption and possession of cannabis for recreational use, formalizing the effective legalization: adults have the right to own up to 50 grams of weed and can grow 2 plants each or 4 per family. Being a federal state, however, this law only involves the territory of the capital although since 2016 the consumption of marijuana for therapeutic purposes has also been legalized.

Legalization in California

California has also gradually adapted to the legalization process for cannabis: starting from January 1, 2019, the recreational use of marijuana became legal following a referendum held in November. Citizens over the age of 21 can freely own up to 28 grams of weed and grow up to six seedlings at home. However, hiring in public places is prohibited.

Legalization in the United States

On June 25, 2019, the Governor of Illinois approved the law by which the legalization of the use and sale of cannabis throughout the state took place in effect, starting from January 1, 2020. To date, this represents the 11th state in the US to have fully legalized marijuana, in the footsteps of Alaska, California, Colorado, Maine, Massachusetts, Michigan, Nevada, Oregon, Vermont and Washington. However, the number of states where it is considered legal to sell and buy marijuana increases if we also include the District of Columbia, where private sale is prohibited, and the territories of the Northern Mariana Islands and Guam. Quite curious if you think that prohibition was first seen in the United States!

THE MODERN MARIJUANA THERAPEUTIC

In the 19th century, European doctors such as William Brooke O'Shaughnessy and Jacques-Joseph Moreau introduced cannabis from a scientific angle to the Western world. They recorded the various therapeutic effects offered by cannabis. Curiously, the substance began to be used to treat various ailments, even after it was forced into hiding in the 20th century.

During that time, the newly founded nation of Israel began researching the molecules and chemical compounds found in the cannabis plant. A team of Israeli scientists, led by Dr. Raphael Mechoulam, discovered how to synthesize cannabinoids such as THC and CBD.

In addition, he studied endocannabinoids and cannabinoid receptors in the human body. These researchers helped reveal the potential of cannabis for treating various ailments and diseases. Today, medical marijuana is used in people with cancer and undergoing chemotherapy; it is used in anorexic subjects because it causes appetite, and in inappetent subjects debilitated by chronic diseases, such as AIDS and multiple sclerosis; because it causes muscle relaxation that fights the stiffness that these diseases cause. It is used against Parkinson's disease. It is also used in the treatment of epileptic subjects. It also plays a role in the treatment of glaucoma, since it lowers intraocular pressure.

CHAPTER 2: LEGAL CANNABIS AROUND THE WORLD: A PATCHY REALITY

Hemp continues to be the most persecuted plant in the world. This seems a strange thing, how can a plant be outlawed? Yet it is.

Cannabis suddenly became public enemy number one in 1937 when America banned the production, trade and use of hemp by enacting the Marijuana Act. The United States was not the first to embark on this reckless war: before them Egypt, Jamaica and South Africa had thought about it, while in Italy it was Mussolini who banned the cultivation and use of cannabis forever. Despite this, the American stance is remembered as the highlight of this absurd prohibition, as the law was accompanied by a shameful press campaign, which forever associated the use of this plant with deviant behavior. Also tinged with a subtle as well as ferocious racism, American propaganda planted the seeds of what, in the following years, became the social and political orientation towards cannabis and those who use it.

The ban quickly spread like wildfire, affecting not only Western countries, but also the states in which marijuana was a full part of the uses and traditions of the peoples who, among other things, had always cultivated it.

Since then, hemp has been the first outlawed plant in history and still is today in most of the world.

Yet, the first timid signs of change appear on the horizon and the debate on the effectiveness, but above all on the meaning, of this new prohibitionism is increasingly lively and widespread.

To date, between quick pushes forward, timid openings and rigid conservatism, the laws on the possession and use of marijuana are decidedly diverse and range from total legalization to the very severe penalties still in force in some countries of Southeast Asia.

Let's see what the situation is in the world.

Legalized cannabis: where to smoke it without problems

To date, the only countries that have fully legalized cannabis are Uruguay and Canada.

The South American country will be remembered in the history books as the first state to have completely legalized the recreational use of marijuana: in 2013, raising a media fuss and a bitter global debate, President Jose Mujica signs a law which, thanks to subsequent changes, leads the country to be the first nation in the world where it is possible to produce, buy and consume hemp freely. But don't rush to buy a plane ticket to Montevideo: the use of cannabis for recreational uses is allowed only to Uruguayan citizens and residents, who must be registered in the national register of consumers.

In Canada, the legalization of hemp came in 2018 thanks to the Cannabis Act, which finally allows recreational use to all citizens of age. In some provinces it is only possible to buy marijuana from state-run businesses, while in others it is also allowed to purchase from individuals. Smoking marijuana is only allowed in private homes, although outdoor use and public parks are tolerated in some provinces. On the contrary, Canadian law harshly pursues those who drive while intoxicated: if you are stopped by the police, you may be subjected to tests to verify that the THC nanograms contained in your blood do not exceed the 5 established by law. Indoor cultivation is almost always allowed, as long as there are no more than 4 plants and strict protocols are followed to prevent children from coming into contact with cannabis.

The panorama of states that are slowly moving towards more permissive legislation, but have not yet made the big leap towards full legalization, is much wider. Here the situation is really confused and each country has adopted its own laws, with more or less paradoxical aspects.

The country that is most open to marijuana smokers, but also the one with the most schizophrenic legislation, is Holland. Contrary to what many of you think, cannabis is illegal in the Netherlands, although its use is tolerated nationwide. Strange, right? But if this sounds bizarre to you, wait until you hear what the real " backdoor problem " is, as the Dutch call it: as everyone knows, Holland is home to coffeeshops, but these businesses have to get their supplies from the black market. In practice, what they buy illegally suddenly becomes legally marketable from the moment it arrives at their facility. Insane? Yes, and this is the reason why, after a short period of tightening of the laws, which led to the closure of many coffeeshops, the situation is back as before and it seems quite obvious that, sooner or later, the government will legalize what has been done for a long time.

In the rest of Europe, the situation remains very varied. Although many states have opened up to the consumption of light hemp and cannabis for therapeutic purposes, recreational use remains strongly repressed. In some countries, such as Spain, the Czech Republic and Switzerland, the process towards legalization is further ahead than in others and, although not legalized, the possession of hemp is tolerated and decriminalized, as long as the quantity is within the limits set by law.

In the rest of Europe, if you want to buy cannabis, you do it at your own risk: the possession of hemp, if it falls within the so-called moderate quantity, is often tolerated by the police, but it is always better not to rely on it. In practice, holding, selling and growing marijuana remains a crime and penalties vary enormously from one country to another.

Where hemp is illegal and the penalties very severe

In the rest of the world, hemp remains totally illegal and penalties for offenders can reach up to life imprisonment, in cases of buying and selling large quantities. The paradoxical aspect of this type of legislation lies in the fact that it is adopted by countries which were traditionally producers and consumers of this plant. The quality of Indian and Nepalese hemp is famous all over the world, yet in these states the law is clear: production, possession and trade are totally prohibited. Just as the penalties are very severe in Malaysia, Indonesia and all of South Asia, countries where the possession of a few grams of marijuana can lead to very long detention, not to mention international drug trafficking, for which the penalties go up to life imprisonment.

In Africa, hemp is illegal everywhere and if it is true that in many countries it is very easy to find it, be careful what you do: the police are usually complacent with the locals, but it is very likely that they are not with you. The only exception in the continent is South Africa, which in recent years has been trying the difficult road towards legalization, starting to decriminalize the possession of small quantities and the cultivation of cannabis inside homes.

The war that America began almost a century ago is not over yet and, although encouraging signs can be seen here and there, the road to the complete rehabilitation of hemp is still very long and full of obstacles. But, as often happens, the positions of governments are always much more backward than those of the voters: the popular consensus towards a decisive legalization of hemp is increasingly broad and it is not excluded that, in the coming years, many countries will find themselves having to do deals with the anti-prohibitionist pressures of millions of citizens, finally clearing the recreational use of a plant that has not received the treatment it deserved.

CHAPTER 3: WHERE IT IS GROWN

The United Nations Office on Drugs and Crime (UNODC) recently released its 2017 World Drug Report - the 20th annual survey on manufacturing, trafficking and eradication and enforcement efforts around the world.

In recent years, the report has sought to quantify the amount of cannabis grown in each producing country - over the past decade consistently placing Morocco first, generally followed by Mexico and Paraguay.

This general trend continues - with some new variations.

The report seeks only to quantify the cultivated area for the best producers.

Morocco is again at the head of the row, with 47,000 hectares dedicated to cannabis cultivation. It is followed by Mexico with 15,000 hectares.

But now the industry has arrived in Nigeria which settles in third place at just over 4,500 hectares. Followed closely by Lebanon with 3,500. Paraguay is just behind with 2,780.

There is some lag time in UNDOC reports, as they are based on the most recent figures available: the 2017 report is based on data collected between 2010 and 2015.

The estimates are based on "direct indicators (cultivation or eradication of cannabis plants) or indirect (seizures of cannabis plants, production of domestic cannabis as a source of seizures, etc.) ..."

The report acknowledged: "The extent is challenging because some countries report eradication in terms of hectares, while others report in terms of the number of uprooted cannabis plants, the weight of seized cannabis plants or the number of sites of cannabis cultivation that have been eradicated. This makes comparisons of eradication difficult".

If you look at the uprooted area, first is Mexico, followed by Morocco and Nigeria, based on the 2010-2015 figures.

The largest number of cannabis growing sites were found in the United States, followed by Ukraine, the Netherlands and Russia.

The largest number of eradicated cannabis plants were reported from Nigeria, followed by the United States, the Philippines and Paraguay.

The largest quantities of cannabis plants seized were reported from Bolivia and Peru, followed by Jamaica.

In terms of tons of "cannabis weed" seized, the United States is in the lead, followed by Mexico, Paraguay, Colombia and Nigeria. For tons of "cannabis resin", Spain is the global leader (contraband from North Africa), followed by Pakistan, Morocco, Afghanistan and Algeria.

Unsurprisingly, more hash is "taken" in the Old World while more herbaceous cannabis is "taken" in the New World. In 2015, nearly two-thirds (64 percent) of the total amount of cannabis flowers seized around the world were seized in the Americas, according to the report.

Cannabis

Consumer market in Europe

It is estimated that more than 80 million adults have used cannabis at least once; of these over 22 million have done so in the last year. Based on these data, cannabis is by far the most widely consumed illicit drug in the EU. On reflection, the estimated market value of cannabis is very high, coming in at over €9 billion. About 1% of European adults are believed to consume cannabis daily, or almost. It is this group of individuals that raises the greatest concern in relation to the potential health and social problems associated with such consumption. National trends in cannabis use highlighted by recent surveys differ from each other, showing both increases and decreases. However, cannabis is currently the most frequently reported drug as the primary reason for first access to drug addiction therapies and the second most frequently cited substance among all patients on treatment. Cannabis is commonly available in Europe in two distinct forms: the leaves and the resin. Either way, it is usually smoked alongside tobacco, creating additional potential health impacts. The reported retail prices for cannabis resin and leaves are currently very similar, typically ranging between 7 and 12 EURO per gram. However, prices vary by country, as does the perceived quality of the product. Although prices have only risen slightly over the past decade, the average potency in terms of tetrahydrocannabinol (THC) has almost doubled over the same period.

Products and market innovation. Cannabis production in the EU over the past decade has led to a change in the market: in many countries, home-made leaf products have become more relevant at the expense of imported resin. That said, imported resin remains important and continues to enter the EU. Cannabis leaves enter from several other potential source countries. Internal production takes place in various forms, ranging from small-scale cultivation for personal use to large plantations. Although some large-scale crops are located outdoors, intensive cultivation sites are often located indoors or underground and can pose a significant fire hazard. The use of intensive and sophisticated in-house production techniques, together with the availability of high-potency strains of the cannabis plant, is probably one of the factors that have led to the increase in potency of both resins and leaf products observed in recent years. It seems that many cannabis users equate potency with quality, thus resulting in a particular demand and appreciation for high potency products. As there is sufficient competition in the market, this phenomenon acts as an incentive for Moroccan resin producers, who have introduced new hybrid varieties of the plant with high potency and high yield.

Although data on other forms of cannabis available on the European market are scarce, evidence from other contexts, in particular that of the United States, suggest that there is ample room for innovation in the future, especially with regard to edible products, and oils or cannabis intended for use in vaporizers. In historical terms, small quantities of cannabis oil have been sporadically available on the EU market; however, recent reports of domestic production using butane gas from the United States are worrying from both public health and public safety standpoints. More generally, the existence of a large legitimate commercial cannabis market in the United States is likely to lead to more product innovation, with a possible ripple effect in the EU. However, EU internal production is already supported from physical sales points and online, that sell products such as audio-visual equipment and lighting, and kits for the production of resin. Some very high potency resins of domestic production have recently been detected and the future commercial production of very potent cannabis resins in the EU is now a real possibility. A link between some cannabis grow shops and criminal groups involved in the trafficking and sale of cannabis has led to recent businesses in the Czech Republic and the Netherlands to target this type of business. Nonetheless, such measures may result in a shift of business to neighboring countries or the online market.

Between cannabis and organized crime

The somewhat benign public image of the cannabis market derived from the activities of hippy entrepreneurs in the 1960s stands in stark contrast to modern reality.

Crime or organized groups currently play an important role in a large sector that generates financial flows associated with violence and other forms of crime.

Furthermore, the vast reach of the cannabis market makes it important for criminal activities at all levels. For example, street gangs are often involved in retail and sometimes manufacturing, which has led to gang conflicts in some European Member States. The negative impacts of the large illicit cannabis market on local communities and law enforcement resources, as well as the resulting costs, are often overlooked. Moroccan organized crime groups, which exploit the links with Moroccan communities in Europe and collaborate with European groups, have an established role in the import of large quantities of cannabis resin. Spain, the Netherlands and, to a lesser extent, Belgium are the main import and distribution points for the entire EU market. These activities continue to lead to gang violence in some countries.

However, it was probably the growth in domestic cannabis production that caused most of the clashes between the groups. Large indoor production sites are linked to violent crime between groups, as well as the theft of electricity, and are also associated with trafficking in human beings. Migrants and victims of human trafficking, as well as other vulnerable people, have been employed, sometimes with coercive measures, to work at production sites. Although many groups are involved, the Dutch and Vietnamese organized crime groups in particular have built up an international reputation as a major player in this sector. Some of these groups have set up their own cannabis production sites outside their home country, while others provide know-how and equipment to groups in other countries, encouraging the spread of domestic cannabis production to new locations.

In terms of market developments, Spain, traditionally the main entry point for resin produced in Morocco, has recently reported an increase in seizures of cannabis leaves, suggesting an increase in local production. Seizures of cannabis leaves are also on the rise in Italy and in Greece. In addition, Turkey reported in 2013 that it seized 180 tons of cannabis leaves, more than all EU countries combined. However, the implications of such seizures for the EU market are unclear. A recent development has also been the limited appearance, in some parts of the EU, of Afghan resin, which Albanian groups are associated with. Albania is also an important country of origin for cannabis leaves arriving in the EU. Some recent interceptions of large batches of cannabis resin moving east along the North African coast are also worrying, as they may signal the emergence of new trafficking routes through southern European countries and the Western Balkans, with potential links to trafficking in human beings, or to unstable regions of the eastern Mediterranean.

188 million people used cannabis in 2017, with production coming from 159 different countries and, mainly,

from the Maghreb, Mashrek and the southern Balkans. A number that makes you think this is the most widely used substance in the world, with a growth trend in North America (up 60% from 2007 to 2017) and in Asia. The Americas are also where the substance is seized the most. South America represented 38% of the world total in 2017, while North America 21%, a figure in sharp decline compared to 2016 mainly due to the effect of legalization for non-medical use of the substance in some states.

The trend also suggests an increase in both indoor and outdoor growing, with indoor growing closely associated with a general increase in THC levels compared to two decades ago.

Furthermore, in the last decade, cannabis products have increased, which tend to be rich in THC (one of the best-known active ingredients in cannabis) and low in CBD. In Europe alone, the average THC content of cannabis resin has doubled from around 8 percent in 2006 to 17 percent in 2016, and the THC content of cannabis herbs has increased from 5 to 10 percent over the same period. According to the World Drug Report 2019, "it is believed that when CBD and THC are administered in balanced proportions, CBD may be able to reduce some of the effects of THC, such as anxiety and paranoia."

The most recent overview of cannabis use in every single country and globally indicates that the strategy of repression and prohibition has failed to prevent the use of THC and other psychoactive substances by the population.

CONSUMPTION OF CANNABIS IS A GLOBAL NEED

Towards the end of each year, local and international agencies release data on drug use, crimes occurring, unemployment rate, fake inflation data, and everything needed to be good informed citizens. The use of all types of psychotropic drugs, legal and illegal, has been steadily increasing for decades in almost all nations. The use of cannabis is rampant as a medicine, spiritual aid, and a substitute for other more dangerous substances. Fun fact: there is no direct relationship between local laws and cannabis use. People consume cannabis all over the world, despite the laws.

The authoritative United Nation Office on Drugs and Crime has just published some figures on cannabis use around the world. Some caution should be exercised in reading these numbers, because they have been obtained with different research methods and come from different agencies. That is why we prefer to aggregate this information to provide an overall picture rather than drawing up a Top 10 ranking. The winner is Iceland, however. Not those stoners you thought.

UNODC data shows that Iceland is one of the countries with the largest number of cannabis users. The reason is unclear, or it could be that beer was made legal 25 years ago and alcoholic beverages are very expensive. The figures indicate that 18.3% of the Icelandic population aged 15 to 64 use cannabis. Not bad as a result, about one in five adult smokers. Even a small African nation shows a high percentage, with 21.5% smokers, or 5.8 million people. Ghana is the sixth largest cannabis user in the world, and ranks second in percentage of the number of citizens. Cannabis is almost as illegal in Ghana as it is in France, where governments continue to increase penalties for possessing cannabis. Despite this, more than 11% of the French consume cannabis, which is equivalent to 6 million smokers. They are among the largest consumers of weed in Europe, and rank 7th in the world. Voila.

Spain, on the other hand, is one of the leading exponents of drug reform, following a model of decriminalization rather than punishment and incarceration. In Spain it is not legal to grow cannabis for personal use, and even cannabis club experiments live in a gray area of legality. Despite the official status of legality, the use of cannabis for personal and social purposes is tolerated, and sometimes the authorities turn a blind eye to patients who grow their own marijuana for medical use.

Official data indicate that 10.6% of Spaniards consume cannabis. Nobody believes it, and some place the figure over 25%, even higher than in Ghana. Spain continues to follow its normalization path: Another major city is regulating cannabis, and the whole nation will prepare a special law to allow cannabis clubs to operate legally.

The policies can lead to different outcomes, such as the Netherlands is around twentieth in the world rankings. In the US, medical cannabis is legal in over 20 states, for a wide range of conditions. Recreational use is legal in four states, and the number will increase over the next few months or years. The percentage of users could be 14% or 16%, lower than in Zambia, which reaches 17.7%. The Americans therefore showed their love for cannabis by smoking it and spreading its derivatives. Translated into numbers, this passion involves around 44 million people. In absolute numbers, this is obviously the nation with the highest number of stoners.

Among the group of nations that report cannabis use by around 15% of the population, we find Nigeria with 14.3% of users. The same percentage of Italy, which is the nation with the highest cannabis consumption in Europe. The possession of small quantities of cannabis is decriminalized, but the trade is fully punished, with the result that 14.6% of Italians smoke cannabis, or 8.9 million people. Italy ranks fourth in the world in terms of number of consumers. New Zealand has roughly the same percentage of smokers as Italy, while Canada only reaches 12%. Here the government issues licenses for medical and industrial use, and the recreational use of cannabis is highly tolerated. Australia has 10.2% smoking users, more than Jamaica, which, believe it or not, only has 7.2% smokers. Some producers don't consume what they produce, others do. It seems that Pakistan has only 3.9% of consumers, not many, but equivalent to 7.6 million people, ranking 5th in the world. Furthermore, only 6.2% of 88 million Egyptians smoke cannabis, or 5.4 million people, at the 8th position in the world rankings. Cannabis is illegal in these countries, as well as in India, where it is widely consumed in various regions. Only 3.2% of Indians smoke cannabis, but the figures are based on a population of over 1.2 billion, so that is 38.5 million people. Albania doesn't even make it into the top 30 cannabis smoking nations, despite being the scene of a bloody war over cannabis.

We therefore draw up a possible list of the 30 main cannabis smoking nations, according to official UNODC data in percentages, referring to the total adult population.

Looking at the figures, we can easily deduce that 10% of the world's population uses cannabis, or would be willing to consume it, if weed were more available. The number of these patients is constantly increasing, and could mean 500 million individuals consuming 1 gram of cannabis per day at an average price of 10 Euros per gram. This would mean 50 billion euros burned per day, over 18 trillion euros per year. This amount is equivalent to the Gross Domestic Product of the entire European Union. Here's what these figures will ultimately mean if the cultivation of cannabis for personal or aggregative use is not fully legalized.

***WHAT** distinguishes legal marijuana from non-legal marijuana?*

In summary, the main difference is simply in the concentration of a substance (THC), which is naturally present in the plant and which must be contained on particularly low thresholds.

In fact, we recall that in legal cannabis this concentration must be equal to or less than 0.6% in Italy, and that on the other hand all products that exceed this threshold are considered illegal, as well as capable of impacting human health with their effects on the body.

The distinction criteria mentioned above should represent a good alarm bell for those who want to buy safe products, as well as a deep line of demarcation between legal products and those that would expose users to prejudicial consequences, from a criminal point of view. In addition, the illegal derivatives often do not carry any information on the packaging, while the safe and legal products have all the real and transparent information on how to use the product, the amount of THC and the origin of the plant (as well as the identification of the manufacturing company).

It does not escape us, in fact, that in the legal marijuana sector it is traceability that is the real strength. In the purchasing process, therefore, maximum attention must be paid to the shop you're in, which is its operational and legal headquarters and, above all, to what information on the treatments and processing processes that the material has received, before hitting the shelves or an e-commerce site.

We also remember some that distribute legal cannabis - and that can sell some of the most purchased types of light cannabis - can also be franchises, and that it is always advisable - even in this case - to find out who the supplier of the products is. This formula allows you to understand who are the operators involved and responsible for each phase of the supply chain that goes from the producer to the purchase order in total transparency.

Well, having introduced the above, in this guide, you will find out everything you need to know about legal cannabis: the legislation, what a shop must do to be legal, what products to choose and how to recognize them, and of course what is the difference between the products for therapeutic use and those for recreational use and how the Italian law works to mark this difference.

LEGAL MARIJUANA: THE LEGISLATION

Legal Cannabis: Difference Between Therapeutic Use and Recreational Use

It is necessary to mention the difference between therapeutic and recreational use of cannabis, which closely follows the distinction between legal and illegal cannabis.

Medical cannabis is in fact the one necessary as an element and raw material useful for creating drugs. Therefore, medical supervision is constant throughout the production process and the presence of this substance is clearly indicated on the packaging and on the product leaflet. In addition, these products are strictly controlled by AIFA, the Medicines Agency and, for these reasons, they are not sold freely on the market, but only upon presentation of a prescription from a specialist. Naturally, it will be necessary to go to facilities managed by the local ASL to proceed with the withdrawal.

Recreational cannabis, on the other hand, is dangerous to health if it exceeds the legal limits. With the term recreational, in fact, we go to classify those products that are used "to have fun", and therefore present themselves as substances that offer the "easy high".

All those products that are ultimately not for medical use, and for which therefore no prescription is required, are classified as legal cannabis. However, they are not for recreational use as they do not cause any effect, and are therefore to be considered fully safe for health. Among the products that fall under legal cannabis in Italy there are perfumers for rooms or for the person, oils, inflorescences and clothing. Their main task is to allow users to benefit from all the relaxing properties of hemp without fear of the negative effects!

CHAPTER 5: COFFEE SHOP, SMART SHOP, DISPENSARIES

Coffeeshop, headshop, smartshop and dispensaries ... All terms that you may have already read and that may have confused you a bit. We will quickly analyze the differences between these types of retailers and what you can expect from each of them.

In some countries, people are still forced to buy weed on the street or through shady back channels, provided you have the courage and / or the desire to break the law. This situation is downright unpleasant for cannabis enthusiasts who live in, or visit, these areas. Thankfully, a growing number of countries around the world are adopting a more tolerant approach to using and buying and selling cannabis.

The type of "cannabis supplier" you will need to interact with depends mainly on the country you are in. Flowers, for therapeutic or recreational use, and in some places even concentrates, are sold in various shops, each following their own rules of engagement.

COFFEESHOPS: DUTCH SHOPS THAT SELL CANNABIS

The coffeeshops are an invention of the Netherlands and a major tourist attraction of the Netherlands. In the 1970s, the Dutch government decided to change its stance on drugs, largely decriminalizing the use of cannabis. This initiative gave birth to the Dutch coffeeshop scene, now internationally recognized.

The atmosphere at the coffee shops varies from place to place, as do the prices and quality of the weed sold. Most of Amsterdam's coffeeshops are located in the red-light district and cater mainly to tourists. However, there are other less touristy coffeeshops hidden throughout the city.

Almost all coffeeshops offer a large selection of cannabis inflorescences, extracts and even edibles. These stores are licensed by the government and must be subject to a number of restrictions. For example, under Dutch law governing coffeeshops, a store can only sell a maximum of 5g of cannabis twice a day to the same person. They also cannot sell cigarettes or alcohol.

HEADSHOP AND SMARTSHOP: FROM PHYSICAL STORES TO ELECTRONIC COMMERCE

The headshop can still be found in many countries. They usually sell bongs, pipes, rolling papers, grinders, and other cannabis-related accessories and tools. In the United States, during the hippie movement of the 1960s, headshops began to appear across the country and many of them had ties to socio-political movements against drug prohibition, the Vietnam War and more.

Smartshops, however, are more recent and usually are dedicated to the sale of psychoactive substances and related products. They are very popular in the Netherlands, where they can legally sell psychoactive truffles and cacti. However, they are also found in Sweden, the United Kingdom, the Republic of Ireland and Portugal. The latter maintains a very liberal stance on drugs.

Today, physical head / smartshop stores have largely been converted into online businesses.

DISPENSARY: THE AMERICAN METHOD

Dispensaries are a commercial reality that exists only in the United States, although in Canada some retailers have labeled themselves as dispensaries. In the United States, dispensaries are regulated by the local government and, according to local laws, can sell certain quantities of cannabis products.

Dispensaries can only sell cannabis to adult customers (in states with laws on recreational use intended for an adult audience) or for therapeutic purposes. In the latter case, cannabis can only be sold to those with a medical prescription or registered as a patient on medical marijuana treatment.

US dispensaries offer a variety of cannabis products, including extracts, tinctures, vape cartridges, food items and, of course, a large selection of dried buds. In some states, dispensaries even sell clones and plants. The amount of marijuana that a dispensary can legally sell in a single transaction varies from state to state.

COLLECTIVES: NON-PROFIT ORGANIZATIONS

Cannabis collectives differ from dispensaries in that they are usually non-profit organizations. Like existing collectives in other sectors, these organizations are made up of a group of people who work for a common goal, which is to provide cannabis to those in need for therapeutic reasons or to adult buyers. Collectives of this type usually offer the same products as dispensaries. However, in some cases, they may only sell cannabis to their members or patients registered within the collective, it all depends on the local laws in which the organization is operating.

CANNABIS CLUB: THE SOLUTION FOR ADULTS ONLY IN SPAIN AND URUGUAY

Cannabis clubs are very popular in Uruguay and Spain. These clubs are usually registered non-profit organizations to produce cannabis for their members.

In Spain, new members can only join a club on the recommendation of another member. In general, members can purchase a maximum daily amount of around 3g of cannabis, in order to prevent resale.

In Uruguay, registered clubs can produce a certain amount of cannabis per month for each member, who usually has to pay a monthly membership fee. These clubs are also registered as private non-profit organizations.

CHAPTER 6: HOW TO GET INTO THE LEGAL MARIJUANA BUSINESS

Entering the marijuana and legal hemp business, therefore light, represents an interesting opportunity, no doubt to be taken into consideration. Light marijuana is a natural product, which is obtained from the female flowers of hemp plants that have a very low level of THC.

Hemp with low or even insignificant THC levels cannot be equated with drugs, due to the fact that it does not alter the psyche. After years of research and attempts, the experts in the field have in fact succeeded in their intent to originate varieties of plants not able to be called drugs.

These plants are cannabis varieties that have a THC value that should not exceed 0.2%, although exceeding this limit by up to 0.6% is tolerated by law.

Marijuana obtained from light hemp is a highly sought-after product, especially due to the fact that it contains CBD (cannabidiol), a substance that gives a feeling of relaxation, and which according to various studies is also able to offer many others benefits.

But how to become a light cannabis reseller? There are various avenues to choose from, between physical and online stores, and there are also various types of opportunities to buy wholesale hemp and then resell it.

HOW TO BECOME A LIGHT CANNABIS DEALER

No special certifications or specific permits are required to become a light cannabis reseller. In fact, it is possible to do it in the same way as you can open a bar, a grocery store, a mobile phone shop, a tobacconist, etc.

However, it is advisable to have specific skills in the sector, such as an in-depth knowledge of the cannabis products sold, and their target market. And it is also crucial to consider whether to sell in physical stores and / or through online stores.

Furthermore, there are also other issues to consider to set up this business:

Cannabis and light marijuana to be marketed must be accompanied by a special certificate of origin, which certifies the place of origin and quality of the seeds used for cultivation. In particular, the plant varieties judged light are those present in the Common Catalog of the European Union: there are 67 different species, all with a very low THC content.

Light cannabis and light marijuana must also have a laboratory certificate, certifying the values of all the main substances they contain. This document must always be attached to the sale, both wholesale and retail.

The packs of light marijuana must also have information relating to the batch of origin.

Such packages must also be sealed and hermetically sealed, whether they are sold individually at retail or in the case of wholesale supplies.

OPEN A LEGAL MARIJUANA STORE

As for the sale of cannabis and light marijuana in physical stores, there are some commercial activities that can do so. If you already have an established business, such as a grow shop, for the sale of products obtained from light hemp you can contact a supplier.

If, on the other hand, you decide to start from scratch, to dedicate yourself to the sale of products obtained with light hemp, in addition to contacting a supplier it is also necessary to take care of the appropriate opening of a physical store.

For example, you can open a hemp shop: it is a form of grow shop dedicated more specifically to the sale of hemp-based products.

To proceed in opening a hemp shop, there are some steps to follow, including:

Open a VAT number and a current account.

Rent or buy a place to do business.

Make the start of business communication (SCIA) to the trade office of the Municipality, which in the case of hemp shops concerns the sale of flowers and products derived from cannabis.

Respect the safety, urban planning and hygiene regulations.

Choose the supplier (or wholesaler) regardless of nationality. However, we must also keep in mind that the further away from the shop, the longer it will take for the goods to arrive.

For completeness of information, below we explain in more detail what a wholesaler does: he sells products in large quantities at lower prices than those found in stores, to allow retailing to those who have a store, physical and / or online.

Retailing, on the other hand, is the activity of the retailer, who must sell the goods purchased by the wholesaler to the final consumer.

Another, more convenient, possibility to open a physical shop than hemp shop is to contact a franchising company: taking advantage of this opportunity, you rely on a company that generally carries out most of the bureaucratic activities for the opening, while the shopkeeper will mainly have to deal with finding a place, managing it, and dedicating himself to the sale of the products that are supplied from time to time.

Buy hemp wholesale and resell it online

In addition to the possibility of opening a physical store, there is also one that allows you to sell cannabis light products through an online store.

Also, with regard to virtual shops, for the sale of the goods it is necessary to contact a wholesaler, that is a supplier who sells products to the retailer.

After purchasing light hemp products to resell them on the net, it is necessary to propose the goods to be sold to the public through a special website.

In addition, taking advantage of the potential offered by the network, it is possible to use various online tools to increase your clientele, with various types of online marketing initiatives that help to obtain greater visibility for your business.

HOW TO BUY WHOLESALE HEMP

Those who choose to become a light cannabis reseller, whether in a physical store, an online store, or both, have a valid ally on the internet. In fact, on the web it is possible to find several sites that offer wholesale sales.

These are usually reliable wholesalers, offering products from legal cannabis grown under controlled conditions or outdoors, in climatic areas suitable for this type of crop.

By doing a search on Google, typing for example "light hemp wholesalers", as results you will get several sites that you can rely on, after registration. By accessing these sites, it is possible to obtain contact details (telephone, e-mail, etc.) with which you can get in touch for precise information on how to establish a collaborative relationship.

Furthermore, starting from each of these sites it is possible to consult the relative pages to see what type of products they offer, how much they sell them, and where their company headquarters and the goods offered are located.

However, choosing the supplier is only one of the steps to be taken in order to resell legal cannabis products online. Another important step is related to the opening of the online store, as better explained in the next paragraph.

HOW TO OPEN A LEGAL CANNABIS ONLINE SHOP

There are two possibilities to open a legal cannabis online store: do it as a franchise or on your own.

In case you already have a business in a physical store, the choice to make may also depend on the way in which you are already operating. While, in the event that you do not have an online store at the same time, perhaps the ideal solution is to rely on a franchising service, also because in the latter case it is not even necessary to establish agreements with a wholesaler. In addition, online wholesalers are sometimes also franchise sellers.

It is good to highlight the main advantages of opening an online store compared to a physical store:

Fewer expenses: there is no need to buy or rent a room, furnish it, and hire staff to manage it. In this sense, the costs are significantly lowered.

Ability to reach a wider audience than those who live nearby. Furthermore, it is also possible to serve a clientele who would never go to a physical store dedicated to the sale of light cannabis.

Opportunity to sell anytime, any day of the year.

Possibility to ask for an e-mail to those who make purchases on the site, so as to send discounts and promotions directly to their e-mail inbox, in order to facilitate the possibility that they return to buy in the online shop.

Here are the advantages of opening an online store in franchising instead of on your own:

The possibility of always receiving the goods from the best producers, and therefore of offering customers a wide choice of very interesting and certainly legal products.

The opportunity to have at your disposal an already known brand, namely the franchising one. All this will have significant implications, since an already known brand is perceived by end consumers as a sign of reliability, right from the first day of opening the online store.

Less stressful management of the warehouse: procurement of goods and management of unsold items can be carried out in a much simpler way, and with less expense.

The possibility of receiving assistance and help in case of need, from competent personnel.

How to increase the visibility and profits of the legal marijuana online store

When opening any website that sells products, of whatever type they are, it is also very important to understand how to encourage the purchase, and how to obtain adequate visibility that allows you to reach a large number of people interested in the goods.

For the purposes described above, the site used should have the following characteristics:

A simple navigation interface: if the site is easy to use, customers tend to buy with pleasure, and the likelihood that they will return to make other purchases in the future increases.

A search box, and a subdivision of products by categories: in this way, anyone who accesses can view the products available in a faster way.

Multiple payment systems: credit cards, PayPal, etc. so that all users can pay in the way that is possible or more convenient for them.

Detailed information on the light cannabis products sold, including the levels of THC and CBD they contain: transparency with respect to what is sold is highly appreciated by customers, who when they see a wide availability of information on what is offered, they feel in safer hands.

Optimization of the site for search through Google and other search engines: as regards this operation, if you are not an expert on the subject, it is better to rely on SEO specialists. Optimizing your site is essential nowadays if the goal is to sell more. In fact, people usually turn to search engines when they search for something on the web, and they generally choose the first results they see appear.

A section in which to offer more information about your account, and from which city the goods being sold come from.

A possible section for a blog, that is, a space for informative articles relating to your business, any discounts and promotions, news on the subject of cannabis, and useful advice for consumers relating to the purchase and use of legal cannabis.

Furthermore, to obtain greater visibility it is also highly recommended to open social channels.

On Instagram it is possible, for example, to periodically publish photos of the products sold, and at the same time illustrate any discounts and promotions in progress.

On Facebook, in addition to what is also possible with Instagram, you can also publish any content from your blog of the online site, the one with which the sale of light marijuana products is also carried out.

Again, with regard to social media, it is very important to publish content with a certain frequency, also because in this way people are able to remember if necessary, the existence of the online store to promote.

Another system to obtain visibility is to make a request to appear on the advertising banners of the various sites with advertising.

Yet another is to be sponsored by influencers (charismatic and / or competent people in a certain topic, who are followed on social networks), or by certain blogs or other sites that practice affiliate marketing, an activity that consists of creating content in which certain products to be purchased are strategically proposed.

CHAPTER 7: WHAT IT TAKES TO OPEN A SHOP

What Does It Take to Get a License to Grow or Sell Cannabis?

Are you thinking of entering the cannabis industry? If you want to become a commercial grower or if you like the idea of opening a dispensary, know that you will have to bear a mountain of costs and legal requirements. Find out what to expect if you want to get a license to sell cannabis in America, Canada and Europe.

The cannabis industry is booming. New cannabis companies and outlets are opening at an impressive pace in many places. It might seem like an easy industry to break into, but the reality is very different. In short: it takes a long time to get a license to sell cannabis, and we're not just referring to very high taxes. Below we discuss the main factors to consider when considering applying for a commercial license for cannabis in the United States, Canada, and Europe.

FACTORS TO TAKE INTO CONSIDERATION IF YOU WANT TO JOIN CANNABUSINESS AND KNOW LOCAL LAWS AND REGULATIONS

It doesn't matter if you want to get a license to farm or to open a dispensary, the starting point is to consider the legal aspects. Despite the "youth" of the legal cannabis industry, the barrier to entry is actually very high and the requirements stringent. That is why it is imperative that you know all local laws and regulations. Markets for legal cannabis vary widely and can either favor or prevent the success of those who accept this challenge.

Criminal background checks are often required, not just for a dispensary owner, for example, but also for all employees and investors. In some places, such as Canada, growing commercial medical cannabis requires all managers to have a valid permit. So, if you have a criminal background, your dreams of hitting the market big as a licensed medical grower may vanish before you even begin.

Then there are the gray areas, which are complex to navigate. "Tolerated" or "decriminalized" does not mean that marijuana is legal. And if it's not legal, or local laws aren't clear and your city council hasn't passed anything explicitly authorizing the cultivation of recreational cannabis, that means a dispensary could be shut down by the government at any time. And you usually don't want to risk an investment in something that is still illegal in the eyes of the state.

You should not only be aware of current laws, but future ones as well. This young industry has a lot of legislative proposals to consider, so there are likely to be changes in the regulations. Staying ahead in this game by trying to understand future developments will make the process smoother.

Likewise, you need to be aware that some places, like the United States for example, have cannabis laws that put individual states in conflict with federal power. At the federal level, cannabis is still illegal and is classified as a Schedule 1 drug in the United States, while legal cannabis flourishes in individual states.

So, first of all make sure you prioritize research. Even better, consult an experienced attorney in the field and follow their advice.

PREPARE A BUSINESS PLAN

On paper, there is nothing more attractive than the prospect of turning a hobby into a business. But with the saturation of numerous niches in the cannabis market, such as the CBD sector, many people who enter the field quickly find themselves in difficulty, not only due to the high requirements and legal uncertainties, but also due to a lack of skills. and professional experience.

If you want to be successful you have to be professional. A solid business plan is a great first step in this direction. A well-made plan will help you in several ways. First, show that you are serious about your business and that you understand the intricacies of what you are about to do. It also works as a personal roadmap for keeping things organized and under control, especially in the early stages. Finally, a business plan is key when trying to get investor finance. These people want to understand if they will ultimately make a return on their investment.

YOU NEED CAPITAL TO START

As a matter of fact, you need capital to start a business. Your business plan should indicate how you will access this capital and what it will be used for. This can be a major challenge as not only is funding of between $ 200,000 and $ 250,000 as a minimum, but also because a bank is unlikely to guarantee a loan. You can thank the legal gray areas for that. Therefore, it is necessary to obtain financing through other methods, for example from investors or private capital.

Your business plan should also list the future running costs for your business. This will include annual license fees, rental costs, employee salaries, transportation costs and any other expenses.

FIND A SUITABLE OFFICE

There are not only special requirements for obtaining a license, but those who start a company in the cannabis sector must also follow some operational rules. To work as a dispensary in California you can't just rent a space wherever you like. There are strict rules on how far cannabis outlets must be from schools, churches and residential areas.

Similarly, it is necessary to maintain a high level of security for any type of premises where cannabis is stored. For example, there are some regulations that dictate that walls must be of a certain thickness, along with other security specifications that add to the cost and energy needed to support the business. To be accepted, your commercial grow license application in Canada must include a detailed description of the site, its floor plans, and the safety measures applied.

FEES AND LICENSE FEES

Aside from the costs of starting and running your business, you will then have to bear all the costs of the license. These, in addition to legal obstacles, are often enough to discourage many would-be dispensary owners. In some places, the license fee can exceed tens of thousands of dollars. Add the annual fee to renew your license and it's clear how quickly the money can be sucked out of your wallet.

OBTAINING LICENSES FOR GROWING CANNABIS IN AMERICA, CANADA AND EUROPE

The above is a snapshot of the different factors you will need to consider on a more or less global basis. We will now shed some light on the specific requirements for licensing in America, Canada and Europe, to help you get an idea of how things are in your area.

UNITED STATES

In the United States, laws and regulations for commercial growing vary from state to state, county to county, and even from city to city. So, before you start making plans for opening a dispensary or large-scale cannabis grow, make sure you know the laws and regulations that apply to you. Licensing fees also vary widely. For example, in Washington state, license fees are only $ 250, with annual fees of $ 1,480. This is a bargain compared to most other states. In Illinois, the registration fee is $ 25,000, with the annual grow license costing $ 100,000. Some states, such as California, Colorado, and Oregon, have variable annual licensing and renewal costs that depend on the size and type of cultivation: indoor or outdoor, number of plants being grown, and so on. In the best cases this can cost you a couple of thousand dollars, but it can go up to tens or hundreds of thousands of dollars just to get and keep your grow license.

CANADA

Canada officially passed the C-45 (Cannabis Act) in October 2018, making it the only G7 country that allows the cultivation and sale of recreational cannabis. This means that cannabis in Canada is federally legal. All aspects of the sale and distribution of cannabis are however under provincial jurisdiction, with different rules for licensing retailers. The Cannabis Legalization and Regulation Branch (CLRB) is responsible for overseeing the licensing process.

Where and how the license is obtained in Canada depends on which province will host the headquarters. For example, in British Columbia it is necessary to obtain a license as a private enterprise from the British Columbia Liquor and Cannabis Regulation Branch (LCRB) by following a detailed application process. In Manitoba, the Manitoba Liquor and Gaming Authority (LGA) issues retail licenses, but individual municipalities can veto the opening of stores in their area.

In Ontario, a license as a dispensary can be obtained by following a detailed application process to be sent to Ontario Cannabis Retail Corporation (OCRC). In Alberta, the application is sent to the Alberta Gaming and Liquor Commission (AGLC).

EUROPE

Unlike Canada and US states where cannabis is legal, all EU member states make possession of cannabis for personal use a criminal offense. However, several countries such as Spain, Italy, the Czech Republic and Belgium have begun to eliminate detention as a penalty for minor offenses.

No government in Europe openly supports the legalization of cannabis for recreational use: the legal cannabis market in Europe exists today only in a medical context. Even dispensaries and coffeeshops in the Netherlands are simply tolerated, as long as they follow strict criteria set by the public authority. This works similar to cannabis clubs in Spain, which are technically private venues, not commercial retail spaces.

Due to the legal status of cannabis in European nations, it is not yet possible to apply for a license to sell recreational cannabis today, although small steps have been taken.

Germany, for example, assigned the first national licenses for medical cannabis cultivation in 2019, although the process has so far been complicated by setbacks and delays. Germany recently restarted the application process, and companies that are eventually selected to legally grow German medical cannabis will have to comply with strict safety requirements and the highest pharmaceutical manufacturing standards.

CANNABUSINESS LICENSE: YOU NEED MONEY, TIME AND ENERGY

If you live in Canada or one of the US states where it is legal you can apply for a license to sell or grow cannabis. This is if you are willing to invest a huge amount of money (and energy, and time) in a very competitive industry where success is far from certain. Here in Europe, things are moving more slowly for aspiring commercial growers. Cannabis is still illegal in the eyes of the law, despite several attempts at decriminalization made here and there. But if the markets where cannabis is already legal teach us anything, it is that things can change quickly.

CHAPTER 8: LIGHT HEMP SHOP IN FRANCHISING

Is it worth opening a light hemp franchise? Are there really good business opportunities in this sector? Or is it a bad investment?

In the guide we will analyze the state of the art of this specific sector, one of the most innovative for those looking for good business opportunities. Cannabis light is liked by many, almost everyone and also allows you to open a business that sells many different products, which can have appeal to many categories of customers.

Let's see together why this could be your next business idea, the one that will be able to lead you into the world of profitable investment, work you like, and business opportunities.

Why cannabis light?

Before going into more specifics, it is more than legitimate to ask why such a sector exists, in fact, the light cannabis franchise, and why it is attracting more and more investors.

While standard cannabis is now on the market almost everywhere in Canada and the US, a little bit all over Europe (except for the Netherlands), there are important restrictions on the marketing of products with a high THC rate.

The problem has been solved by creating hemp species that contain very low percentages and that can be sold freely.

It is not just about food or smoking hemp, but about products that use this extraordinary plant as a raw material, such as oils, creams and incense.

The sector is very diverse and allows everyone to find products suitable for their needs - light cannabis shops have become meeting points for enthusiasts and less enthusiasts and bring home pretty good profits.

A premium product, with high costs and revenues

This is by no means a product for everyone - average prices are over 10 euros per gram, with significant markups for both producers and those who trade the product. This means that those who choose a light hemp franchise can count on a product capable of filling the cash register even with sales volumes that are not exactly big scale.

This particularity of the market must also be taken into consideration with regard to the choice of location: cannabis shops are more than good in selected urban contexts, where those who frequent them are able to spend without too many thoughts.

A growing market for some years now

If the wide margins enjoyed by the products were not enough, it is worth remembering that the cannabis light market has been growing steadily for some years now, which also attracts customers who have never consumed the illegal product.

It is no longer a niche product, but a legitimate product for many customers, with different personal stories, but united by a passion for legal marijuana.

The law is clear: it can be opened and operated without problems

When we talk about legal cannabis and the convenience of opening a franchise or not (or even a shop on your own) it is more than legitimate to worry about the legality of the product.

For a few years, smart shops have been in a gray area, which has led managers to have major problems, which in many cases have led to the closure of businesses.

Today things, at least as regards light cannabis, have definitely changed and there is finally a certain law that protects all operators in the sector:

Marijuana can be sold freely, as long as it has a THC concentration of less than 0.2%;

In any case, between 0.2% and 0.6% are exempt from any penal consequences;

The law is clear and further jurisprudential rulings have helped to define the boundaries of the legality of such a business.

To understand this, today you can open your own light cannabis franchise shop without any consequences, without risking anything, operating like any other entrepreneur.

If you want to sell cannabis light - better go to a good franchise

If you want to sell cannabis light, we advise you to choose a good franchise offer, which guarantees you among other things:

A quality product, which is able to satisfy your customers and to remain within the strict limits set by law;

Intelligent warehouse management, with the right assortments, the possibility of returns and possibly also with the sales account;

A brand known as much as possible: even if there is a premium price to pay, a known brand allows you to operate on the market with greater ease - also avoiding start-up costs in the advertising sector;

By focusing on these characteristics, you will be more than certain to be able to identify a really convenient franchise and that it will give you good support for your entry into the sector and for management once the business is actually started.

CHAPTER 9: LICENSES AND BUREAUCRATIC PROCEDURES IN THE USA

Eleven states in the United States have so far legalized cannabis for non-medical use by adults, with many more ready to follow. With cannabis still federally illegal, a series of natural experiments are taking place, each presenting a different model of how cannabis can be regulated, thus providing important lessons for policymakers looking to pursue similar policies. In this report, we compare regulation across states, taking into account key objectives, including public health and social justice, and consider lessons that can be learned for future policy reform.

The transition from the market to therapeutic use

Cannabis is now legal for medical purposes in most of the United States, so many states have drawn the architecture of their non-medical cannabis distribution system on existing models. Illinois, for example, implemented an "early demand" system for companies already licensed to retail medical cannabis in the area, before sales began in January 2020. In Michigan, the Marijuana Regulatory Agency has made having a state operating license for medical cannabis a requirement to obtain certain types of licenses.

While such strategies simplify the administrative process of developing a new retail market, they also create significant barriers to entry, particularly for small businesses and suppliers based in local communities. The existing medical cannabis production and sales infrastructure therefore does not offer the best platform for non-medical procurement if the goal is to promote local involvement. The investment necessary to start structures oriented to medical production inevitably excludes small producers, even if giving priority to activities active in the therapeutic field allows for a smoother regulatory transition.

Granting of Licenses

Licensing is the key mechanism for regulating sales and checking product availability. States have adopted a number of different licensing systems, leading to different results.

Cannabis licensing in the USA

All states have tried to give municipalities and local authorities some degree of autonomy in regulating non-medical cannabis within their communities: including the flexibility of zoning rules or the option to ban retailers altogether. In California, this has resulted in 76% of cities turning down cannabis shops, leading to criticism that the patchwork of bans is undermining regulatory efforts in tackling the state-level illegal market. States attempt a balance in ensuring access to retail markets by taking into account the concerns of municipalities and have responded in several ways. In Oregon, for example, cities and counties had direct authority until December 2015 to implement local bans if their residents voted at least 55 percent against legalization, although only five cities did.

Taxation

Legal regulation allows you to tax profits from cannabis markets. The collected tax can be spent in various ways in addition to financing the implementation of the regulatory framework, including social projects (if desired). However, it is also a key lever for influencing the retail price.

Some states have tried to allocate revenue (or "mortgage it") for social purposes. In Illinois, 20% of state cannabis taxes goes to basic services to "tackle substance abuse ... prevention and mental health problems" and 2% goes to the Drug Treatment Fund to help with its public education campaign and consequently, analyze the public health impacts of regulation. In Oregon, 20% of the taxes goes directly to the Mental Health Alcoholism and Drug Services Account that provides care for prevention, intervention and treatment of drug abuse and a further 5% goes to the health authority for prevention and of alcohol and drug abuse.

State Excise Other taxes

Washington 37% 7-10% additional state and local sales tax.

Colorado 15% Additional 15% 'special marijuana sales tax' and additional 2.9% state sales tax.

Illinois 10% for THC <35%

25% for THC> 35%

20% on all cannabis infusions

Additional 7% cultivation tax on gross income.

Municipalities and counties can add additional taxes to stores up to 3% and 3.75% respectively.

Nevada 15% off the wholesale price (paid by the grower)

10% on retail

Tax on retail sales at the local rate.

Oregon 17%. Up to 3% additional local taxes.

Massachusetts 10.75%. Additional 6.25% state general sales tax and up to 3% optional local tax.

Maine 10%. Additional 10% sales tax on grower-to-retailer or derivatives producer sales.

California 15%. Growth Fee per ounce of dry produce: $ 9.25 for flowers; $ 2.75 for the leaves or $ 1.29 for the cannabis plant.

Local governments can apply additional taxes.

Michigan 10%. Additional 6% state sales tax.

Alaska Buds: $ 50 per ounce, and Ripe Flowers: $ 15 per ounce.

Abnormal / immature buds and flowers: $ 25 per ounce.

Cuttings: $ 1 per cuttings.

Vermont N / A

PACKAGING, ADVERTISING AND MARKETING

All states have packaging controls, including the definition of various "universal symbology" systems to ensure that it is clear when a product contains cannabis, as well as the inclusion of warnings about potential driving hazards or the need to keep away from children. In some states there are specific restrictions to prevent accidental use by children, which include a ban on the use of characters that children like, such as cartoon characters.

All states require the THC content to be specified on the packaging. All states also require that cannabis be contained in resealable and child resistant packages and in all states, except Oregon, they must be opaque. The degree of uniformity on this issue reflects a certain consensus on the common objectives of regulation, especially in relation to public health and the protection of minors.

Removal from criminal records (expungement)

The moves to regulate represent a radical change in social views on cannabis use; however, previous criminal records remain an enduring stigma that people carry with them. The so-called "expungement", which means the destruction or deletion from the criminal record of an individual's background, allows states to remove this burden from individuals and, to some extent, recognize the errors of previous policy. The expungement is technically different from the "Record sealing", a process according to which the precedent in the criminal record is not canceled, but hidden from the public record and therefore can only be recalled in certain situations.

Status Type of previous penalty removal - Automatic?

California Record sealing Yes

Oregon Record sealing

Individuals can file a motion to request a court order to set aside convictions for now legal conduct. A law in 2020 removed the demand for fees to be paid.

Nevada Record sealing

Individuals can request a court order to set aside convictions for now decriminalized conduct.

Vermont Expungement / Record sealing

Individuals can file a petition requesting Expungement or Sealing from the criminal record if the conduct is no longer prohibited by law or defined as a criminal offense.

Washington Record sealing

The individual can file a request with the court to overturn convictions for minor offenses related to cannabis. An expedited pardon by the Governor is also possible.

Washington State law does not allow expungement, so cancellation is not the same as expungement.

Colorado Record sealing

At the state level, only record sealing is allowed, but in Denver and Boulder, minor offenses related to cannabis no longer punishable (such as possessing less than an ounce of cannabis) can be overruled.

Massachusetts Expungement

The court can order the cancellation of a "crime at the time of registration which at the time of the cancellation is no longer a crime", but an individual petition is required.

Illinois Expungement

The penal system is obliged to automatically delete any possible annotation that is no longer condemned within specific dates. The Governor can grant pardon by authorizing the cancellation for penalties for possession, production, and possession with the purpose of selling up to 30 grams of cannabis. For higher quantities, the subject can file a motion for cancellation to the State Attorney (up to 500gr).

For certain violations

In Maine, a law has been proposed that would oblige "the Department of Public Security to cancel, by July 1, 2020, all criminal recordings related to crime for conduct now authorized by the regulations on the use of marijuana for adults." But the bill was later declared "dead".

The removal of criminal records can be complicated, and administrative and economic barriers can prevent people from deleting their records from the records, even where technically possible. One way to solve this problem is to automate the elements of the process. In California, Bill 1793 requires the Department of Justice to review past convictions related to cannabis to determine all cases that qualify for the withdrawal or revocation of a sentence, revocation and " sealing " or redefinition, by 1 ° July 2020. In this case, record sealing is effective and automatic: the execution of the operation is entirely the responsibility of the Department of Justice, rather than requiring interested parties to submit their applications.

Social equity measures

Legal regulation of cannabis supply offers states the opportunity to begin repairing the harm to individuals and communities disproportionately affected by the cannabis ban. Legal cannabis is a potentially lucrative sector, and proactive measures are needed to ensure that the benefits are not only widely shared, but directed towards the communities that have suffered the most under prohibition. In some (but not all) states, social equity measures have become a key feature of cannabis regulation to ensure market access for disproportionately affected groups.

As companies need a license to produce or sell cannabis, social equity measures can be integrated into license application procedures to promote access for affected individuals disproportionately. In Nevada, "business diversity " (i.e. the presence in the company of people of different ethnic, cultural, social, age and gender, ed) is required and counted when license applications are evaluated, and ends up in the Overall Applicant Scores. In Illinois, up to one-fifth of points in the dispensary license application scoring system are eligible for social equity applicant status. Additional measures to facilitate market access include exemptions and loans. Illinois has proposed a low-interest loan program in areas where prohibition has had a disproportionate impact, with funding of $ 30 million, as well as licensing tax cuts of up to 50 percent. Loan programs also help mitigate financial obstacles to business startups. This is particularly important since the lack of banking services available to cannabis companies (given the ban on banks from having dealings with "illegal" companies at the federal level) has been reported as an "effective blockade for almost everyone," if not rich and well connected, from entering and benefiting from the industry". While loans and tax exemptions are key to promoting early access to the industry, training, technical assistance and mentoring - such as that offered by the Massachusetts Social Equity Program - are key to ensuring long-term success.

Conversely, some states have no social equity schemes at all. Washington state, for example, has been criticized for failing to support minority groups in the cannabis industry. In response, it detailed new proposals to increase business diversity, but it is unclear how practical they are, especially since it is currently not accepting new license applications. The difficulty of retroactively applying equity measures highlights the fundamental importance of putting business diversity and equity at the center of the regulatory framework from the outset.

Lessons learned

The legal regulation of cannabis is still relatively new. We cannot know the full impact until the policies have had time to roll out and the longer-term market readjustments have taken place. In the United States we are seeing a number of approaches, with large differences between states but also a high level of "policy transfer". It is unclear how these approaches will shape the size and pattern of markets in the long term; however, we can already begin to see how different regulatory models lead or facilitate different results. For example, the system shift directly from medical to non-medical retail may exclude smaller operators; allowing the possibility of local prohibition, while creating local democratic accountability, can also create regulatory patchwork; the availability of " expungement " processes can be compromised if these are excessively complicated; and failing to establish proactive measures of social equity from the outset can reinforce inequality in the new market and create an environment in which those most affected by the previous system are excluded from reaping the benefits of change.

The United States is undergoing a revolution in their approach to cannabis. Like all revolutions, however, the results are uncertain. Legal regulation offers a unique opportunity to address the dire injustices that prevent normalization, but it can also transfer financial benefits away from local communities and into the pockets of large corporations. Regulation should not replace one set of inequalities with others. Looking through the experiences of states that have legalized so far, we can see the drift in both directions: corporate dominance and the lack of market access to groups that have been disproportionately impacted by prohibition in some cases, careful efforts to ensure the economic inclusion and addressing historical injustice in others. Getting the best results is often a question of detail: how are licensing systems built in relation to entry costs? What are the systems for handling past convictions? What are the precise rules on marketing and promotion? As we move through high-level debates for change in a world where it is already happening, these details matter. Therefore, while we are still awaiting evidence of some long-term consequences, this report suggests that there are essential considerations that must be part of the regulatory design from the outset if the goals are to be realized - improving public health, protection of the human being, his rights and the promotion of social justice in the best possible way.

CHAPTER 10: THE DISPENSARY FOR MARIJUANA

Do you want to start a medical marijuana dispensary in the United States? If YES, here is a detailed guide on how to obtain a dispensary license in Texas, California, Florida, Michigan, and Maryland. Marijuana is steadily gaining ground in the United States, although it still remains federally illegal. States have now begun to enact laws regulating the marijuana industry. These laws determine who can grow or sell marijuana and under what conditions they can do so. Aside from medical and research purposes, most states have made the affairs of the marijuana dispensary legal. For this reason, many entrepreneurs are now considering owning marijuana dispensaries. To own and operate a marijuana dispensary in the US, you need to obtain a license. The type of license and documentation your marijuana company requires will depend on both the location of your operation and the type of business you are running. This is why you need to do a lot of research before starting. If you are looking for ways to obtain a marijuana dispensary license in the United States, we have listed the states that have legalized marijuana dispensaries. We've also included where you can get these licenses and some of the guidelines you need to follow when applying.

ALASKA

A Detailed Guide to Obtaining a Marijuana Dispensing License in the United States: Alaska.

It has been confirmed that Alaska is one of the states in the United States that allows the use of marijuana, but only for those 21 years of age and older. This state authorizes companies to grow, produce and sell marijuana. If you want to open a marijuana dispensary in Alaska, you need to apply for a license, and this can be done online at the Department of Commerce, Community and Economic Development, MARIJUANA ALCOHOL CONTROL OFFICE. Fingerprints must be submitted with each application. Fingerprint cards cannot be sent electronically to AMCO but physically. Applicants must use an approved agency to obtain their fingerprints. They can also get marijuana growing permits, product manufacturing facilities, testing facilities, retail stores here.

ARIZONA

In Arizona, registered patients can possess and use medical marijuana. Licensed state-owned companies can grow, process, transport and distribute medical marijuana. All marijuana dispensary license applications must be filed online with the Arizona Department of Health Services. The site also lists the requirements for the application. Additionally, Arizona requires all cultivation facilities to be licensed as dispensaries. The Department will first determine if there is a county where there is no dispensary registration certificate. If there is one, then it would be easier to get a license there. All the necessary information about this is available on the website.

ARKANSAS

According to the dispensary licenses in Arkansas, all individuals with legal prescription can possess and use medical marijuana. Licensed state-owned companies can grow, process, transport and distribute medical marijuana.

The Arkansas Medical Marijuana Commission is responsible for the states' medical marijuana program. The commission had established strict guidelines for obtaining a dispensary license and they included: No more than 32 dispensary licenses will be awarded within the "8 dispensary zones" Dispensary location cannot be less than 1,500 feet from a school, one church or kindergarten. No more than 1 license should be issued to any entity. The application fee for dispensary licenses is set at $ 7,500 (half of the application fee will be refunded if the license is not granted). There is a two-tier licensing system for dispensaries: A tier of those dispensaries intending to grow marijuana will be included - a dispensary can choose to grow fifty (50) mature marijuana plants. A second tier will consist of those dispensaries that do not intend to grow marijuana. The applicant must declare their intention to grow or not to grow at the time of submitting the application. Within 7 days of receiving the commission's written notice of the selection, the selected applicant must submit a licensing fee of $ 15,000.00 in cash or certified funds, as well as a performance bond in the amount of $ 100,000.00.

CALIFORNIA

In California, the Bureau issues temporary cannabis control marijuana dispensary licenses, cannabis growing licenses of CDFA, and cannabis safety branch produced by CDPH. Growers, producers, retailers, distributors, micro-enterprises, test labs and event organizers can apply for their licenses from these offices. Applications for annual licenses will be accepted through an online licensing system - the Manufactured Cannabis Licensing System (MLCS).

This application will require information about the company, owners, financial interest holders and operating premises, as well as the description of procedures for waste disposal, inventory and quality control, transportation and safety. More information can be obtained on the California cannabis portal.

COLORADO

If you intend to own a Colorado Retail Marijuana Business you should also visit the Colorado Marijuana Owners and Investors page. Licenses are available for both medical and recreational marijuana. The guidelines for obtaining a retail license in Colorado include that applicants must apply to the state for a retail license before selling marijuana, must confirm that the local authority in which it is planned to operate allows retail marijuana stores to operate within their jurisdiction. Applicants must be resident in the state of the Colorado for at least 2 years before applying for a license. Number of retail stores licenses are limited by the local government Applicant must submit a non-refundable application fee of $ 4,500.

CONNECTICUT

In Connecticut, all qualified patients with legal prescriptions can be in possession of marijuana and licensed state companies can grow, process, transport and dispense marijuana. The Connecticut Department of Consumer Protection is responsible for the States Medical Marijuana Program, and all applications are filed there. from authorized manufacturers, to patients and qualified healthcare professionals. During the application, there is a non-refundable application fee of $ 1,000 payable at the time of application and a non-refundable application fee of $ 5,000. All marijuana businesses must be located at least 300 meters from places used primarily for religious worship, public or private school, convent, charitable institution, supported by public or private funds, hospital or veterans' home or from any military camp or establishment.

Documentation that must be provided when submitting the application; Personal Information, Latest Employment Information, Dispensing Facility Information, Licenses, Permits, and Records, Professional History, Criminal Actions, Photo Identification, (Passport-sized Photograph and Copy of Valid Government-Issued ID) License Fee, Initial Tuition Fee: $ 1,000 [non-refundable] Registration fee: $ 5,000 [non-refundable] Renewal fee: $ 5,000 [non-refundable] License and renewal fees: $ 100 each Registration / renewal of dispensary technician and dispensary staff: $ 50 Registration / Dispensary Facility Supporter Renewal: $ 100 Dispensary

Name Change Application: $ 100 Dispensary Facility Manager Change: $ 50 Location Change or Expansion Application: $ 1,000 [plus $ 1,500 if approved], Application of physical, non-cosmetic modification of the structure [other than expansion]: $ 500. Questions and materials support must be delivered by hand according to the instructions in the application request, along with an application fee of $ 25,000.

DELAWARE

In Delaware, all persons with legal prescriptions can possess and use medical marijuana. Licensed state companies can grow, process, transport and distribute medical marijuana. The Department of Health is responsible for issuing this license through the medical marijuana program. The state only grants licenses to compassion centers and has strict guidelines for opening these centers.

They include; a compassion center must be run on a non-profit basis. A compassion center must not be located less than 300 meters from the property line of an existing public or private school. New applicants for a Compassion Center license will only be accepted during an open application period announced by the Department. A non-refundable application fee, made payable to the Division of Public Health, Medical Marijuana Program, in the amount of $ 5,000 will be required at the time of application. There is currently one compassion center and another opening soon.

FLORIDA

Licensed distribution organizations are licensed to cultivate the process and dispense medical marijuana. These are the only companies in Florida licensed to distribute medical marijuana to qualified patients and legal representatives. The Office of Medical Marijuana Use (a division of the Florida Department of Health) is responsible for drafting and enforcing the department's rules and licensing activities for dispensing, processing and growing medical marijuana. The Office is not currently accepting applications for medical marijuana treatment centers.

HAWAII

In Hawaii, anyone with a legal prescription can possess and use medical marijuana. Licensed state-owned companies can grow, process, transport and distribute medical marijuana. The Hawaii Department of Health Medical Cannabis Dispensing Program is responsible for licensing. The dispensary licensing guidelines for Hawaii are therefore; Non-refundable application fee of $ 5,000. An application must state that applicants have resources in the amount of $ 1,000,000, plus a minimum of $ 100,000 for each retail location the applicant wishes to operate. A distributor licensee can manage up to two retail distribution points. If an applicant intends to operate two retail distribution points, the total money an applicant must have in reserve at the time of application is $ 1,200,000. Applicants can apply for more than one license, but only one license can be issued. If an applicant is entitled to more than one license, they will need to choose the county in which they want to operate a dispensary.

ILLINOIS

In Illinois, all individuals with a legal prescription can possess and use medical marijuana. Licensed state-owned companies can grow, process, transport, and distribute medical marijuana. The Illinois Department of Financial and Professional Regulation is responsible for licensing dispensaries. At the moment they do not issue any licenses.

IOWA

In Iowa, qualified patients can use, possess and access low-THC cannabis oil. The production, delivery, transportation and dispensing of cannabidiol are permitted by authorized license holders. The Iowa Department of Public Health is authorized to select and license five medical cannabidiol dispensaries in Iowa. Dispensaries selected through the competitive process will obtain licenses from the department to legally provide medical cannabidiol to patients and primary caregivers with valid medical cannabidiol registration cards. Licensed dispensaries must be ready to begin providing medical cannabidiol by December 1, 2018. The law sets the non-refundable application fee for a dispensary license at $ 5,000.

LOUISIANA

In Louisiana, people with a legal recommendation from their doctor can be in possession of medical marijuana, and licensed state pharmacies can dispense medical marijuana.

The Louisiana Board of Pharmacy is responsible for licensing. The state has a number of laws for opening dispensaries, and one of their laws limits the number of licenses to be distributed to 10. Others include; Only existing pharmacies are allowed to dispense medical marijuana a single manufacturing facility will be responsible for growing, which one or both Louisiana State University and Southern University have the first right of refusal to grow medical marijuana collaboratively or separately. No more than 10 pharmacies can obtain licenses to dispense marijuana within the state. In the state, pharmacists can only dispense marijuana grown in state universities. Those wishing to prescribe medical marijuana in Louisiana must pay an application fee of $ 5,000 in addition to a licensing fee of $ 150 to become one of the 10 marijuana pharmacists in the state. The $ 5,000 application fee is non-refundable and only applies to marijuana pharmacies, not regular drug stores.

MAINE

In Maine, all individuals can be in possession of marijuana. The state is currently working on rules to establish a system for state-owned companies licensed to grow, process, transport and distribute recreational marijuana. License applicants must be at least 21 years old, citizens of Maine and have a verifiable SSN. Their businesses must be a corporation, association, LLC or organization. If the applicant is a corporation, all board members must meet the criteria above. Also, criminal convictions punishable by five years or more may automatically disqualify candidates, provided they have not elapsed 10 years or more since have occurred. Licenses for dispensaries are provided but are rarely available. The retail marijuana store license is as follows: license fee of $ 250- $ 2,500; non-refundable application fee of $ 10- $ 250

MARYLAND

In Maryland, all individuals with a prescription can possess and use medical marijuana. The Maryland Medical Cannabis Commission is responsible for developing policies, procedures and regulations for the use of medical marijuana, as well as licensing. It has issued medical cannabis dispensary pre-approvals to 102 companies, with 22 approved and the others in phase 2 of the approval process.

MASSACHUSETTS

In Massachusetts, people over the age of 21 can own up to one ounce of marijuana, keep up to 10 ounces of marijuana at home, and grow up to six plants. Licensed state-owned enterprises can grow, produce, distribute and sell marijuana. All information on licensing marijuana establishments through the Cannabis Control Commission must be obtained on the Commission's website Applicants are required to pay $ 1,500 for the intent request and $

30,000 for the management profile application and Operations Applications can be submitted by mail to the Cannabis Control Commission, 101 Federal Street, 13th Floor, Boston, MA 02110. In order to obtain a license in accordance with the Adult Use of Marijuana Act passed in 2016, you must apply for the Cannabis Control Commission.

MICHIGAN

In Michigan, people 21 years of age and older can possess and use marijuana. Licensed state-owned companies can grow, process, transport and distribute marijuana. Here are some of the requirements to apply for a marijuana dispensary license in Michigan; An applicant may have to pay a fee to their local city / municipality of up to $ 5,000 and a non-refundable state application fee of $ 6,000. The applicant, if an individual, must have been a resident of the State of Michigan for a continuous period of 2 years.

This requirement does not apply after June 30, 2018. The applicant is ineligible if he has been convicted or released from incarceration under the laws of this state, any other state of the United States (federal law) within the past 10 years or has been convicted of a controlled substance-related crime within the past 10 years. The applicant is ineligible if he has been convicted of a crime involving a controlled substance, theft, dishonesty or fraud in any state within the past 5 years. Must apply for a procurement center license with the local city and state before selling marijuana and marijuana products. The Regulations. of the Office of Medical Marijuana is responsible for the supervision of medical marijuana and is composed of the Medical Marijuana

Program and the Facility Licensing Division. The Licensing and Regulatory Affairs Department is currently accepting applications for growers, processors, transporters, procurement centers and safety compliance facilities.

MINNESOTA

Minnesota On May 29, 2014, Governor Mark Dayton signed a bipartisan medical marijuana proposal that was drafted by a House and Senate conference committee, making Minnesota the 22nd state to exempt some sufferers and their caregivers from penalty for using marijuana with a medical certification. Licenses for marijuana companies are not available. The Department of Health has selected two companies as registered marijuana producers and distributors.

The state has 8 dispensaries, which are called centers for cannabis patients. A non-refundable application fee of $ 20,000 is required for registration.

MONTANA

In Montana, only registered cardholders are allowed to own and use marijuana. The Montana Department of Public Health and Human Services is in charge of the States Medical Marijuana Program. Questions for the provider, test lab, and dispensary licenses are available periodically. The proposed test rooms or laboratories may not be less than 150 meters away and on the same street as a building used exclusively as a church, synagogue or other place of worship or secondary school or post-school other than a commercially operated school.

NEVADA

Nevada legalized medical marijuana on November 7, 2000, when 65% of the population voted yes on question 9. The Nevada Tax Department is responsible for licensing and regulating retail marijuana businesses and the state medical marijuana program. As of November 2018, only holders of existing medical marijuana establishment certificates can apply for a retail marijuana establishment license. Fees you may incur in attempting to open a dispensary in Nevada: Medical Marijuana Institution Registration Certificate: $ 5,000 [non-refundable, applies to all of the following in addition to lower fees]; Pantry Registration Certificate: $ 30,000; Pantry Certificate Renewal: $ 5,000; Growing Facility Registration Certificate: $ 3,000; Growing Facility Certificate Renewal: $ 1,000; Facility producing edible marijuana or marijuana products - Certificate of Registration: $ 3,000; Edible Manufacturing Facility Certificate Renewal: $ 1,000; MM Agent Registration Card: $ 75; Card Renewal Agent: $ 75; Certificate of Registration of independent testing laboratory: $ 5,000; Renewal of certain Independent Testing Lab Fee: $ 3,000; Some guidelines include that applicants must submit a non-refundable application fee of $ 5,000.

They must show proof of the amount of taxes paid or other beneficial financial contributions paid to this State or its political subdivisions over the past 5 years by the applicant or persons who purport to be owners, officers or board members of the proposed marijuana business. Again, the retail marijuana store must be at least 300m from a public or private school and 30m from a community facility. Not more than 80 licenses issued in a county with a population of less than 700,000. No more than 20 licenses issued in a county with a population of less than 700,000 but more than 100,000. Not more than 4 licenses issued in a county with a population of less than 100,000 but greater than 55,000. No more than 2 licenses issued in a county with a population of less than 55,000.

NEW HAMPSHIRE

In New Hampshire, anyone with a legal prescription can possess and use medical marijuana. The New Hampshire Department of Health and Human Services is responsible for managing the cannabis therapeutic program. The Department established New Hampshire's terms for 4 Alternative Treatment Center (ATC) dispensaries. These centers are the only ones needed to own, grow, acquire, deliver, produce, transfer, supply, sell, distribute and transport cannabis and other related supplies, as well as provide educational materials for both eligible patients and other alternative treatment centers.

NEW JERSEY

In New Jersey, anyone with a legal prescription can be in possession of marijuana, and licensed state companies can grow, process, transport, and dispense marijuana. The New

Jersey Department of Health is in charge of the States Medicinal Marijuana Program. State licensing firms called Alternative Treatment Centers (ATCs) for the production and distribution of medical marijuana. Six ATCs have been licensed. Once the initial six are opened, the state will evaluate the program and determine whether or not expansion is needed. At present, however, the state does not license any medical marijuana business.

NEW MEXICO

The New Mexico Department of Health is responsible for overseeing the medical cannabis program. To produce, distribute and distribute medical marijuana, you must be a licensed nonprofit producer (LNPP). A non-profit producer operates a facility and, at any one time, is limited to a combined total of no more than 450 mature female male plants, seedlings, and plants.

In this period, LNPP application is closed and the department is not currently accepting applications for medical marijuana production and distribution. Currently, there are 50 licensed cannabis dispensaries in New Mexico with an estimated 50,954 registered patients. At the end of 2016, the cannabis market in New Mexico exceeded $ 50.6 million.

NEW YORK

The New York Department of Health is in charge of its medical marijuana program. Only registered organizations can produce and distribute medical marijuana. The Department began accepting applications for registration as a registered organization on April 27, 2015. Each applicant was required to submit two fees with their application: a non-refundable application fee in the amount of $ 10,000 and a registration fee for an amount of $ 200,000. The $ 200,000 registration fee is to be refunded to the applicant only if the applicant has not been issued a registration. The Department does not currently accept applications to become a registered organization.

NORTH DAKOTA

The Division of Medical Marijuana (part of the North Dakota Department of Health) is in charge of the state's medical marijuana program. Compassion centers are dispensaries or facilities for marijuana growers / producers. The application period for compassion centers is currently closed. Some of their application guidelines include that: Compassion centers are required to maintain adequate security, including well-lit entrances, an alarm system that contacts law enforcement, and video surveillance. They may not be within 1,000 feet of a school and will be subject to inspections and other regulations.

There is a $ 5,000 non-refundable application fee to submit a proposal (application) and a $ 90,000 certification fee upon issuance of the license. Compassion Center licenses will be granted on the basis of a merit-based application procedure, which will consider: the suitability of the proposed venue; the character and competence of applicants in related fields; proposed center plans, including those related to record keeping, security, personnel and training, to prevent diversion. Every staff member of a compassion center must apply for and obtain a registry photo ID card. They must be at least 21 years of age and must not have been convicted of a crime of barred crime or a recent drug. Compassion Center membership fee is non-refundable.

OHIO

Under new regulations, enacted September 8, 2016, Ohio is ready to welcome medical marijuana businesses. While the state has already licensed a limited number of growers, dispensaries, and other businesses, it can issue multiple licenses as needed to meet demand.

OKLAHOMA

With the death of SQ 788 in June 2018, Oklahoma became the 30th state in the United States to legalize medical marijuana. Oklahoma residents over the age of 18 with a valid medical recommendation can apply for a license for a medical marijuana patient. If approved, they can purchase medical marijuana from licensed dispensaries across the state. Dispensaries in Oklahoma must be located at least 300 meters from a public or private school. This is measured by a straight line (the shortest distance) from the dispensary property line to any school entrance.

The Oklahoma State Department of Health is responsible for approving licenses and they have some application criteria which include; The applicant must be twenty five (25) years of age or older; Any applicant, presenting himself as an individual, must exhibit residence in the state of Oklahoma; All applicant entities must demonstrate that all members, officers and board members are resident in Oklahoma; An applicant entity can show ownership of non-Oklahoma residents, but this percentage cannot exceed 25% (25%). All applicant persons or entities must be registered to conduct business in the state of Oklahoma; All applicants must disclose all ownership; Applicant (s) with only convictions for nonviolent crimes in the past two (2) years, any other felony convictions over five (5) years, inmates or any other person currently incarcerated are not eligible for a medical marijuana dispensary license.

OREGON

In 2013, Oregon House Bill 3460 became law, allowing medical marijuana dispensaries to be registered. The legislation went into effect on March 1, 2014. Licenses are mandatory and available for medical and recreational marijuana companies. The state requires separate licenses and registrations for growers and dispensary operators. The Oregon Liquor Control Commission (OLCC) license accepts applications for marijuana licenses. The application fee is usually $ 3,500 and the application fee is $ 500. There is also an annual tracking system fee of $ 480. Each applicant must also pay $ 35 for a background check. Furthermore, there will be a huge capital of up to $ 500,000 to open a new cannabis dispensary.

RHODE ISLAND

According to state law of Rhode Island, cannabis businesses such as dispensaries, must be defined compassion centers. A compassion center in the state of Rhode Island can do any of the following: growing, processing, transporting, as well as selling cannabis to all registered patients and registered primary care providers. Applications can only be submitted during an open application period announced by the state if necessary.

The state has 3 licensed compassion centers currently in operation. Each application for a compassion center must include: A non-refundable application fee paid to the department in the amount of two hundred and fifty dollars ($ 250); The proposed legal name and proposed incorporation of the compassion center; the proposed physical address of the compassion center, if a specific address has been determined or, if not, the general location where it would be located. This may include a second location for medical marijuana cultivation; A description of the closed facility that would be used in the cultivation of marijuana; The name, address, and date of birth of each principal officer and board member of the compassion center; Proposed safety and security measures that include at least one security alert system for each location, planned measures to deter and prevent unauthorized entry into areas containing marijuana and theft of marijuana, as well as a draft, instruction manual for employees which includes security policies, personal safety and security procedures, and crime prevention techniques; and proposed procedures to ensure accurate record keeping.

TENNESSEE

In 2014 the state approved SB 2531, a limited medical bill for cannabis, which allows the use of cannabis oil containing CBAAD as part of the Aa clinical research study on its effects on patients with seizure disorders. Tennessee Tech has the opportunity to grow, process and distribute CBD. In Tennessee, qualified patients can own and use CBD extracts. Current law does not provide for a state-regulated dispensary system.

TEXAS

In Texas, only clinically qualified people are allowed to own or use CBD oil. Licensed state-owned companies can brew, grow and process low-THC marijuana.

The Texas Department of Public Safety (DPS) issues the license. The license will authorize organizations to cultivate the process and dispense low-THC cannabis to prescribed patients. The department under the state bill is required to license only three donor organizations, and these organizations have already been licensed. For now, the state is not receiving applications.

UTAH

In Utah, qualified registered patients can possess and use medical marijuana. Authorized state agencies can grow, process and distribute medical marijuana. The Utah Department of Health is responsible for licensing. The applicant will need an operational plan that includes operational procedures that comply with the law; Including financial statements showing that the applicant has a minimum of $ 500,000 in liquid assets available to each cannabis growing facility for which the person applies, or a minimum of $ 100,000 in liquid assets available to each processing facility, cannabis or independent cannabis testing laboratory for which the person applies.

VERMONT

The Department of Public Safety is responsible for the marijuana registry and issues dispensary registration certificates. The Department has issued 4 dispensary registration certificates and 1 conditional certificate. The Department plans to announce an application period for a sixth dispensary once the number of registered patients reaches 7,000. Currently, dispensaries are the only types of licensed marijuana companies in Vermont. Licensees can run two dispensaries with the same license. It is advisable to understand state regulations and also to treat the marijuana business in line with local laws. Application fees are as follows: $ 2,500 for dispensary application; $ 50 for caregiver enrollment application. Licensing fees include: $ 20,000 Initial

Waiver Registration Fee; $ 25,000 Renewal Waiver Registration Fee.

WASHINGTON

In 2012, Washington became the first US state to legalize the recreational use of cannabis after more than a decade of medical legalization. With the demise of Initiative 502, adults over the age of 21 were legally allowed to purchase and own cannabis products from licensed distributors. The Washington State Liquor and Cannabis Board is responsible for licensing marijuana; however, it is not currently accepting license requests.

Washington DC. While it is legal to use marijuana recreationally, there are no businesses that sell marijuana for recreational use. The DC Department of Health has a medical marijuana program, but is not currently accepting applications for medical marijuana facilities.

WISCONSIN

In Wisconsin, qualified patients can own and use CBD extracts. State-licensed doctors and pharmacies can dispense CBD extracts to patients. The state of Wisconsin is not currently accepting applications for marijuana companies. West Virginia Governor Jim Justice signed Senate Bill 386, known as the Medical Cannabis Act, on April 20, 2017, making the medicinal use of marijuana legal for qualified patients in West Virginia. Patients will be able to obtain medical cannabis in the following forms: pill, oil, topical forms including gels, creams or ointments, a medically appropriate form for administration by vaporization or nebulization, tincture, liquid or dermal patch.

The state intends to issue around 30 dispensary permits to individuals. Individuals wishing to obtain a West Virginia dispensing permit must submit an application that includes the following: Verification of all principal, operator, financier, or employee of a medical cannabis grower / processor or distributor; a description of your responsibilities as a principal, operator, financier or employee; any releases required to obtain information from government agencies, employers and other organizations; a criminal background check; details of any license, permit or other similar authorization obtained in another jurisdiction, including any suspension, revocation or regulation in that jurisdiction; a description of the business activities in which it intends to engage as a medical cannabis organization; application for grant permit will require specific business plans.

A statement that the applicant: has a good moral character; possesses the ability to quickly obtain the right to use sufficient land, buildings and other premises and equipment to properly carry out the activity described in the application and any proposed location for a facility; is able to maintain effective security and control to prevent diversion, abuse and other illegal conduct related to medical cannabis; is able to comply with all applicable state laws and regulations relating to the activities in which the applicant intends to engage under this act.

Name, residential address and title of each lender and principal of the applicant.

Any other information requested by the Office of Public Health States without laws on the use of marijuana for medical or recreational use.

States that currently prohibit the use of marijuana or severely restrict its use include: Alabama Georgia Idaho Indiana Kansas Kentucky Mississippi Nebraska New Hampshire North Carolina South Carolina South Dakota Wyoming

CHAPTER 11: OPENING A DISPENSARY

The recent legalization of marijuana in several states was an unprecedented process. By legitimizing both recreational and medical marijuana, states have opened up a new industry, one that people are clamoring to take advantage of.

We spoke to two dispensary owners from pioneering states: Mitch Woolhiser, owner of the Northern Lights Cannabis company in Denver, Colorado, and Lincoln Fish, CEO of OutCo Labs, which runs the Collective Outliers dispensary in San Diego, California. While the details of their experiences are very different, their general attitude was similar: opening a dispensary is not for the faint of heart. It is a job that takes a lot of hard work and time before it becomes profitable.

"It's one of the hardest things you can do," says Mitch Woolhiser. "It can't just be this fun thing. It has to be taken seriously." In addition to requiring a lot of effort, opening a clinic requires careful compliance with laws and regulations, as well as a large amount of start-up capital. "You won't make any money if you don't follow these rules," says Lincoln Fish. "It's an expensive business to run."

But if hard work, cash up front and bureaucratic red tape don't put you off, opening a dispensary is an opportunity for you to be a pioneer in what will soon be a huge, national industry. Marijuana Business Daily estimates revenue generated by dispensaries and retail stores to reach between $ 6.5 and $ 8 billion by 2019.

"It's still on the ground floor entirely, considering the federal lawlessness of it," Mitch says. "It's still a good time to get in."

STEP 1: ASSESS YOUR COMMITMENT AND ELIGIBILITY

Lincoln Fish moved into the medical marijuana industry to challenge hypocrisy.

"I was with a lot of people. I thought, 'These are drugs, this is bad,' " Lincoln says. "Then you start to realize how much hypocrisy surrounds marijuana. Alcohol and tobacco are much more harmful and much more addictive. Schedule 1 Narcotics by legal definition are highly addictive, prove to have no medicinal benefits, and can be harmful to lethality. Alcohol and tobacco meet all three of these requirements and marijuana does not meet any of them. "

Mitch Woolhiser saw a magnificent and unusual business opportunity in the budding marijuana industry in 2010. "This is something that, as a businessman, you can do almost revolutionary," he says. "It's the chance of a lifetime. What product suddenly becomes legal when it hasn't been for a long time? Not since the alcohol prohibition has such a thing happened and it probably won't happen again in my life."

But Mitch and Lincoln warn against opening a dispensary just for financial gain. "If the only reason you're dealing with this is money, you're not going to have fun," Mitch says. "It's not a get-rich-quick scheme. It's a long game. You have to have something extra to motivate yourself."

It is also important to recognize that background checks are often required, not only for a dispensary owner, but also for investors and employees. If you have a criminal background, you may not be eligible to open a dispensary.

Also, if medical marijuana isn't legalized in your state, any dispensary could be closed by the federal government. If there are no existing laws or regulations in your area, opening a dispensary is probably not a good idea. "If the city or county hasn't gone through anything, the state's default position is that there's nothing legal there," Lincoln says. "You have to be very careful. This could be a problem. You could be turned off."

Considering the money spent to open a dispensary, trying to run one illegally is not worth the risk.

STEP 2: DO YOUR RESEARCH

The dispensary business is full of laws and regulations. To be successful as a dispensary owner, you need to understand not only the existing laws on growing and selling marijuana, but also the proposed laws and changes that will come into effect in the coming years.

Lincoln Fish recommends reading Cole's Memorandum, which provides guidance to US state lawyers on how to prioritize the enforcement of marijuana laws. If you are in California, he also recommends that you read Proposition 215 and Proposition 420.

"In most cities and counties, it's very easy to study and see what the legislation is," says Lincoln. "Either it's banned altogether, [or] if it's not, they've already issued ordinances and guidance."

The National Organization for the Reform of Marijuana Laws, or NORML, has a database of detailed marijuana laws and sanctions for every state in the U.S. These tables from the National Conference of State Legislature are also helpful.

"There are a lot of rules to follow and I highly recommend that people get help right from the start: a lawyer and a CPA attorney," says Lincoln. This will help you comply with the law and access permissions and licenses. NORML has a database of lawyers from all over the United States who specialize in the marijuana industry.

Both Mitch and Lincoln recommend a thorough study of US 280E, a deceptive tax code that can bring dispensary owners down, particularly on the budget.

"If you're dealing with a Schedule I narcotic, which is marijuana, you can only deduct the cost of the goods sold from your income before you do your taxes," Lincoln explains. "Suppose you buy the product for $ 500, put it on the shelf, sell it for $ 1000. You would have to pay taxes on the profit of $ 500 before you can pay the rent, the employees, and so on. What's happening to many dispensaries is that they are driving themselves crazy with huge taxes. This is another reason why opening a dispensary is not necessarily as profitable as people think. "

STEP 3: FIND A RENTAL PROPERTY

"The key is really just to find a compliant property," says Lincoln. In San Diego, a compliant property has many requirements: "To be a compliant property, it must be more than 1,000 feet from a church, 1,000 feet from a school, 1,000 feet from a residential area, and 1,000 feet from another compliant property, "says Lincoln. "There's an online map showing all San Diego County compliant properties."

It is important to remember that due to the ever-changing environment of the marijuana industry, a property that is now compliant may not be in two years. "Make sure when you access a property that it will be consistent with the new laws that come into effect next two years, " says Lincoln. "Make sure you don't open one and close it because they clash with the new laws."

Compliant property means different things in different places, and even if you find a compliant property, you need to be honest with the landlord about your plans to open a dispensary there, and they may not be supportive. Mitch Woolhiser took care of this while looking for space for his dispensary in 2010. "Some owners just didn't want to take care of it and still won't," Mitch says. "Some of these are due to federal lawlessness and the liability they may have."

Owners are sometimes under pressure from law enforcement. Mother Earth Collective, which used to operate in the space that is now Outliers Collective in San Diego, was indirectly forced out by the DEA. "The DEA sent letters to homeowners across the country and said, 'Hey, if we decide to get off on these guys, you can be responsible if you're renting them.' The landlord threw them out and the collective shut down." Lincoln explains.

When looking for a place to open your practice, also consider whether it is convenient for potential clients. "For planning purposes, location is the most important thing on the business side," says Mitch. "People come to you because you are a destination or because you are convenient." Identifying a target market can help you choose a good location for your store.

It is also important that most, if not all members of your community (even non-users who will not be your customers) are comfortable with a dispensary in their area. If your county or city has had proposals to vote on marijuana laws, Mitch recommends accessing the ballot results for any area where you are considering a property.

"In Colorado, in 2012 we voted on Amendment 64, which is the recreational law, " he says. "I visited the Secretary of State's website and got the election results for Edgewater [where the Northern Lights Cannabis Company is located]. In Edgewater it went up to 70%. Any other community, you can find out that information too. You can find out about the results of these questions and decide, on the basis of this information, whether the community will be welcoming or not. "

STEP 4: WRITE A BUSINESS PLAN

When an industry is saturated in the way the medical marijuana industry is, it's all the more important to appear professional and prepared with a solid business plan.

Mitch, who used Bplans to write his dispensary business plan in 2010, says a business plan can separate you from the crowd. "Write a business plan, " he says. "There are a lot of people who get involved in this business and they're not very serious. Understand what you are getting into and don't just listen to someone who is high in the sky."

Access capital

Any good business plan will start with how to access capital, which is one of the most challenging parts of the marijuana industry.

"The barriers to entry are still quite high," says Mitch. "It's going to take a lot more money than it used to. We got in with about fifty thousand dollars and some credit cards. Now, you wouldn't be able to introduce it without at least half a million because of the regulations. Also, because there is a lot of competition. "

Due to the federal illegality of marijuana, it is not possible to obtain a bank loan for a dispensary. Lincoln recommends sticking to personal funds for your starting capital. "You are better off now that you really focus on angelic investors, friends and family to get to the point where you can acquire a property," says Lincoln. "Many investors won't talk to you until you have a lot of pieces under your belt. If you have compliant ownership, it gets easier."

Determine your budget

Another consideration in your business plan is a clear and concise budget.

"You have to create a budget and take 280E into account, Lincoln says." You won't be able to do it with little money. You have to be prepared for it to grow slowly. "

Consult wholesalers in your area to find out the cost of the products. "For the business plan itself, you need to know the costs in regards to the cost of getting the product," says Mitch.

In addition to product costs, there are other considerations for your budget:

- Cost of rental
- Cost of the license
- Cost of the license application
- Salary of the employees
- Transport and storage of the product
- Safety

Competition search

In addition to knowing the licensed competition in your area, opening a dispensary requires thinking about another competitive demographic that presents more challenges: unlicensed operators.

"Understand the landscape of unlicensed competition in that area," says Lincoln. "What is law enforcement doing about it or planning to do? The truth is that unlicensed people are allowed to ramp up. Law enforcement is working to shut them down, but it's not a high priority because they cannot get any sentences ".

Search local publications for pantry ads, both home and delivery. This will give you an idea of the unlicensed operators in your area. Furthermore, the search will focus on unauthorized operations in your area. Are unauthorized dispensaries allowed to function freely, or are law enforcement agencies working to get rid of them? This will be good information to inform your business plan.

"It is very difficult to build a patient base when there are nearby people who are open 24/7, which you won't be able to do, who aren't paying taxes or social security for their employees, they're not paying federal taxes, "Lincoln says. "This will kill you. You have to play by the rules and they don't."

Conduct market research

Your business plan offers you an important opportunity to identify your customers. This will help inform your dispensary's marketing and pricing strategy. "Know your market," Lincoln says. "You know your demographics and psychographics. Is there a consumer demand? Where is it? That will also determine some of your prices."

STEP 5: GET A LICENSE

Getting a license to open a medical marijuana dispensary is usually difficult and expensive. "I've known people who spent up to three or four thousand dollars in legal fees to get their license," says Lincoln. For example, in Colorado, the registration fee for a medical marijuana dispensary can cost up to $ 15,000.

"Be prepared to spend a lot of time on compliance and have a lot of resources for it," says Mitch. "A lot of consolidation has gone on here because a lot of small operations can't keep up with compliance. It's a full-time job."

Take a look at the retail and medical marijuana license application process in Colorado to get an idea of what your application process might look like.

STEP 6: GET PRODUCT

Getting good product for your marijuana dispensary, and making sure you do so legally, will be a central part of opening a successful dispensary. Many dispensaries grow their own marijuana, and in some states this is mandatory. Mitch Woolhiser has his own grow facility for the Northern Lights Cannabis Company and says it should be on the horizon for every dispensary owner.

"First open a retail facility and then have an eye on your grow facility," he says. "Get your sales off the ground with wholesale products. I'd recommend it."

Opening a dispensary doesn't mean you have to sell marijuana in its typical form. Many patients prefer edibles, oils, tannins and concentrates. Mitch says vendors of these forms of marijuana are easy to find and bargain with. "When it comes to edibles and concentrates, these companies have sales forces," he says. "Just reach out to them and make contact."

STEP 7: MARKET YOUR DISPENSARY

Decide what your competitive dispensary does and sell it.

"You can compete on price or other things, and I chose other things," says Mitch. "We try to be more boutique. For us, ask all the questions, smell and look at each type before deciding which one to buy. Create more of a unique shopping experience."

The Outliers collective is also involved in advertising to a more mature audience. "We are looking for long-term customers who come to us because they want service, quality and consistency," says Lincoln. "We want to spread the word to a different type of patient, people who care about all the things a licensed place represents."

Your target market will inform some of your marketing choices, but Lincoln says there are a few necessities for marketing your new dispensary. "You have to be on Weed Maps and Leafly, " he says. Weed Maps and Leafly are applications that allow patients to search for dispensaries in their area. Lincoln also uses some magazine advertisements and has a billboard on California State Route 67.

Mitch recommends marketing through social media accounts like Instagram, encouraging customers to give reviews on Google and keeping your website up to date with the correct SEO strategies.

It is also important to check your dispensary's marketing regulations. There are many methods Mitch can't use in Colorado: "You can't advertise on radio, TV, billboards," he says. "There are a lot of restrictions. You can't market to out-of-state people. You can't advertise pop-up."

Mitch and Lincoln both use loyalty programs that help market their dispensaries by word of mouth. A program that offers customers store credit when they refer a new customer, such as the Outliers Collective Jane Dough program, will expand your customer base.

Stay informed

With this information you have a good chance of opening a successful, profitable dispensary program.

Lincoln Fish encourages those with the right motivation to enter the relatively new medical marijuana industry: "I'd like to see more responsible and credible people come into our space and open dispensaries and do a good job with it, " he says. "The more we do to show the general public how important and how responsible we can be and how much good can be done, the more we will get public opinion on our side."

With marijuana legislation changing often, it's important to keep up with new information even after you've opened your dispensary to ensure you are operating safely and legally.

CHAPTER 12: HOW MUCH DOES IT COST AND HOW TO OPEN A CANNABIS SHOP IN ITALY?

Following the approval of law 242 of 2016 which protects and encourages the cultivation and processing of hemp, the cannabis market in Italy has seen thousands of companies "flourish" with not a few satisfactions. In fact, opening a cannabis shop can become a very profitable business and can make you good money. Anyone over 18 can become an entrepreneur in the hemp market.

There are basically three ways to open a cannabis shop:

- In autonomy (from scratch)
- In franchising
- Intermediate formula

1) **Open a shop selling legal hemp products from scratch.**

This is certainly the most complicated way but it can give various satisfactions to an entrepreneur. There is nothing of your company, you will have to create it from scratch, step by step.

You will therefore need to:

- do a market research
- draw up a business plan with objectives and forecasts for the return on investment (ROI)

Finding the funds to invest

Open a VAT number by creating a customized company (sole proprietorship or company) with the help of an accountant

- ✓ Find the right place where the shop will be
- ✓ Renovate or furnish it to make it functional for your purpose
- ✓ Find a name
- ✓ Create the brand
- ✓ Create a corporate image and a marketing strategy
- ✓ Search and compare suppliers
- ✓ Choose and buy products to resell
- ✓ Investing in communication and advertising to promote the brand

The cost to open your own hemp products retail shop from scratch ranges from approximately € 30,000 to € 50,000.

Pros:

- Autonomous choice of name, products and suppliers.
- Total independence of the company
- Greater profits should the company grow over the years

Versus:

- High opening costs
- Greater business risks

Greater efforts in terms of time and resources to create and make known a new brand and position yourself on the market (at the beginning you are literally nobody).

Long time to open the shop

2) Open a cannabis shop in Franchising

One choice you can make is to open your company, your shop, relying on a brand that already exists and is known in the market. The name, the brand, the products will be provided to you directly by the "parent" company with which you will continue to have commercial relations dictated by a contract that will bind the two parties.

The cost to open a cannabis shop in Franchising is around € 20,000 / € 25,000

Pros:

- Slightly lower initial investment costs
- Brand already known and placed on the market
- Faster opening times
- Initial training and coaching

Versus:

- Total dependence on the "parent" company in business decisions.
- Affiliate fees.
- Royalty (percentage of turnover to be paid to the franchisor).
- Little flexibility.
- Advertising rights to be recognized to the Franchisor

3) Open a cannabis shop with an intermediate formula

An excellent compromise between opening your own company from scratch and Franchising is the intermediate formula. In this case, an existing brand offers its know- how, logo, graphics, products, initial training and support for starting a business. Unlike franchising, however, it is very flexible. I can therefore also choose only some of the components offered by the "parent" Brand. There is the possibility for example to choose your company name, logo etc. You will then be helped with the opening procedures, any public funding if present, shop setting up, product supply etc.

The cost to open a Cannabis Shop with an intermediate formula varies from € 5,000 to € 20,000

Pros:

- Total flexibility (I can choose whether to be helped totally or only in certain areas).
- Lower initial costs.
- Initial training and coaching.
- No commission on sales.
- Good profit margins.
- Short opening times.

Versus:

- Dependence on the "parent" company in the initial stages.
- Limited decision-making powers regarding company choices.

CHAPTER 13: CANNABIS LIGHT AND MEDICAL CANNABIS.

For cannabis light we mean all those preparations in which the concentrations of THC, or the substance responsible for the psychotropic effect (responsible for the "high" effect), are between 0.2% and 0.6%. It is defined light precisely by virtue of the low concentration of THC when compared to that present in illegally purchased cannabis or cannabis sold in pharmacies and intended for medical use. To convey the idea, the most used product for therapeutic purposes, Bedrocan, has a THC percentage of 22%.

In an interview with Wired, Vincenzo Di Marzo, director of the CNR molecular chemistry institute that has been dealing with the physiological effects of cannabinoids for over 20 years, said:

"The claimed content of Thc is actually very low by comparison, the substances that were smoked in the 60s and 70s contained between 2 and 4% Thc , while the most potent modern herbs, such as skunk, exceed 20% ". And since Thc is the active ingredient responsible for the psychotropic effects of cannabis (and for the damage to neurodevelopment in adolescents and children), it is likely that a "legal joint" has negligible effects.

"However, there is a strong individual variability in the response to the substance, and a certain difference linked to the way the substance is taken, which make it difficult to give a single answer. Much also depends on how the cannabinoid content is measured. In fact, in the plant they are not contained in an active form, but in a non-active, or carboxylated form, which does not produce effects on the nervous system. The transition to the non-carboxylated form occurs with drying and heating, and therefore one should be sure of the percentages of Thc in active form present at the time of consumption, which often involves heating the substance, in order to hypothesize the possible effects on the nervous system ".

The expert concluded his interview by stating that there are not many studies on the pharmacokinetics of Thc , and it is therefore difficult to understand how the repeated consumption of many joints containing very low amounts of Thc would affect the body , compared to the use of smaller doses. of more concentrated substance (typical of currently illegal recreational consumption).

But Marijuana is not all THC, in fact we must not forget about cannabidiol. The situation when we talk about cannabidiol becomes clearer. It is a perfectly legal substance, which has proven antiansiolytic abilities and excellent tolerability. On this Vincenzo Di Marzo declared:

"Studies to date show that it has very few side effects, even at extremely high doses, much higher than those found in cannabis. Suffice it to say that today it is being tested as an antiepileptic for pediatric use. And in some researches, it has been used in doses of 800 milligrams to verify the possible antipsychotic effect, without finding any harmful effects ".

Is there a difference and between medical cannabis and light cannabis?

Medical cannabis and light cannabis differ mainly in the amount of THC and CBD present. This difference means that the therapeutic one can be considered a drug in all respects useful for the control of nausea, vomiting, lack of appetite mainly in patients undergoing chemotherapy and for the control of some forms of chronic pain such as neuropathic pain. Not only that, another indication is that in the treatment of muscle spasticity pains and in cases of fibromyalgia. This effect can only be achieved by consuming cannabis with precise concentrations of THC and CBD.

Furthermore, there is a legal difference between the two types of cannabis. Light hemp can be purchased by any adult, both in physical outlets and in online cannabis stores. Medicinal cannabis can only be bought with a prescription and from pharmacies, and as is well known, the sale is very complex.

The therapeutic effects of hemp are consequently clear and scientifically proven. Light hemp, thanks to the high concentrations of CBD, has or can have positive and relaxing effects that exclude the contraindications and consequently also the therapeutic functions of a high presence of THC, the psychotropic substance that gets you high. Basically, cannabis light thanks to CBD have relaxing and anti-anxiety functions, the therapeutic one is used in a wide range of more or less serious pathologies as a symptomatic treatment.

THE EXTRACTION OF THC RESIN BY THE BUTANE PROCEDURE

Last October, some newspapers began to report this new "trend": the extraction of THC from the inflorescences of light cannabis with butane. As mentioned, the concentration of light cannabis must be less than 0.6%, but according to what these newspapers said, the result would also be 10 times higher (we therefore assume 6%, therefore still much lower than a therapeutic hemp, which is around at 22%). In other articles, however, it was written that the resin produced was about 98% pure by extracting the substance from about 20/30 grams of cannabis light. The article reported that a "doping dose" was formed from 20/30g of light cannabis.

But what is cannabis resin extracted with butane? This resin has a name, BHO or Butane Hash Oil, also known as budder, honey oil, shatter and dab, and is a very powerful cannabis concentrate obtained by butane extraction. This gas is injected under pressure into an elongated, cylindrical container containing marijuana. In this way, the butane is forced to pass through the entire plant material of marijuana, bringing with itself the cannabinoids present in the grass before it is released as a mixture of butane and cannabis. Subsequently, it is left to stand for a few moments to allow the gas to evaporate and, at a later time, it undergoes a purging process, to remove the toxic residues present (such as butane itself) and thus obtain a concentrate of the purest BHO possible.

It is not in our interest to know the extraction procedure, but looking for many more reports and articles, we can say with certainty that this system has been used for many years in the production of BHO with plants that normally have a very high concentration of THC. So what we assume has happened, is that some people have decided to try to use the same procedure on cannabis light to create a finished product, to be considered illegal in the Italian legislature.

However, we believe alarmism is foolish. As stated in various articles and newspapers, for a dose of resin considered illegal it takes about 20/30 grams. On the internet, in one of the online stores, it can be seen that light cannabis costs around 70/80 euros for 10 grams. So to create this narcotic dose, of which the newspapers are so terrified, the cost would be around 150/200 euros. The articles underline the fact that the kit costs 80 euros and the butane cylinders only one euro, but they seem to totally forget the cost of the raw material.

In conclusion, cannabis has carved out a small space in society year after year, moving from taking care of the health of our patients to the recreational use. I am sure that the butane extraction method, which could be useful from the point of view of therapeutic formulations for some of our patients, is not currently a risk or a danger to our society.

In summary. In the United States, medical marijuana growers continue to benefit from the constant aging of the population. Chronic diseases have become more common as the population ages, driving the demand for medical marijuana.

2.6 million people are estimated to use marijuana for medical purposes and this segment of the US population is expected to increase dramatically over the next five years.

More than two-thirds of Americans now live-in jurisdictions that have legalized the medical or recreational use of marijuana.

The industry's revenue is estimated to grow at a rate of 33.5% annually for a turnover of $ 15 billion through 2021.

As of 2016, there are approximately 148,294 companies engaged in the industry in the US, contributing $ 957.6 million in wages and salaries to the nation's economic growth.

As of 2018, 223,123 companies operate in the sector, with approximately 763,189 people employed.

Medical marijuana patients with chronic pain are the largest market segment for the cannabis industry, accounting for 64.6% of the market in 2016, with recreational users accounting for only 14.1% of the market.

The remaining market share is shared by consumers who purchase products for the treatment and management of other pains.

According to data released by Forbes, in 2017 the trade in legal marijuana around the world grew by 37% and was worth $ 9.5 billion.

With sales of approximately $ 8.5 billion, the United States accounts for 90% of the medical cannabis market.

With a turnover of around €0.6 billion Canada's market shares in 2017 was 6%. The rest of the world holds the remaining 4% of the market.

CHAPTER 14: WHAT TO SELL IN A GROW SHOP

Opening a grow shop is one of the business opportunities that at the moment seems to involve and interest various people throughout Italy. In fact, these shops dedicated to the sale of legal cannabis, its derivatives, marijuana-based foods and products and oils for physical well-being and beauty always deriving from cannabis.

But are grow shops legal? More and more people are wondering if the sale of light cannabis is really legal and if opening one of these shops does not lead to problems with the police. This activity in Italy is legal, or rather there is no law prohibiting the sale of cannabis inflorescences with a THC content lower than that considered illegal by law.

The limit THC content is 0.6%, so in these shops you can sell all products that derive from hemp, as long as their content of this cannabinoid is below the limit imposed by law.

HOW TO OPEN A GROW SHOP: PROCEDURE AND LEGAL PRECAUTIONS

Being a relatively recent activity, opening a grow shop is considered a good form of investment, but before opening a shop of this kind it is necessary to take into consideration some precautions that allow you to start a totally legal business and that does not risk closure. In fact, unlike other shops dedicated to the trade of traditional goods, grow shops are considered to be at risk of illegal activities, for this reason they are constantly monitored by the police who control the type of goods sold.

Given this particular attention of the police forces, to open a grow shop in addition to having to follow the classic bureaucratic process required for the opening of a commercial activity (Registration with the Chamber of Commerce, opening of Inps and Inail positions, municipal authorization permits etc ...) you must also pay attention to the products you buy.

All products should only be purchased from vendors who can certify that all hemp products do not contain a THC value greater than 0.6%. Furthermore, it is always recommended to keep all invoices, receipts and documents certifying that the cannabis you are selling is light and that the product has been purchased regularly.

As we have mentioned, grow shops can sell all light cannabis products. These stores are primarily supposed to market light cannabis growing and gardening equipment. In fact, you can sell seeds, the right land, lamps to encourage growth, irrigation systems, etc.

In addition to gardening products, you can also sell inflorescences, and specialize for example in the sale of items for smokers, choosing to also market lighters, bongs, hookahs or vaporizers, but also papers and everything you need to smoke.

In addition to these products, you can also choose to sell food products such as: hemp flour, beer and marijuana drinks, cannabis jam, supplements, etc. For the sale of these products, however, it is necessary to ask for permits for the opening of a commercial activity, also the permission to sell and supply drinks and food.

Finally, many of these stores also offer a wide range of beneficial products made with marijuana, in fact it is possible to sell oils, creams, ointments, make-up and cosmetics.

What Is A Grow Shop?

A grow shop is a retail store specializing in the sale of equipment and supplies for growing plants especially indoors.

Although grow shops are known as specialized shops for growing cannabis, in reality the products marketed are suitable for all types of crops such as horticulture.

The grow shop has an extensive catalog ranging from various substrate soils, to fertilizers, lamps, hydroponic systems, etc.

In addition to all the growing material, grow shops often offer other products such as hemp food, cosmetics and the now famous cannabis light.

The first grow shops were started in the USA during the 1950s during the first marijuana boom, a phenomenon that arrived about 20 years late in Europe, especially in countries more tolerant of DIY cannabis cultivation such as Spain and Holland.

Grow shops are an example of contradiction in a country like Italy where certain activities such as the cultivation of cannabis is prohibited in theory, but in parallel has a thriving sector such as grow shops.

Finally, after decades of contradictions, the European law 242 of December 2016 has brought some certainties about the cultivation of cannabis.

Despite continuing doubts and legislative interpretations, the first clear stakes have been defined and that is, that in Italy the cultivation of cannabis is allowed as long as the plant derives from a certified seed with a special tag that certifies the origin of the seed that was originally selected, to contain a percentage lower than 0.6% of THC, the psychoactive substance of cannabis present in the inflorescence.

Despite decades of scientific literature, we have now shown that THC is a substance that is not only harmless, but even beneficial for the treatment of many diseases, in Italy there is still an obscurantist lobby that fights against complete legalization.

We must understand this timeless lobby, it is now an active part in the defense of certain clear and obvious interests such as the multinationals of pharmaceuticals and plastics that fear the spread of a plant that is not only harmless, but capable of undermining the monopoly of certain characters.

In fact, hemp produces medicines, fabrics, building materials, bio fuels, seed oil and much more.

Despite the lobbying that attacks hemp, the law is now on the side of producers and therefore the road to the future has been traced as Canada, California, Uruguay, Holland and Spain have already shown.

Pending a complete legalization, today the legal situation of the grow shops is absolutely calm as long as you follow the law and market products normally on the market.

If there are no problems with regards to the equipment, if the trader decides to sell inflorescences of light cannabis, he must pay attention to the producer and always ask for the analyses that certify the level of THC contained.

CHAPTER 15: OPENING A DISPENSARY IN ILLINOIS COST

What are the costs of opening a cannabis business in Illinois?

Opening a cannabis dispensary in Illinois costs $ 500,000 to $ 1,000,000.

Opening a Cannabis Dispensary in Illinois will be expensive due to the costs of security, capital requirements, licensing, consulting, and legal costs, which continue in your company's operations.

Get ready and build a great team and a business plan and get the right consultants and resources for your success.

The experts we spoke to believe that the costs to open your cannabis business in Illinois will range from $ 400,000 to $ 1,000,000 for a dispensary and from $ 1.5 million to $ 3.0 million for artisanal grow shops, depending on your location and size of buildings.

Each state is a little different, but if you want to open a dispensary or a grow shop in Illinois, the regulations and limited number of licenses add to the cost more than on the West Coast.

What are the costs of opening a dispensary?

Here is a quick rundown of the startup costs for opening a cannabis dispensary or craft growing in Illinois:

- Statutory commissions
- Costs of compiling the application
- Legal fees
- Cannabis Operations Advisor Fees

- Fees for accountants and other professionals
- Insurance premiums
- Community outreach costs
- Properly capitalized requirements
- Construction of buildings and fixed rental costs
- Employees
- Costs of flowers and inventory
- Renewal license fees
- Taxes (IRC 280E)
- Marketing
- Professional commissions in progress
- Licensing fees for your cannabis dispensary or Craft Grow

These are the simplest costs: the taxes you pay to the state of Illinois. They are provided for by statute and have a number. Simple to plug into your budget, but that's just the tip-to-toe cost of your cannabis companies to open their dispensary or grow artisanally.

For dispensaries:

- Non-refundable application fee of $ 5,000.
- $ 60,000 registration fee (renewable for the same amount every two years.)

For Craft Grows:

- Non-refundable application fee of $ 5,000.
- $ 40,000 application fee (becomes renewable fee)

Location of your cannabis dispensary or craft cultivation

Real estate is all about location, so where you open your cannabis business is important. Rent, because cannabis businesses cannot finance a mortgage for them

Your dispensary square footage will impact your double taxation under IRC 280E and also your rental costs. Although growers are not impressed with IRC 280E, they must maintain buildings within closed loop system buildings if they are to maintain the highest quality product.

You have to plan and imagine your cannabis business very precisely, with the help of talented designers and architects, to determine not only your startup needs, but also your daily operating costs.

Expect a market rent premium and possible zoning problems. Fortunately, dispensaries in Illinois have six months from the granting of their conditional use dispensing license to provide the state with its address.

Also, the security issues regarding the location of your property should be explored and discussed in your question because security is an important point under your score. The same goes for the configurations and security features needed to be integrated into your craft dispensing or growing business, which isn't as stringent in West Coast states. The costs of furniture, fixtures and equipment (FF&E) in Illinois are higher due to the precise level of security built into the law to prevent the diversion of cannabis from the supply chain or the robberies of adult-only cannabis-using money.

Complete the application for an Illinois Dispensary or Craft Grow

The consultants will help you put together your cannabis license application, business plan, financial plans, security plans, social equity plans, and numerous other things. The completed question will resemble what was known as a "rubric" in the 20th century. The phrase means that a high-scoring application's stack of papers will be large, perhaps hundreds of pages.

The reason for the length of the application has to do with the promises your cannabis business is making to the State of Illinois (and your state if you are elsewhere) about its application. Upon issuing a license to grow or distribute cannabis in your business, all the terms and conditions and promises regarding your cannabis business that you have made in the application actually become requirements to run your business!

Your application requires employee training policies, public awareness plans, security design and protocols, sophisticated business operations, property and financial contracts, and important record keeping systems and procedures employed in growing or selling the adult who they use cannabis. No other company has so many pre- plans to be licensed to open its doors.

If you've ever heard an entrepreneur complain about overly burdensome regulations, ask if they're in the cannabis industry.

The application process can cost tens of thousands of dollars and will be described in more detail below. The important thing your business can do when taking the risk of applying for a license is at least to purchase a good application. Illinois has very few places open for the first wave of the industry. Maybe you will do the first wave, or the second, or the third.

If Illinois becomes like Colorado, the number of dispensary and craft production licenses will have to triple about the current legal maximums, which means people like you will need to continue lobbying the state to update and amend the law to more players.

CANNABIS BUSINESS (TEAM) PLAN

When drafting your business plan, use this team mindset when combining: your culture, your key legal, tax, security and operational advisors, your investors and, of course, your clients.

Illinois adds a new wrinkle to the traditional cannabis business plans of other adult consumption states: social equity. You can use social equity goals to open up the cannabis industry to those who have been most influenced by drug laws over the past 80 years. Perhaps your cannabis company will come up with a plan to hire 10 full-time candidates for social equity so that your company can be proudly recognized for helping meet the state's goals in its new adult use law.

Of course, the business plan should have traditional revenue and expense projections and a financial planner or CPA with previous retail experience, and hopefully cannabis, the experience will bring your company's most reliable data. Cannabis business plans, unlike simple business plans, often have to address aspects of the business resulting from regulatory compliance. For example, you will have compliance costs to ensure that your operations comply with new and evolving laws in its operations and how they can be detailed as those managed by software or human resources.

SAFETY PLAN FOR THE DISTRIBUTION OF CANNABIS OR ARTISANAL CULTIVATION

Security doesn't just mean having a burly guy with a gun. Security blends best practices in technology, structural design, and law enforcement surveillance to implement a system that, if something goes wrong, who did it, when it was done, and what exactly happened is all captured in high definition, printed and provided to law enforcement authorities.

Security is also built into your property in its layout, customer experience stream, doors, cameras, strobes, building materials, and even employee training policies and procedures. The security plan aspect of your application counts for many points. Cannabis businesses cost a lot to open, but the initial cost is to fill out the right safety plan so that it meets your state's approval and high score.

Record-keeping plan to prevent the diversion of cannabis or money

Many companies have proprietary software that was invented before Illinois even became a medical cannabis state. These are the ancillary activities that arise when cannabis becomes a legal activity. The software you will use to track product supply and sales will depend on the consultant you choose. You don't want your Point of Sale (POS) system to be a real, well, POS.

If your business plan includes developing such technologies in its five-year plans to create additional revenue streams by selling licenses for what it creates, then you should call me unless you are thinking of doing it in C #. Then you can hire someone else or provide a detailed reason for your choice of that language.

Employee training plans and policies should also have best practices in place that provide accurate cannabis registration. These procedures must be followed and include training with whatever software your business has decided to use to track their inventory and sales. Familiarity with your systems is key to preventing cannabis from being hijacked down the supply chain or going bad by taking up shelf space with products that should have cleared faster.

FINANCIAL ABILITY TO DESIGN, BUILD AND MANAGE CANNABIS BUSINESSES

The application to obtain your license to grow or dispense cannabis includes many projects and plans for your facility and perhaps the packaging and labeling of the product. Designers are very important to the image and look they can convey for your new cannabis brand. So having them draw up plans for your property or product packaging won't be cheap. But if your application is successful, it gets even more expensive because projects now have to be built and used.

With or without access to loans and grants available to "qualified social equity applicants", all licensed cannabis companies must prove their financial capacity to carry out their projects and make them a reality. This cost is specific and unique to your particular brand, its design and the location of the properties.

Regardless of whether your cannabis business is highly cost-conscious or well-funded, you need to be able to demonstrate that you have the money to carry out your projects and application specifications, including payroll financing for your operations.

Employee Handbook and Educational Policies Required by Illinois Cannabis Law

Many companies build their employment practices and manuals as they grow over time, but cannabis companies need to have them in place before opening their doors.

Training your cannabis employees is another step in setting your brand for the customer experience, but it also draws on your safety policies by teaching practices for observing the person's body language and actions to remember certain details in case something goes wrong.

Further employee education and training can guide policies to reduce and recognize theft and protect employees and customers in the event of a robbery.

Of course, budtenders should have knowledge of the flower and its extracts, terpenoid profiles and strains so that they can advise clients on what kind of experience they intend to gain from cannabis.

Employee training policies can help you make your customers happy, state regulators happy, and your business safe.

Community Commitment / Social Equity Plan to Achieve the Goals of the Illinois Cannabis Law

While not many points are specifically enumerated for community outreach, and in some cases the points are simply bonuses in the event of a tie, which means you should still do it. If you tied and didn't include it, but the other candidate did, bad luck!

What does your cannabis company do to give back? There are many things you can do to educate people, or help those harmed by the damage caused by the war on drugs, or another woman, minority, veteran or disabled group.

Provide funding for this engagement plan in your business operations budget, as it should be an ongoing expense that your business continues to make to enrich the community it serves.

COSTS FOR CANNABIS EMPLOYEES

Dispensary managers must keep the business running smoothly in a compliant manner. They deal with employees, customers, vendors, state regulators, business owners, perhaps even investors. They are in demand due to the scarcity of the industry, but consultants estimate that for a dispensary, annual staff costs can reach the range of a quarter of a million dollars.

There are both upfront costs and ongoing costs. You need a lawyer, an accountant, an operations consultant and you need to be properly insured. Annual budgets for these range in the tens of thousands of dollars.

COSTS TO PROMOTE YOUR CANNABIS BUSINESS

Not just SEO, social media outreach, design and YouTube, you can sponsor community outreach events to build your brand. Our favorite is sponsoring expungement seminars and job fairs in partnership with local lawyer associations, politicians and cannabis companies. Remember to include these things into your plans and set yourself apart from the competition.

Summary of the costs of entering the legal cannabis market in Illinois

So now you understand why we said it would average around $ 500,000 to open a cannabis dispensary in Illinois. We didn't actually get into all the costs of the growing equipment that can mount due to the various HVAC and machinery, and the safety, construction requirements of a craft grow. That average will likely be around $ 2,000,000, but it depends on the characteristics the grow wants to offer.

CHAPTER 16: HOW TO OBTAIN A COMMERCIAL LICENSE FOR CANNABIS IN NEW JERSEY

The people of New Jersey voted and a new cannabis legalization law passed! - Get ready to receive your licensed cannabis business to start operating in New Jersey.

New Jersey immediately got new legislation to codify people's votes. Question 1 was approved with 66.91% of the votes. The cannabis market is opening up in the state, it is your opportunity to start preparing your license application to open your cannabis business.

The cannabis industry is changing a lot when it comes to its regulations, New Jersey is no exception. The regulations are still being drafted and there are many important details to be determined, so we can expect many updates on legalization in New Jersey in the coming months.

CONSTITUTIONAL AMENDMENT FOR THE LEGALIZATION OF MARIJUANA

Do you approve of the Constitution amendment to legalize a controlled form of marijuana called "cannabis"?

Only adults 21 years of age or older could use cannabis. The state commission created to oversee the state medical cannabis program would also oversee the new cannabis market for personal use.

Cannabis products would be subject to state sales tax. If authorized by the legislature, a municipality can pass a local ordinance to charge a local tax on cannabis products.

INTERPRETIVE STATEMENT

This amendment would legalize a controlled form of marijuana called "cannabis". Only people 21 years of age or older could legally use cannabis products.

The Cannabis Regulatory Commission would oversee the new adult cannabis market. This commission was created in 2019 to oversee the state's medical cannabis program. The scope of the new Commission authority would be detailed in the laws enacted by the legislature.

All retail sales of cannabis products in the new adult cannabis market would be subject to state sales tax. If authorized by the legislature, a municipality can pass a local ordinance to charge a local tax on cannabis products.

CHAPTER 17: IDEAS FOR WORKING WITH LEGAL CANNABIS

If you are passionate about cannabis, this is probably one of the most exciting times you can live in. The legal marijuana industry is growing like wildfire, creating new businesses and numerous job opportunities.

So, if you've always dreamed of working with marijuana (instead of just smoking it) now is the time to step forward. Here are some business ideas for the cannabis industry to help you get your creativity flowing and kickstart your life as a cannabis entrepreneur.

1. DESIGN OF SALES POINTS

Legalization is showing us that the term " stoner " should be banned and marijuana accessible to all. More and more people, from the parents of footballers to the most skilled professionals, are showing greater openness to cannabis. As a result, people expect a lot more from cannabis shops.

That's why we're starting to see a complete revamp of dispensaries, coffeeshops, and other cannabis retailers. Dispensaries in the US and coffeeshops in the Netherlands are decorating their interiors with increasingly modern styles and furnishings to attract a new type of cannabis customer.

Stores that sell cannabis are changing their strategies to present themselves to the public through novel design. This has created a growing demand for talented designers with professional qualifications and a broad understanding of this particular industry, but also for international designers who are passionate about cannabis and eager to work in this environment.

2. COSMETICS

If you've been living in a cave for the past couple of years, here's some outdated news that might interest you: Cannabis cosmetics are hugely successful.

The benefits of cannabis cosmetics and the compounds they contain are amply demonstrated by a solid research base. Furthermore, the therapeutic properties of cannabinoids such as THC and CBD (pain relievers, anti-inflammatory, etc.) are supported by a lot of research and our body can benefit from them topically in the form of balms, sprays, lotions and more.

These important developments have given birth to a new and gigantic market for medicinal and beauty products. In fact, there are many brands specialized in cannabis-based beauty products on the market. Lord Jones, Khus Khus and Vertly are only a small part of those now established in this niche market.

The Body Shop brand has also caught on in the industry with its new line of cannabis creams and balms, not to mention actress Whoopi Goldberg who launched her medical marijuana products, including bubble baths, body balms and more.

As the cannabis industry grows and becomes more and more competitive, companies do their best to make their business more effective and outperform the competition.

And just as companies in other sectors rely on branding experts, designers, copywriters and advertisers, cannabis companies target the same professionals. From dispensaries to seedbanks, and everything in between, companies are constantly looking for tailor-made services to develop attractive brands and drive sales of their products / services.

This is very encouraging news for marketers looking to expand into a new industry. If you fit into this professional profile, working as a freelancer or starting your own agency could be a very promising business idea.

3. CONSULTING

There are, of course, endless regulations drawn up to legally produce, manage and sell cannabis. Not to mention the regulations for its marketing, for the places where it is consumed and much more. If you live in the United States, these regulations can drastically change from one state to another.

Above these legal gray areas, the production and sale of cannabis-related products remains a challenge in itself. Cultivating the plant alone is quite challenging, especially for those who are unfamiliar with the plant but still want to compete on the commercial playground.

This situation is worrying young entrepreneurs looking to enter the marijuana market. Fortunately, in these cases a consultant may be the most sought-after professional figure.

There is an increasing need for consultants with expertise in the cannabis sector who are able to help new businesses overcome market obstacles.

If you are an experienced grower, for example, you could advise emerging producers on the deep and growing developments in professional cannabis cultivation. If you're a cannabis lawyer, you have what it takes to help companies navigate the treacherous sea of legal minutiae.

4. TECHNOLOGY

The legal cannabis industry is still quite recent. While the technology of many other sectors has evolved for centuries, technological solutions for the cannabis industry have only been openly developed in recent years.

Of course, some have already begun to adopt technology solutions for businesses and, for example, have created comprehensive technology packages specifically designed to help dispensaries and other cannabis businesses automate and optimize their businesses, using technology for e- commerce, CMS and more.

Other examples of how companies are renovating the cannabis industry include agencies developing software for marijuana outlets.

And while the cannabis industry is becoming increasingly competitive, there are still many ways the technology could help track the management and sale of this plant more quickly. If you are tech savvy, get your ideas together and step forward.

5. CANNABIS EVENT ORGANIZERS

We have written about the extension of cannabis communities on repeated occasions and that is why we see so much excitement among the agencies that organize cannabis events.

Cannabis users are constantly looking for fun gatherings where they can share their love of weed and do different activities, such as painting under the effects of marijuana or cycling tours in favor of the legalization of this plant.

But there are still tons of other job opportunities for creative event organizers where they can come up with the best tactics for combining cannabis with other exciting activities. So if you have a penchant for organizing large events, this might be your chance.

6. EDIBLES AND CANNABIS-BASED COOKING

If there's one thing we all agree on, it's that cannabis and food are like peaches and cream. If you think like us and are passionate about finding new and intriguing ways to combine cannabis and food, this professional profile could be for you.

Like cosmetics and concentrates (which we'll discuss in the next section of this list), the cannabis market for edibles and other food products is huge. In addition to producers of cannabis-based foods, even the most creative entrepreneurs are starting to give cannabis cooking classes, seminars on how to combine the various foods and more.

This is an extremely exciting way to enter the legal cannabis market, without necessarily becoming a grower or a retailer of buds.

7. CONCENTRATES AND EXTRACTS OF CANNABIS

Another huge chunk of the cannabis market revolves around extracts. " Dabbing " is certainly one of the most popular trends in the industry, another quite creative alternative to get into this business.

The concentrate market offers the most diverse job opportunities. Of course, you could create your own brand of extracts. However, it is also possible to specialize in the production of machinery and equipment for extraction, or to advise those who would like to enter the market. There are numerous business ventures involving the creation, management and sale of concentrates.

8. ART AND CANNABIS RELATED ITEMS

The cannabis industry has supported the rise of extraordinary artists, including Tony Greenhand, the artistic joint rolling professional, and numerous other glass artists who specialize in producing carefully crafted items sold at exorbitant prices around the world.

Cannabis has also made its way into high fashion and among the giants of "fast fashion", with some clothes that can reach unprecedented figures. Currently, the art world is experiencing a major resurgence in marijuana-inspired projects across various disciplines. If you are a creative person interested in combining your passion for art and cannabis, this is yet another field of research to consider to be successful in the "cane business".

9. OPEN A BED & BREAKFAST FOR CANNABIS LOVERS

In countries where marijuana regulations have changed in recent years, more and more cannabis tourists are looking for comfortable accommodations to spend their holidays. If you live in one of these places, you may want to set up a facility to accommodate cannabis smokers.

Decorate the rooms according to what you think a cannabis lover might appreciate and always offer something special. You could possibly sell local handicrafts.

So, if you have a passion for cannabis and have always wanted to be part of this industry, now is the time to step up. The market is booming and if you think you have the necessary requirements, please jump at the opportunity.

CHAPTER 18: HOW TO OBTAIN A MEDICAL MARIJUANA CARD IN THE UNITED STATES

As of 2019, 33 US states have legalized some form of medical marijuana. Each state has a different legal framework governing medical marijuana. Therefore, it is important to be aware of all local marijuana rules, laws and requirements before you can obtain a card and purchase medical marijuana.

Despite the fact that it remains federally illegal, medical marijuana is now legal in 33 US states, and Washington DC Each state has developed its own legal framework for governing the medical marijuana system. While there are similarities between the legal frameworks applied in each state, there are also important differences. It is incredibly important to make sure you understand your state's rules and regulations.

Having a medical marijuana card exempts you from most statewide marijuana possession and consumption laws. However, the qualification conditions and the process for obtaining a card differ from state to state. If your state does not recognize your specific illness, buying outside of the state is not an option.

The following states have legalized medical marijuana:

Legal Medical Cannabis

Alaska (1) - Arizona (2) - Arkansas (3) - California (4) - Colorado (5) - Connecticut (6) - Delaware (7) - Florida (8) - Hawaii (9) - Illinois (10) - Louisiana (11) - Maine (12) - Maryland (13) - Massachusetts (14) - Michigan (15) -

Minnesota (16) - Missouri (17) - Montana (18) - Nevada (19) - New Hampshire (20) - New Jersey (21) - New Mexico (22) - New York (23) - North Dakota (24) - Ohio (25) - Oklahoma (26) - Oregon (27) - Pennsylvania (28) - Rhode Island (29) - Utah (30) - Vermont (31) - Washington (32) - West Virginia (33) - Washington DC (34).

WHAT DO YOU NEED TO GET A MEDICAL MARIJUANA CARD?

The answer to this question will largely depend on the state you live in. However, there are some things that will be required of you in every state. Regardless of the state you are in, you will be required to: know the requirements, prepare the correct documentation and obtain a legal prescription.

LOOK FOR THE REGULATIONS AND RESTRICTIONS OF YOUR STATE

Make sure you have a thorough understanding of your state's medical marijuana regulations, requirements, and restrictions. Having this information in advance can help you avoid potential obstacles or surprises in the future. It will also allow you to carry out the application process in a faster and more peaceful way.

To get a medical marijuana card, you must have a qualified medical condition. The conditions required for a medical card can vary extremely from state to state. Your state's health services office will most likely be able to provide you with an up-to-date list of accepted conditions.

COLLECT THE REQUIRED DOCUMENTATION

You will need to provide adequate medical and legal documentation. During the process, any previous medical records documenting your illness may be helpful or even necessary. Your physician or a representative of your state's health department may be able to tell you exactly what documents will be needed in your jurisdiction.

You will also need proper legal identification, such as a driver's license or passport. Additionally, you will need to provide proof of residency.

GET A PRESCRIPTION FROM YOUR DOCTOR

You need to get approval from a registered doctor, which may not always be an easy thing to do, as many doctors are not yet willing to prescribe medical marijuana. In these situations, you may be able to find a clinic or doctor who specializes in medical marijuana prescriptions. Having a medical document to support a claim for a disease can be helpful in obtaining a prescription.

In most states, medical marijuana cards are only valid for a specific period of time. Remember the expiration date of your card and take some time to look for your state's renewal process. Doing this in advance can prevent you from finding yourself without a valid card for any length of time.

WHAT MEDICAL CONDITIONS QUALIFY YOU FOR MEDICAL MARIJUANA?

The qualifying medical conditions required to obtain a medical marijuana card differ from state to state. Here are some of the most common diseases that medical marijuana is prescribed for in the United States:

ANXIETY, ANOREXIA AND DIETARY PROBLEMS, ARTHRITIS, AIDS / HIV, CHRONIC PAIN, CANCER,

EPILEPSY AND CONVULSIVE DISORDERS, GLAUCOMA, MULTIPLE SCLEROSIS, NAUSEA, NEURODEGENERATIVE DISEASES, POST-TRAUMATIC STRESS.

HOW CAN YOU GET THE MEDICAL MARIJUANA CARD ONLINE?

In some states, such as California and Florida, you may be able to get a medical marijuana card online. This process will save you time by connecting directly to a doctor who specializes in medical marijuana. In addition, it will allow you to get a card from the comfort of your home. Some online clinics may even give you an immediate recommendation, allowing you to purchase legal marijuana on the same day. If you're looking to get the procedure done as quickly and conveniently as possible, an online clinic may be your best choice.

In most cases, the process is very quick and straightforward. After providing your identification, medical information and proof of residency, you will be subjected to a personal online assessment. These assessments typically last from 5 to 15 minutes and involve a series of questions. The main purpose of these assessments is to clearly establish your medical situation and why marijuana could improve it.

Once your request has been accepted, you can expect to receive your card in the mail within a few days. However, in some states you will be able to legally purchase medical marijuana immediately after receiving an email confirmation. Often this means being able to purchase marijuana on the same day as the valuation. Talk to your doctor and local dispensaries to find out what their exact policy is regarding email recommendations.

CAN YOU TRAVEL WITH MEDICAL CANNABIS?

CAN TOURISTS QUALIFY FOR A MEDICAL MARIJUANA CARD?

No. The United States requires proof of residency when licensing medical marijuana. Hence, out-of-state tourists will not be able to successfully obtain medical marijuana licenses.

However, in some states, tourists from other states who have valid medical marijuana cards and identification can purchase marijuana legally. States like California, Arizona, and Washington sell recreational or medical marijuana to all tourists of legal age. However, traveling from state to state with legally purchased marijuana is not yet recommended.

In September 2018, the Arizona Appeals Court ruled that out-of-state medical marijuana licenses would be recognized within its state. If you're traveling to a state that has recreational marijuana, your medical state doesn't matter. However, if you intend to purchase medical marijuana, check local laws and regulations to make sure your medical license is accepted in the state you are visiting.

CHAPTER 19: DO YOU WANT TO GROW HEMP LEGALLY? HERE ARE SOME TIPS AND INDICATIONS

Nowadays, light hemp is undoubtedly one of the trendiest crops in Italy, and it is enough to take a look at the latest cannabis cultivation statistics to realize how thriving the market is.

To demonstrate this, it is also useful to share some reflections with the main associations that bring together small farmers and large farms: they will confirm that there are more and more operators who declare themselves extremely interested in participating in this sector, and that they are always more people who have decided to discover how to grow cannabis in order to benefit from the many beneficial properties that this plant substance is able to give us.

In fact, despite the countless criticisms that come from some of the media and public opinion, not everyone knows that light hemp can bring many advantages: we remember that this plant has pain-relieving, anti-nausea, anti-inflammatory properties and, moreover, can be a great help against migraines.

Growing cannabis, so many benefits from growing weed!

According to some scientific studies, moreover, it would seem that the results of cannabis cultivation can inhibit tumor growth since it causes apoptosis, or the death of malignant cells (but, beware, further studies are needed to be able to consciously ascertain this and, therefore, we cannot do more than advise you to talk to your doctor for the latest updates on this topic!).

Precisely for these reasons there are so many people who have discovered how to grow cannabis legally and have chosen to enter this sector in a lawful way, obtaining their evident satisfaction.

It is by virtue of the above that hemp crops are growing more and more all over the world: in the United States there has been a significant increase in crops, constant in recent years, but at the same time - driven by more favorable legislation - also in Italy, companies that know better and better how cannabis is grown and how to make use of these experiences.

Hemp cultivation, a simple and affordable practice for (almost) everyone

On the other hand, light hemp is a very simple plant to grow, since it grows easily and produces inflorescences for a good part of the year. Furthermore, this plant does not need particular climatic conditions to grow luxuriantly, and for this reason it can be grown in any suitably equipped space, even indoors.

As far as the legal aspects are concerned, nowadays installing a legitimate hemp cultivation is very simple, considering that it is sufficient to go through a rather lean authorization process to be able to obtain the licenses that allow you to start a cannabis cultivation business without running into any problems of a legal nature, and therefore being able to conduct an agricultural entrepreneurial initiative that has the same characteristics as any business linked to the "land".

Of course, before embarking on this area it is necessary to be aware of all the regulations in force, in order not to risk making mistakes and having to deal with drastic "corrections".

To grow hemp legally it is therefore necessary to take into account simple but fundamental precautions, which we will summarize below, inviting all those who are interested to get very well informed, in advance, to know how to grow light hemp legally or to understand how to produce it at home.

Cannabis cultivation: how to grow cannabis seeds in Italy without risk

The first thing to do, if you want to find out how to grow cannabis at home, is to find out about the laws in force in Italy in relation to hemp plants. In this context, it should be remembered that nowadays it is no longer necessary to have the authorization for the cultivation of cannabis legally by the police and that, therefore, you can therefore begin to produce it at home without being afraid of legal repercussions. Therefore, you no longer need to hide: light hemp can also be grown in the home, if all the other requirements set by current legislation are respected. Good news for those who are trying these days to evaluate whether or not this can be a profitable path for their professional interests. Furthermore, there are numerous varieties available that are sold in Italy and that come from certified seeds, thus allowing the satisfaction of any declination - even the most specific - of one's cannabis cultivation business.

The origin of the seeds

We recall in this regard that everyone can start the cultivation of cannabis as long as the latter is characterized by seeds certified by the European Union.

If, on the other hand, the seeds are not present on the "approved" list, then it will not be possible to cultivate them fully legally, therefore making it necessary to proceed with the selection of another variety (considering the vast range available today, we are sure that you will have no problems in identifying the one for you!).

To choose a light hemp variety, however, you must also understand what result you intend to obtain, since they are all different in terms of cultivation characteristics. Usually, the most used variety in recent times is the dioecious, which is able to develop both male and female varieties, but on different plants (therefore both characters will not be produced on the same plant). If you want to produce the inflorescences you will need to proceed with a job called unmasking, which basically consists in eliminating the males from the field, since it is the female plants that produce the largest and best inflorescences, if these are not pollinated by their male colleagues.

The above is an extremely important process, since preventing the male from pollinating the female allows the female plants to raise their quality to a much more appreciated and sought-after stage.

If, on the other hand, a person wants to produce hemp from seed, he can prefer both dioecious and monoecious varieties: the latter are used to reproduce the seed of a certain genetics while the former are usually used to have a seed to be used in the cosmetic field or food.

<u>What are the regulations that allow you to grow hemp legally?</u>

Having clarified the above, let's try to take another step forward in deepening cannabis cultivation and ask ourselves what are the regulations that today allow us to grow hemp legally.

We therefore specify, as you should have well understood by reading the previous lines, that to grow hemp legally at your home it is advisable to know the regulations in force on the subject and the latest updates on the subject. Fortunately, however, today the Italian legal discipline is much more generous than in the past, and it is certainly more open to this world than it was in the past.

In addition to doing what we have already mentioned, which is to grow the seeds on the list approved by the European Union, you will also need to make sure that the seeds do not contain THC higher than 0.2%.

Remember that if your seeds do not contain more than 0.2% THC you will not need any authorization to grow cannabis. You must also keep in mind to always keep the tags of the seeds you buy (along with the invoices) for at least twelve months.

What if you go over the 0.2% THC limit?

If, on the other hand, the plants that will be obtained from cultivation contain a THC value lower than or equal to 0.6%, the farmer will still have no legal repercussions, but will have to proceed towards a more specific authorization process.

In particular, it is also possible that the authorities want to carry out tests to see if the THC value is actually within the norm. In this case, however, they will have to leave a sample to the grower so that they can perform possible counter-checks, for their own protection.

We also note that according to the law in force, and according to subsequent clarifications by the Ministry of

Agricultural Policies, it is possible to grow light hemp without the need for authorization but cultivation by cuttings is prohibited: this term indicates a part of a plant which is introduced into the soil and which can create another individual plant.

Those who want to produce inflorescences can decide between different varieties. The most used are Carmagnola, Eletta Campana, Finola, Kompolti and Tisza. You have to keep in mind, however, that Finola is used more for late sowing since it has an extremely short cycle and therefore allows you to have a harvest three months after planting.

Those who want to grow light hemp outdoors, on the other hand, can use other varieties that have a greater development such as Kompolti which can reach up to seven meters in height and can be grown in 130 days depending on the area in which the cultivation takes place. If, on the other hand, you want to produce a seed that can be used for food or cosmetic use, you can use varieties such as Fedora, Uzo 31 or Felina.

Where to get the seeds to grow light hemp legally

In the last few lines, we have focused on the fact that in order to grow light hemp in a legal way it is necessary to buy seeds certified by the Ministry of Agricultural Policies and by the European Union.

Today, the purchase can take place in two ways: in the shop or at agricultural seed dealers. The latter, in fact, have most of the hemp varieties or at least the most used ones. Another very simple way to buy seeds is to use the internet: online there are many retailers of light hemp seeds that also come from abroad (many varieties in fact originate both in Eastern Europe and in France) and that they will open the door to a range of alternatives that you probably never suspected could exist!

However, it is good to remember that before making the online purchase it is advisable to carefully check that the seeds are actually legal in Italy. Furthermore, we must not forget that it is not possible to use the cuttings except for ornamental purposes. Therefore, if you want a cutting to create a hemp plant to display in your home as a decorative object, you will have no problem, but if you need the cuttings for the production of hemp you will have to abandon the idea and use seeds or sprouts instead.

Choosing the right terrain

The right soil is also an element that should not be underestimated when you want to grow this type of plant. It is usually advisable to choose a medium-textured one, which is therefore composed of sand, clay and silt divided into equal parts. Of course, the soil must also be well prepared and worked in such a way as to be able to adequately accommodate the cultivation of hemp. The latter also does not need a lot of water; therefore, it is not mandatory to irrigate. However, it is always good to keep in mind that climatic conditions can change and therefore a drip irrigation system could be the ideal solution. For fertilization, on the other hand, it is possible to use manure or a phosphorus-based fertiliser that can significantly promote flowering. Also remember that more and more people are discovering the possibility of growing cannabis thanks to coconut fiber, as we documented in our recent study, or growing cannabis in aeroponics, without soil.

What you need to know for growing light hemp

Finally, it must be remembered that light flowering hemp must be harvested manually and in a delicate way, since it is necessary to preserve its quality and value. If you use machinery, in fact, you could risk ruining the inflorescence! Seed hemp, on the other hand, can be harvested either manually or by means of machines that are made specifically for the cultivation of hemp.

Furthermore, in both cases it is advisable to create dryers, since the seeds need to be dried after harvesting. You must remember that to carry out this operation you will need a professional dryer as this is one of the most important processes that will help you to obtain quality light hemp.

To grow light hemp legally at home, you can use different methods. One of the simplest to put into practice concerns the use of LED lamps and grow boxes. The latter are basically greenhouses that have particular ventilation systems and that can also be kept safely at home.

The use of LED lamps, on the other hand, can also bring various benefits to those who grow light hemp. First of all, this system involves a lower expenditure of electricity which therefore translates into a lower cost on the bill. In addition to this, LED lamps allow for a higher quality of light: this means that the harvest will also be significantly better. Finally, with Led lamps it is also possible to cultivate in all months of the year without the need for particular climatic conditions. No less important is the reduced risk of pest attacks that could ruin the cultivation of light hemp.

Conclusions

In short, if you want to grow hemp at home, and you want to do it legally, today you have many possibilities at your disposal.

The regulatory interventions that have occurred over the last few years have increasingly favored the possibility of independently starting the cultivation of legal cannabis, provided - of course - you respect the regulatory requirements in force, which in any case are not excessively stringent and they will therefore allow you, if you are interested, to be able to start this type of business.

CHAPTER 20: GROWING HEMP IN THE USA

Industrial hemp is the fastest growing crop in American agriculture. The US defines industrial hemp as cannabis sativa plants containing 0.3% or less of THC. Prior to 2015, hemp was virtually non-existent in terms of U.S. agriculture because the Federal Controlled Substances Act prevented it.

Then, in 2014, a new agricultural law opened the industrial cultivation of hemp in experimental form and for pilot programs controlled by the state. The following year, 1,500 acres of hemp were planted in the United States. Today, after hemp was removed from federally controlled substances thanks to the latest Farm Bill of 2018, according to new data from the United States Department of Agriculture (USDA), crops have increased 100 times and have reached 146 thousand acres, about 60 thousand hectares. To make a comparison throughout Europe, 47 thousand hectares were cultivated in 2017.

In 2018 hemp was planted in 18 states and in 2019 that more than doubled, with 37 states growing it for a 350% increase in acreage in December 2018. Leading the way is Montana (over 44,000 acres), which has more than double the area of the second state - Colorado - when it comes to growing hemp.

Meanwhile, the US Department of Agriculture is rolling out a new pilot hemp insurance program, which will provide Actual Production History coverage under the agency's Multi-Peril Crop Insurance program. The new insurance program comes on top of federal crop insurance, to which the USDA has said hemp growers will have access in August.

In Arizona a specific law to identify the pesticides allowed for the cultivation of cannabis for therapeutic purposes

A panel of the most reputable operators in the cannabis sector has been defined to determine which pesticides can be allowed in the industry of the sector. Any final decision must be approved by the Department of Health Services.

Under a law passed last year in Arizona to test cannabis-derived products before they are displayed in retail outlets, a 12-member panel will determine which chemicals can be used in the industry. Proponents of the bill, however, call the plan akin to "the fox watching the chicken coop" since six of the panel members are representatives of the medical cannabis business, the Arizona Capitol Times reports.

Majority leader Sonny Borrelli (Republican) said he would prefer an outright ban on certain chemicals rather than leave it all to the panel which, in addition to six industry members, includes the owner of an Arizona-based cannabis testing lab, an assistant, a caregiver, a laboratory scientist, a health care provider, and a representative of the State Department of Public Safety.

Borrelli has set his sights on the Eagle 20 fungicide, which has been defined as banned on tobacco and a 'heavy carcinogen' but is allowed to be used for growing cannabis in the state under the current regime.

Borrelli introduced a bill that would specifically ban the use of any pesticides except those that the Federal Insecticide, Fungicide and Rodenticide Act claim are benign and require no regulation at all: castor oil, cinnamon oil, garlic, lemongrass oil, rosemary, sesame and white pepper.

"Suppose the card we put together this year shows up and says, Well, are you allowed to use Eagle 20 (in) a certain amount? Antifungal pesticides are needed because all these growth structures are indoors. So they want to be able to mitigate the mold that is found on marijuana," Borrelli told the Capitol Times.

Pele Peacock Fischer, lobbyist for the Arizona Dispensaries Association, said that while the organization is "trying to put together a testing regimen that is extremely safe for patients," it is also trying to find a balance "that you work in the industry so that laboratories can meet demand, [and] that dispensaries can implement". Additionally, Fischer said even if the panel does approve a pesticide that could be potentially harmful, the Department of Health Services has the final say in what is or is not approved.

CHAPTER 21: INCOME FROM CULTIVATION

The food, beverage and bakery products industry is constantly looking for new ingredients and preparations of a vegetable nature, rich in active ingredients with a strong innovative and functional value.

Among the requirements of industry, above all, is safety for humans and animals, which, in other words means:

- absence of heavy metals and contaminants (in general, agricultural land contains many that are absorbed by plants);
- cultivation without pesticides, herbicides, pesticides;
- without aflatoxins;
- without gram negative microorganisms, molds, fungi.

To avoid soil contamination, it must be removed. To eliminate soil, there are two solutions: Hydroponics which contains substrate, and aeroponics without any substrate: the roots are suspended in the air.

Aeroponics is the most advantageous technique, as it is possible, thanks to the apparatus, to customize the vegetable product, increase yields, vary the aromatic character and the active ingredients present in the vegetable biomass and in the flowers. In other words, it is possible to enrich the flower and fortify it with active ingredients to prevent pathologies or fortify diets.

Among the medicinal plants with the highest added value there is hemp with low THC content and about 400 bioactive substances. The plant produces flowers which, like saffron and truffles, are sold by the gram.

A factory of 1026 square meters of aeroponic technology cultivation, in a controlled environment (CEA), aseptic greenhouse in polycarbonate and premises of 196 square meters for processing, employs 6 employees and an annual yield of over 2300 kg distributed in 4 cycles per year.

The flower biomass as it is (without processing) can be sold for 2.5 euros per gram on the wholesale market. The average price is € 5 per gram.

With less than 200 ml of cannabis oil one liter of water, a soft drink can be enriched and help the consumer to sleep well at night.

In this regard, we have built a business plan that takes into account everything that is happening globally, the uses, the problems it solves, the profits it can generate.

<u>What are the profits?</u>

This amounts to millions of euros in the space of a year.

Through aeroponic technology it is possible to obtain 150 grams of dry inflorescence from a single cannabis plant compared to 50 grams of traditional cultivation. The proposed structure, in an aseptic environment, in a greenhouse with natural ventilation, (patented) hosts from a minimum of 3900 plants to a maximum of 6 thousand every 3 months. The germination of seeds is planned in the technical rooms.

Growing legal or light or low-THC cannabis plants, with an aeroponic system, speeds up growth times and increases yields by at least 10% compared to hydroponics and 150% compared to the open field, as well as reducing water inputs, fertilizers, substrates, manpower, the risk of diseases and mold due to excess water, without residues.

The production cycles are distributed 4 times a year, with low plants and adoption of fertilisation techniques aimed at exclusively enlarging the inflorescences with the desired aroma.

This is an innovative cultivation that can be financed by the start & smart measure (with 70 percent mortgage interest-free) or by crowdfunding or through the measures of the 2014-2020 RDP: sub- measures 6.1, 4.1, 4.2.

Or create an operating group and start a test with sub-measure 16.2.

We have prepared a fairly complete version for those who want to diligently investigate the opportunity to grow legal cannabis and maybe someday, when legalized, medical and recreational cannabis.

It is necessary to hurry up, to start experimenting, to start entering the market. The Germans assessed the sector and decided to take the lead in Europe.

You can find online a business plan designed for students, which contains:

1) The document, in addition to the calculation of the individual investment items and related costs, contains a comparison between the yields of the major international players and our system. Well, despite having fixed a lower yield per square meter, our project remains sustainable.

2) I propose the project for a collaboration, to marketing managers or decision makers of the agri-food and cosmetics

sector in order to develop new products with cannabis flowers (chocolate bars, fruit juices, enriched bread, enriched breadstick, enriched flours, ice cream, etc).

3) The system is scalable and flexible (cultivation of other medicinal products or baby leaves destined for the IV range market in the event of a market crisis).

4) The system implements product sterilization innovations and the cultivation and processing environments and related equipment (Sterilization from hospital operating room)